WATER UNDER THE BRIDGE

Gwilym D. Williams

By the same Author

FROM THE CAPTAIN'S TABLE
Tales of a Master Mariner

WATER UNDER THE BRIDGE

First published by
Bernard Durnford Publishing
457 Upper Shoreham Road, Shoreham-by-Sea, West Sussex,
BN43 5WQ
England
2004

© Gwilym D. Williams
All rights reserved

This book is sold subject to the condition that
it shall not, by way of trade or otherwise, be lent,
re-sold, hired out, or otherwise circulated without
the publisher's prior consent in any form
of binding or cover other than that in which it is
published and without a similar condition
being imposed on the subsequent purchaser.

A catalogue record of this book
is available from the British Library

ISBN 1 904470 02 5

Format, design and cover by StewART

Printed and bound by Antony Rowe Limited
Eastbourne, England

WATER UNDER THE BRIDGE

Gwilym D. Williams

Published by

Bernard Durnford Publishing

CONTENTS

Dedication	7
Acknowledgements	9
Foreword	11
The Patagonia Connection	15
E.S.P. (Extra-Sensory Perception)	72
The Briefest Encounter	88
The Mills of God	99
A Little Old Lady	109
The Master and His Ship	119
A Charismatic Skipper	120

The Christmas Spirit	129
Unashamed Name-Dropping	143
The Brooch	155
Easter Sundays	186
Obsession	190
The Arab Beggar	195
My Lucky Star	201
What Price Loyalty	209
Of Affluence and Effluence	216
Decline of the Old Red Duster	272
Epilogue	280

DEDICATION

This book is dedicated to all my former shipmates whose loyalty to their employers was never in question, but who's loyalties were often taken too much for granted.

GDW
Mersea Island
August 2003

ACKNOWLEDGEMENTS

I am grateful to my cousin Huw Williams for his detailed contribution to the 'Patagonia Connection'. To Captain Ken Goody, Harbourmaster, Colchester, Hythe Quay. Also Denis Horrigan, MBE, East Donyland Council. Squadron Leader James Wellerd was especially helpful in aiding the typography and layout of my original collection of stories that form the basis of this book. To Bernard Durnford, my publisher for his invaluable advice during the long gestation period of this book.

My grateful thanks to cousin Huw Williams for much of the details, letters and the Family Tree, the relevant section of which is included in this narrative.

And, thanks to the good offices of a local Councillor, Dennis Horrigan I was able to contact my old friend Captain Ken Goody at his home in Old Heath, Colchester where he now lives in retirement. Ken made me most welcome and within the hour I spent with him I was able to glean all the information I required in preparation for this narrative. A short but accurate account of my career from 'Affluence to Effluence'.

Gwilym D. Williams
Mersea Island
August 2003

FOREWORD

My greatest pleasure is reading of the sea, the ships and of those who have sailed around the world. The tales of the early explorers, who, often at great peril, charted the distant lands; the epic stories of the fighting tall ships in Elizabethan times; the tragedies and bravery shown, in convoys, during the First and Second World Wars. Sea romances and reminiscences are compulsive reading.

Not myself a seafarer, it was my good fortune to have spent all my working life in shipping and to have been closely associated with the navigators, the apprentices, the junior and senior officers and the Masters, who, like the Author of this book, rose to take command of their own cargo and passenger ships. Friendships formed fifty and more years ago have remained and now, long retired, count among my closest friends.

The experiences of Captain Williams and his commentary on shipping will give pleasure to all and will strike a special chord in: -

'They that go down to the sea in ships
And occupy their business in great waters,
These men see the works of the Lord
And his wonders in the deep.'

Gerry Dalton
Operations Manager
Cunard Line

The Author as an apprentice aged 17

He stoops to conquer

"The Patagonia Connection"
INTRODUCTION

From circa 1853 onwards the Argentine Government devised various measures to attract immigrants from all over Europe with promises of huge grants of land to families prepared to cultivate the barren wasteland steppes of Patagonia.

An ardent Welshman, Michael D. Jones succeeded in persuading several others to join him in this adventure. History records that 153 of these courageous folk sailed from Liverpool in the 'clipper-ship' "Mimosa" on the 25th May 1865 for Puerto Madryn.

They must have been heartbroken when they arrived at this so-called 'Promised Land' in the middle of a Patagonian Winter. Their earliest crops were a disastrous failure and were it not for occasional 'hand-outs' by the Argentine Government they would have starved.

But with typical Welsh stubbornness and perseverance their little settlement began to prosper until today their territory in and about the Chubut Valley contains over 12,000 descendants from those original pioneers.

Although Spanish is now their native tongue taught in all the schools thousands of these descendants still speak Welsh fluently. Among the present population of over 150,000 the names of 'Evans', 'Jones', 'Hughes', 'Parry' and 'Williams' can be found everywhere while the town of Trelew is named after Lewis Jones one of the original settlers. And the largest building in the town is Saint David's Hall where each November the annual Festival and Eisteddfod is held.

"The Patagonia Connection"

In a corner of the churchyard surrounding St. Cynog's Church, Ystradgynlais, there lies a grave, on the headstone of which, neatly and clearly engraved, is the following inscription: -

IN

LOVING MEMORY

OF

WATCYN WILLIAM PRITCHARD WILLIAMS
Who died April 20th. 1912 Aged 80 Years

Also MATILDA His Widow
Died June 22nd. 1921 Aged 62 Years

Also GWILYM THOMAS WILLIAMS Their Son
Died & Buried in Ashanti, West Africa
November 18th. 1916 Aged 36 Years

Also WATCYN WESLEY WILLIAMS Brother
Of the First-Named-Died April 30th. 1915
Aged 77 Years

"Each Call Was Short & The Shock Severe,
To Part From Those We Loved So Dear,
Our Loss Is Great, We Won't Complain,
We Hope, Through Christ, To Meet Again."

The Above Brothers & Their Sister Formed Part of 150 Welsh Settlers in the Chubut Valley, Patagonia, 1865

"The Immediate Williams Family"

GWILYM THOMAS WILLIAMS. Father.
Born - July, 1881, Pontypridd, Glamorgan, South Wales.
Died - 18th. November, 1916 - (Malaria) Obuasi, Gold Coast, (Ghana),
West Africa. Buried in European Cemetery. Ashanti Gold-Fields.

MARGARET ADA, (neé Evans). Mother.
Born - 14th. May, 1882 - "Rose Cottage', Ynyscedwyn, Ystradgynlais, Breconshire, South Wales.
Married - 24th February, 1906. 'St. Cynog's Church, Ystradgynlais.
Officiating Clergy, Rev. E.J.D. Glanley & Rev. D.J. Teague.
Died - 8th. March, 1959. Manor Park, East Ham, London, E12.
(Ashes at Romford Crematorium, Essex).

EVA WINIFRED MAUDE.
Born - 8th July, 1908 at 'Pelresfa', Ystalyfera, Glamorgan, South Wales.
Married - Major Kistrick - (Divorced), Married II, James Day Esq. No Issue.
Died - 29th August, 1983. (Ashes in St. David's Church, Ystalyfera).

CEDRIC WATCYN.
Born - 1st. February, 1910 at 'Pelresfa', Ystalyfera, Glamorgan, South Wales.
Married - Helen (neé Morgan).
Issue, Edward Tudor.
Died - 25th. August, 1940 - Squadron Leader, Royal Air Force.
(Battle of Britain - One of 'The Few')

MATILDA GWENLLIAN.
Born - 30th. January 1912 at 'Pelresfa', Ystalyfera, Glamorgan, South Wales.
Married - 1937 Robert Pearson, Rowhedge, Nr. Colchester, Essex.
Issue - Two daughters, Wendy and Leslie Veday.
Died - 8th May 2001

GWILYM DENNIS. (Author)
Born - 7th. May, 1915 at "Glanffrwd', Ynyscedwyn, Ystradgynlais.
Married - Joan Novello (nee Mathews) 5th October 1948 Lawford Church, Essex.
Issue - Three Daughters Carol-Anne Margaret, Twins - Jane Denise and Julie Novello.

OBITUARY

Death of Old Welsh Patagonia Colonist

1912

At the advanced age of 80 years the death occurred on Saturday morning at Penrhos, Ystradgynlais, of Watcyn William Pritchard Williams. He had been in declining health for some time but only confined to his bed about two months ago.

Deceased was a native of Barmouth, North Wales but when a young man he had moved to Liverpool where he became apprenticed to the grocery trade. After serving seven years he became a grocer's traveller for Liverpool and District a vocation he followed for several years.

Mr. Williams was an ardent Welshman and when the movement for establishing a Welsh colony in Patagonia was started about the year 1862 he threw himself enthusiastically into it. Eventually a Committee was formed which finally decided that Patagonia, a province in the southern part of Argentina in South America, offered the best inducement.

Deceased took a very active part in the work of the Committee, others being, Professor Michael D. Jones of Bala, Mr. Hugh Hughes of Cadfon, Mr. Owen Edwards of Liverpool and another Mr. Hughes, a coal merchant who assisted the project financially. In 1865 a party of 153 men, women and children, all of Welsh extraction left Liverpool in the sailing vessel 'Mimosa' bound for Puerto Madryn in Patagonia. Together with his brother Watcyn Wesley and his sister Elizabeth Louise, (the late Mrs. Humble) Mr. Williams lived in the Chubut for two years then left for Patagonia 200 miles to the north where they remained for nine years.

In 1870 Watcyn William Pritchard returned to Wales where he married Miss. Matilda Fisher of Pontypridd. After a few months sojourn in his native land he returned with his bride to Patagonia for another three years. Once again he returned to the old country and spent five years in Pontypridd but the longing for his adopted country was so strong that he again returned there, now with his little family of two boys, Edwin, Gwilym Thomas and their little sister Elizabeth Louise, back to the Chubut Valley. And remained there until 1890 when they left for Chile where they engaged in wheat-farming for nine years.

Eventually they returned to Wales in 1899 to finally settle down in Ystalyfera in the Swansea Valley where he became proprietor of an 'ice-cream & soda-fountain shop and billiard-hall. Watcyn William Pritchard Williams will long be remembered for his great interest in mathematics and he became a keen advocate of the metric system, translating it into Welsh. Later still he became interested in the dozenal system and published an explanatory treatise even designing an ingenious system of numerals with special figures being manufactured in order to illustrate and demonstrate his new revolutionary ideas.

In this respect he received many letters of acknowledgement from eminent scholars including President Roosevelt and ex-King Alfonso of Spain together with dozens of letters from heads of several universities throughout Great Britain.

In disposition the deceased was a quiet and genial gentlemen who readily earned the respect of all with whom he came into contact. His enthusiasm for the Welsh Colony in Patagonia was ever aflame and he would talk for hours on the glorious prospects of that country made fertile by his fellow-countrymen. He leaves a widow and a family of three, two sons and a daughter. His brother Watcyn Wesley now aged 71 lives with his eldest son Edwin in Ystradgynlais.

The Patagonia Connection
PREFACE

Patagonia is the southernmost province of Argentina. The territory stretches southward from the 45th. parallel for over six-hundred miles to Tierra Del Fuego and the Magellan Straits. From the Atlantic seaboard westward to the Andes mountain-range and the border with Chile on the Pacific coast.

Vast beds of gravel, six-hundred miles long, two-hundred miles wide and approximately fifty feet deep are a result of huge mountain-ranges worn down glacially.

The three members of the Williams family who sailed from Liverpool to Puerto Madryn on the clipper-ship "Mimosa" in May 1865 were the two brothers, Watcyn William Pritchard, Watcyn Wesley and their sister Elizabeth Louise.

In 1870, leaving his brother and sister in Patagonia, Watcyn William Pritchard returned to Pontypridd to marry his childhood sweetheart Matilda Fisher. Over the next eight years their union was blessed with two boys and a girl. The eldest boy Edwin (my Uncle), Gwilym Thomas (my Father) and Elizabeth Louise the second (my Aunty Elw).

Twenty years later, in 1890, Watcyn William Pritchard and family and the brother Watcyn Wesley returned home to Wales and settled in the Swansea Valley. Meanwhile, the older Elizabeth Louise had married a local general-practitioner, Doctor Jorge Humble. To repeat what may be construed as a family tradition their union was also blessed with two boys and a girl, Jorge Guillermo, Charles Arturo and Marie Lellita thus establishing for all time the Williams' "Patagonia Connection".

"Mimosa"

LLOYD'S LIST INDEX

(Clipper-Ship 'Mimosa')

Built 1853 by A. Hall of Aberdeen, Scotland.
Official Number 1973 Identity 'Clipper'.
Wooden Ship Copper-Sheathed.
Length 139 feet 9 inches. Beam 25 feet 5 inches.
Height 15 feet 5 inches.
410 Gross Tons.

1854 Departed Shanghai Destination Unknown.
12th. Sept. 1856 - 18th. Jan. 1857 Shanghai to London.
24th. Oct. 1863 - 3rd Mar. 1864 Foochow to London.
20th. Feb. to 4th. Apr. 1865 Converted to Passenger Ship.
25th. May 1865 Sailed from Liverpool to Puerto Madryn,
Patagonia, Argentina.
153 Welsh Emigrants.

Arrived Puerto Madryn 22nd. July 1865.

Captain Pepperill-Montalvo. Master.

"The Patagonia Connection"

By
Gwilym D. Williams
(Master Mariner)

After nearly half-a-century of a seagoing career I had finally "swallowed the anchor", my wife and I retired to the attractive bungalow we had bought on Mersea Island. The island lies just off the coast of ESSEX to which it is joined by a narrow umbilical causeway known as "The Strood" and nine miles from the town of Colchester (the oldest recorded town in Britain). At high water (springs) the tide covers the Strood to a depth of several feet when all traffic is brought to a halt thus making Mersea an island in every respect.

It was two years later, Sunday 1st March, 1980 (St. David's Day) Joan and I settled-down in our respective arm-chairs to watch a television programme entitled "A Valley In The Desert" produced by Selwyn Roderick for the BBC and a running commentary by Sir Huw Wheldon in his most inimitable style.

The programme was devoted to the development of Patagonia by a group of Welsh immigrants who had sailed from Liverpool on 28th May 1865 on board the converted clipper-ship "Mimosa". It told the story of how, after years of blood, sweat and tears, they turned this bleak, barren and hostile wilderness into what is today a flourishing, fertile and rich province of Argentina.

The programme held a special significance for me as my paternal grandparents were among those courageous pioneers. My Father, Gwilym Thomas Williams; his older brother, (my Uncle Edwin) and their sister Elizabeth Louise (my Auntie Elw) attended school when old enough to do so and helping with the domestic chores at all other times. It was a hard, tough life for them all.

My 'nostalgia cup' overflowed as the programme with Huw Weldon's commentary described how, within three years of occupation in the Chubut Valley of Patagonia these Welsh pioneers were producing their own newspaper. My admiration for them knew no bounds when Sir Huw went on to say the editor of its successor "Y Drafed" is now Señora Irma Hughes de Jones. And that a second publication called "Ein Breiniad" was the first 'printed' newspaper in the whole of the South Americas!

Year after year, with increasing numbers arriving in Patagonia from Wales and other European countries, the earlier settlers sought pastures further westward right up to the foothills of the mighty Andes Mountains. Here they found rivers, mountain streams and lakes surrounded by trees and verdant green pastures. Someone was heard to exclaim, "Oh, what a beautiful valley" - and from that very moment it was given the name "Cym Hyfred" where, today, lies the town of "Trevelyn". Here also are the two large freshwater lakes "Perin" and "Padern" that nestle under the towering peak they named "Gorsedd-y-Cwmwyl" (The Throne of the Clouds).

Sir Huw even mentioned a street in Gaiman called "Michael Jones" where now stands a Secondary School above the door of which is inscribed, "Nyd Byd byd heb Wybodaeth", (There would be no world without Knowledge). And the headmistress Señora Roberto de Gonzales speaks fluent Welsh! As a matter of fact the deeper one travels in Patagonia the more one hears Welsh spoken. And in nearly all the chapels in the country the Big Day of the Year is July 28th. The anniversary of the arrival of the "Mimosa" at Puerto Madryn in 1865.

In his commentary Sir Huw described how the past and present now co-exists in Gaiman and that the very first house built in the village, 'Number 234' in John C. Evans Street, is still occupied. Furthermore, the railway these pioneers built from the Chubut

Valley to Puerto Madryn, fifty miles away, was the southernmost railway in the whole of South America.

And when Sir Huw Wheldon pointed out the Memorial erected to the memory of Richard Davie, John Hughes and John Parry the inscription records in Welsh that they had been killed by native Indians in 1885. I remembered my Mother telling us how my Father had described how some Indians had been friendly while others had been downright hostile. A lump came into my throat when Sir Huw described how these early pioneers had harnessed the waters of the River Chubut by digging hundreds of canals with their bare hands and the most primitive tools.

Now, over a hundred years later the descendants of those early Welsh pioneers enjoy the fruits of their labour. Where the more modern towns and villages in Patagonia have the comforts of electricity brought over five-hundred miles from the Andes Mountains and to supply the huge aluminium smelter by the sea near Puerto Madryn. Maybe very few workers there today speak Welsh but in the towns and villages nearby the Welsh Founders are officially remembered. As, for instance, the name Lewis Jones is found in dozens of places - hence the name, "Trelew" is a town much larger than any in Wales itself.

When the programme ended I sat staring at the television screen for minutes without saying a word. I felt mixed emotions of pride and sadness for what those Welsh Pioneers had suffered and achieved. But most of all a certain feeling of guilt when realising how close to Patagonia I had been on numerous voyages to the Argentine in the early 1930's but, in those days, air travel was yet to come.

The next day, with the television programme "A Valley in the Desert" still lingering on my mind I began rummaging through boxes of photographs and memorabilia until I found what I'd been seeking, a photograph of the grave in St. Cynog's Churchyard in Ystradgynlais. And it was that which inspired me to write to Selwyn Roderick to congratulate him on his splendid programme and the sincere commentary by Sir Huw Wheldon.

In my letter to Selwyn Roderick I also mentioned having seen a very interesting article in the popular nautical magazine "Sea Breezes" dated February 1986 a part of which I quoted: -

".... and on September 25th. 1965 the Argentine Government issued an 'Eight Peso Stamp' to commemorate the centenary of the Welsh colonisation of Patagonia. The stamp design shows the tea clipper "Mimosa" which had been especially converted into a passenger-carrying vessel for this voyage and it is shown against the background of the Province of Chubut where these Welsh folk had built their first settlement."

Needless to say I was delighted to receive a reply from Selwyn Roderick which is reproduced within this narrative. I now became obsessed with the desire to write my own version of these events, not necessarily with ambitions of having it published but for the interest of my children - and their progeny!!! Perhaps it is understandable I am a little saddened that our marriage, although blessed with three beautiful daughters, fate has denied us the prospect of continuity with a male heir.

Be all that as it may, a great deal has been written about Patagonia and the early Welsh settlers there. Much of it by more accomplished writers and in more detail than I could ever hope to achieve. This narrative concerns itself narrowly with my forbears who were among the 153 Welsh pioneers who sailed in the "Mimosa" but more especially with my grandfather's sister Elizabeth Louise who married Doctor Jorge Arturo Humble, thus forging the link I chose to call "The Patagonia Connection".

If one is tempted to ask, "From what date does one begin to trace a 'Family Tree'?" - one might just as well ask, "How long is a piece of string?" It is possible my family name 'Williams' is derived from 'William, Duke of Normandy'. And his marriage to Matilda of Flanders may account for the number of ladies in my family who bear that name. And is my given name of 'Gwilym' a mere simplification of the French 'Guillaume'?

As a schoolboy I remember the seasonal arrival in the Swansea Docks of the French sailing-cutters whose crews would then cycle up the valleys in South Wales and, from their broad shoulders would be slung strings of onions which they would sell door to door. Their Breton patois so like the Welsh language they could converse freely with the valley folk. During school holidays I would often stay with relatives in Swansea and nothing gave me greater pleasure than a stroll around the docks admiring the French luggers moored alongside and to smell the heavy mixture of tarred-rope tarpaulins, pitch and the all-pervading smell of onions!!

For the purpose of my narrative and the Patagonia Connection I had to start my quest somewhere, and where better than with the marriage in 1758 of a certain wine-merchant, Thomas Williams living at Number 13 Whitechapel, Liverpool, to a very handsome young Welsh lady named Elizabeth. And that union was blessed with the birth of a son who was baptised in her home town of Llanaber, North Wales on March 2nd. 1788.

When old enough, young Watcyn decided on a seagoing career and eventually, having obtained the necessary qualification became a certificated watchkeeping ship's 'Mate'. In those days Barmouth was a thriving seaport on the Cardiganshire coast. And the famous Penrhyn Quarries supplied much of the world's roofing slate a large proportion of it exported from Barmouth. Little did Watcyn know one of his descendants would have his memoirs published entitled "From The Captain's Table" (although the author would have preferred "The Reluctant Sailor"!!!).

But Watcyn Williams had problems of his own. It was at some time during this period that Watcyn the elder was captured by the French during the Napoleonic War (1803-1815) and became a prisoner-of-war.

He met and courted Mair (Mary) Huws, known to her intimates as "Mair Gwilym" and on 7th. February 1829 they were married and settled in a house called 'Glanyglasfor' in Abermaw near Barmouth. While Watcyn was away at sea in 1837 Mary wrote the song "To Hope" which is included in "A Scrapbook of English Poetry" now held in the 'National Library of Wales' (Mss 109310 - 314).

In 1843 Mair translated into Welsh the book "Heavenly World" written by J. Edmonson and the book is inscribed by her to her brother Gwilym and sister Elizabeth Huws a copy of which is held by my second-cousin Huw Williams, (Uncle Edwin's grandson) and Alun's father.

But to return to Watcyn and Mair. They had six children, three boys and three girls, all of whom were baptised in Llanaber Parish Church by the then incumbent rector John Jones in manner following: - Elizabeth was baptised July 4th. 1830, - Watcyn Pritchard on April 15th. 1832, - Mary Nancy on October 9th. 1833, - Elizabeth Louise 1834, - Watcyn Wesley on April 11th. 1838 and Charles Thomas in July 1839. Sadly, of the six children born and baptised only three survived to maturity, Watcyn Pritchard, Watcyn Wesley and Elizabeth Louise.

It is recorded he was Master of the sloop "Valiant" when he died November 2nd. 1862 at the age of 74 and was duly buried in the churchyard at St. Asaph. There is no record of how, where or why the family removed from their home, "Glanyglasfor" to Birkenhead.

There is even less known of the three surviving children after their parents, Captain Watcyn and Mair were dead and buried. There is however, mention of a grocery business in Birkenhead so it is assumed the two boys, Watcyn Pritchard and Watcyn Wesley looked after the business while their unmarried sister Elizabeth Louise kept house for them.

From about 1853 onwards successive Argentine Governments had devised various measures with which to attract agricultural workers from various European countries. Contracts were made in which there was a promise of grants of land. An ardent Welsh Nationalist, Michael D. Jones had for years been convinced there must be somewhere in the world where a Welsh colony could be established to preserve the Welsh language, customs, culture and their Non-Conformist religion.

He had been impressed by the Argentine Government's tempting offers of land, sheep, horses and grain for a whole twelve months from the date of landing in the Province. And Patagonia seemed ideally remote from other peoples and cultures in which to preserve the Welsh culture he so ardently championed. But our Mr. Jones had never been to Patagonia so he had no idea about the bleak, desolate nature of the country he was now choosing, other than that it 'appeared' to be ideal for the purpose!

To their unbounded joy they discovered the tea-clipper "Mimosa" was available in between the tea trade from China and the wool trade from Australia. She had been built by Alexander Hall of Aberdeen in 1853 - of 410 tons gross with a length of 139ft. 9ins. a beam of 25ft. 9ins. and a depth of 15ft. 6ins. She was a fully rigged ship with a raised fo'c'sle and a raised quarterdeck. Her official number was 1973 and her signal letters HFMN and with a fair wind astern she was capable of up to sixteen knots.

Cabin spaces had been improvised by dividing the cargo holds with stout timbers and boards, but without the provision of port-holes her passengers would not enjoy the benefit of natural light. Certainly no cruise ship her passengers were to be carried at 'steerage rates' of £12.0s.0d per adult. Within a relatively short time the number of volunteers had grown to over two-hundred but as alterations to the "Mimosa" neared completion the enthusiasm began to wane.

It would appear the two Williams brothers and their sister became drawn into the orbit of these gullible people who were over-eager to take up the apparently-generous offers from the Argentine Government. A committee was formed led by Michael D. Jones, with Huw Huws Cedron, Owen Edwards of Liverpool and a coal-merchant named Hughes who promised financial support.

For a variety of reasons, including fears of the long and tedious passage southwards, with the prospect of seasickness began to take its toll. Some were fearful of having to endure hardship and privation in an unknown and hostile country. There were others who were dissuaded by friends and relatives, as witness the letters received by the Williams trio: -

(Letters to to Watcyn Wesley Williams from his relative John Jones "Talaharin" - the originals of which are held in the National Gallery of Wales, Aberystwyth, voicing his concern about the intended emigration to Patagonia.) : -

2 St. Helen's Place;
LONDON,
Good Friday 1865

Dear Watcyn;

I enclose my 'carte visite' (it is the last one I have). Of all the wild mad schemes that have turned-up of late, the wildest and maddest is this 'Patagonia Scheme'. Against enthusiasm I may hold my tongue therefore, I can but hope (hoping against hope) that you will be successful, comfortable and happy. I also hope the Indians (who will eat you bodily just to confound their indigestion). And with every kind wish for your welfare,

I remain faithfully,
Your Uncle or Cousin, (whichever you choose)
Ino Jones, "Talaharin".

And another: -
The reader will appreciate the Welsh language is very expressive, even musical, and when translated into English it gives the impression of being somewhat 'quaint' Thus: -

2 St. Helens Place;
LONDON, E,C.
21st. April, 1865

Dear Cousin;

I duly received your farewell note on your approaching departure for Patagonia. I know too little of the country and of the object of the intended Welsh colony there to be able to offer any kind of advice. May you and your fellow-migrants prosper and be happy there, and I shall be glad to hear that you will be also. With kindest regards to your sister and brother, wishing you all a safe and pleasant voyage to your new home.

I remain, etc etc etc

Little wonder by the time the conversion of the 'Mimosa' from tea-clipper to passenger-ship was completed, and in all respects ready for sea, the numbers had dwindled to a mere 153. The conditions on the passenger tickets specified that the ship owner would provide each person with 'three quarts of water daily (apart from that allowed for cooking) - and a weekly allowance of 3½ lbs. of bread or biscuit, 11 lbs. wheat-flour, 1½ lbs. oatmeal, 1½ lbs. sugar, 1½ ozs. mustard, ½ oz. white or black pepper, 2 ozs. salt, and a gill of vinegar.

Well, at least, they were not going to starve!!!

And so it was, with the conversion of 'Mimosa' completed and, in all respects ready for sea, she slipped her moorings and sailed from Liverpool on the 25th. May 1865. On board were 153 intrepid Welsh emigrants bound southward into the unknown - but history records they were singing their favourite hymns all the way down the River Mersey and well beyond "Bar Lightship".

Even then it was with great difficulty they were able to tear their eyes away from the rapidly fading coastline of North Wales and the mountains of Anglesey. Ahead of them now lay over 7,000 miles of ocean before their eventual arrival at their destination. Down the Irish Sea, St. George's Channel and across the Bay of Biscay for over a week the 'Mimosa' would carry a 'bone in her teeth' under a full press of sail and the brisk north-east trade winds.

Then would follow days of laying becalmed in the pitiless glare of the sun between the Tropic of Cancer and the Tropic of Capricorn in the area known as 'The Doldrums' with torrential rain one minute and a relentless sun the next. This is the area loved by the Dolphin, the Porpoise and the Flying-Fish. It had been early Spring when they waved farewell to friends and relatives in Liverpool but it would be in the depths of Winter in the land to which they were now heading.

After a passage of 83 days at a poor average of less than 4 knots, they landed at Puerto Madryn on the 28th July 1865. They must have been heartbroken when they reached this 'promised land' in the middle of a Patagonian Winter. Although the Argentine Government had stipulated 'agricultural workers' only four of these settlers came under this category. So, needless to say, they were an ill-selected company for an agricultural settlement and as a result they suffered terrible privation for several years. Their early crop-planting was a calamitous failure and they would certainly have starved but for the regular supplies of food sent them annually by the Argentine Government and occasionally by a British warship.

There is a letter in the National Library of Wales in Aberystwyth written by Watcyn Pritchard Williams in which he describes the voyage of the 'Mimosa' from start to finish. There is also mention of these Welsh colonists in the book "This Way Southward" written by A.F. Tschiffly, and another study of the colonisation of the Chubut Valley in that period from 1865 to 1915 entitled "The Desert and the Dream" written by Glyn Williams. Much more detailed accounts and by more competent writers than I because my narrative is a blinkered vision focussed on my immediate family.

As the gallant band of Welsh folk on board 'Mimosa' gazed with considerable dismay at the forbidding coastline bordering on Puerto Madryn, how could they have known that 33 years earlier His Majesty's Ship "Beagle" had anchored in this identical spot? Or that the ship's Master, Captain Fitzroy and the world-famous scientist Charles Darwin had both formed a very low opinion of such desolation?

On 'Mimosa' 153 pairs of eyes grew thoughtful and troubled. Had they, after all, made the right decision in coming to this God-Forsaken country? But, they had come this far and it looked as though they would have to make the best of it. After all, the Argentine Government had advertised for agricultural workers and only four of them came within this category. Their prospects must have seemed appalling, for all they found beyond the beaches was desert covered only by a thorny scrub and without signs of water anywhere.

After days of exhausting marches, and approximately forty miles from Puerto Madryn across this arid plain, they came across the Chubut River. And it was here they decided to establish the first Welsh Settlement. There were no mechanical implements to help them till the land - So in the first few years when their crops failed they would have starved but for the food regularly supplied by the Argentine Government.

A small group of the Welsh party that sailed in the Mimosa. Arrowed in the back row Watcyn William Pritchard and brother Watcyn Wesley Williams.

The Chubut River winds and twists its sluggish way through the arid desert plains and these early settlers all but starved before learning how to harness and utilise its crystal-clear waters. Almost with bare hands and the most primitive tools they dug a system of irrigation canals and ditches which, ultimately ran for fifty miles to the sea. And all of it by blood sweat and not a few bitter tears.

For those first years there were few if any farm implements and the first machinery to arrive was owned, not by individuals, but by the co-operative Welsh farmers, each of whom had been granted a hundred acres of valley land. Their circumstances and sheer isolation forced them to work together for survival - and by the Grace of God they certainly survived.

It was the local Araucanian Indians who helped them the most, teaching them how to use the 'lasso' and the 'bolas' when hunting wild animals such as the Guanaco. In return, the settlers taught them agriculture, how to prepare and cook healthy balanced meals, until there grew a firm and lasting friendship between them.

Strictly speaking however, not all the Indians were friendly, some were downright hostile, some even murderous, but all tended to be thievish. One of the many tales handed down by the family tells how Elizabeth Louise had made a delicious tart and had put it on a window-sill to cool. And later, when she went to retrieve it the tart had disappeared!

And while her brothers toiled in the fields of their one-hundred acre plot and helped with the canals and irrigation ditches, Elizabeth Louise busied herself from dawn to dusk taking care of their creature comforts. Although there was little time for socialising the brothers could not help noticing that their sister had become attracted to the local general-practitioner Doctor Jorge Arturo Humble who noticeably returned her affections!

Of the three members of the Williams family who sailed to Patagonia in the 'Mimosa;' May 25th. 1865 Watcyn William Pritchard, Watcyn Wesley and their sister Elizabeth Louise. It was she who married Doctor Jorge Humble and established the Argentinian branch of the family.

"THE PATAGONIA CONNECTION"

Elizabeth Louise Williams

M

Doctor Jorge Humble

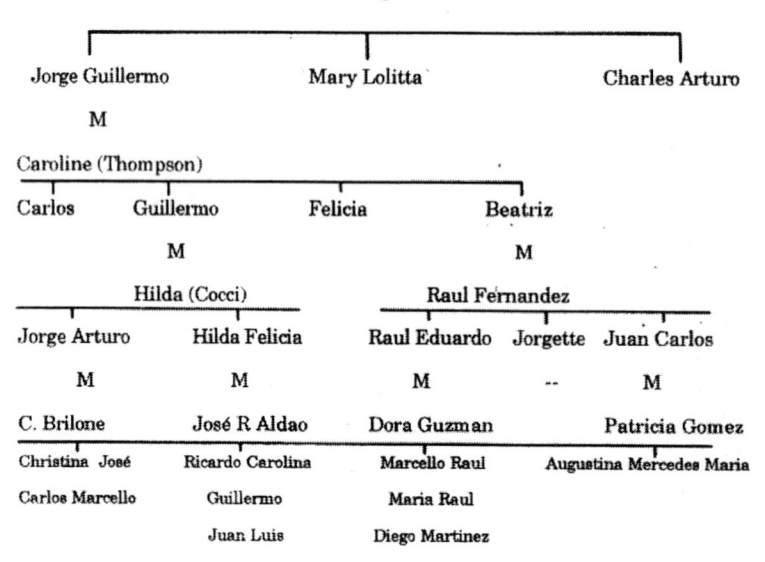

Jorge Guillermo	Mary Lolitta	Charles Arturo
M		

Caroline (Thompson)

Carlos	Guillermo	Felicia	Beatriz
	M		M
	Hilda (Cocci)		Raul Fernandez

Jorge Arturo	Hilda Felicia	Raul Eduardo	Jorgette	Juan Carlos
M	M	M	--	M
C. Brilone	José R Aldao	Dora Guzman		Patricia Gomez
Christina José	Ricardo Carolina	Marcello Raul		Augustina Mercedes Maria
Carlos Marcello	Guillermo	Maria Raul		
	Juan Luis	Diego Martinez		

ET - SEQ

The Indians seem friendly

Mothyr,
Trelew, Chubut,
Argentinia, S. America
July 10th, 1887

By PEREDUR EVANS

DEAR TOMOS,
It is now three months since our departure from Liverpool and I can assure you that a great deal has happened since then.

As you know, The Mimosa was the name of the ship and I am full of praise to its builders for designing such a remarkably strong ship.

It carried us across the ocean and bore many violent storms and apart from an unfortunate man who died from dysentery, the journey was successful. It took us over two months altogether and we landed in Argentina three weeks ago.

We landed in Port Madryn, which is named after one of the first Welshmen who arrived here. It is an ideal place for landing and situated on a beautiful beach that stretches for miles on each side. We were amazed at the sight of the setting sun on the horizon and the sea seemed to be glistening in the powerful rays of the majestic sun.

However, we were soon disappointed when, after travelling a mile or two inland found not the lush green grass of the prairies, but an empty country of mile upon mile of dust and dry land.

At first, we scanned the horizon for any sign of civilisation but only the flat, dry land was to be seen with an occasional scrub-like bush to break the monotony.

The Quechua Indians seem very friendly although we haven't talked to them yet. They are a light-brown coloured tribe and are to be seen galloping in great clouds of dust across the barren landscape.

The Indians ride handsome horses and wear nothing more than a colourful garment from their waists to their knees. I was astonished when I first saw them, for they are so wild-looking and yet so spectacular to watch.

We are, at the moment, waiting for one of the Welshmen from the first group of settlers to come and lead us to the new village. To do this, we will have to travel on foot along the winding Chubut River and eventually reach our longed-for destination.

Many of our party have already lost confidence after the shock of the first sighting of the land.

To be honest with you, my heart sank too when I first saw the desert-like land, but after reminding myself of the severe living conditions in Wales, I soon became excited at the prospect of joining a new colony of Welsh people in a far away land.

A feeling of homesickness comes over me every night as I lie awake staring up at the crystal stars.

I cannot stop my mind from wandering to Wales and to the comfortable bed in which I used to lie. I often hear Mam's voice still ringing in my ears and Dad's deep voice persuading me to stay in South Wales. Then, after I refuse, I hear Mam crying and Dad comforting her.

Those sudden pains come to me often and although I am glad of my freedom from Wales, I long for my parents and the friends I left behind.

On this note, I'll finish my letter and send my regards to everyone in my homeland.

With loving memories,
Dai Ty Mothyr

Extracts From the Diary of
WATCYN WILLIAM PRITCHARD WILLIAMS
(Grandad)

Translated From the Original Welsh

1891

Thurs. 3rd. Sept. I worked with wood, making a chair and worked some more after lunch. Gwilym shepherding. Elw preparing food. We put in eight more furrows to finish the beans. A cloudy seasonal morning. Edwin starting to plough the land ready for next season. Me still working at the chair. Matilda and Elw doing housework. Gwilym doing the shepherding. The chair is almost finished. It rained a little later.

Fri. 4th Sept. We had showers before and after lunch but it turned fair after a heavy shower. I've started to hew wood for the second chair. Rowland John and son Frank, with Howard Davis have gone to fetch firewood. When they were coming home the cart sank and six oxen couldn't move it. We had to unload some of the wood. I saw them pass by the hill here. After lunch I went into town, Gaiman, seeking a cow. I had the history of one and I'll see it tomorrow to decided whether to buy it. Matilda weeding. Edwin Shepherding. Gwilym and Elw brought their Mother home from the field. A very pleasant afternoon. There's a new moon tonight. A good sign I hope.

Sat. 5th. Sept. A very cold foggy morning. After milking and eating breakfast I put bread in the oven. Matilda and I went to town and bought cow for 53 pesos. A man named Jose Valmar will come and buy the ram. He brought the cow and calf to join other animals. We saw another too we'll hear more in our cicle? sic again. After gathering in the animals I went into the house but Gwilym didn't say Eurig hadn't gone with Gordon and Coluido. He went to work in the town.

Sun. 6th. Sept. A cloudy morning again but fairly seasonal Eurig was here again today and took two oxen to town with

Paraese and Rinaldo. In the afternoon Anselmo came very late indeed with brother Oliver, a girl and her father. Anselmo told the story of the uproar that had been in town yesterday. They had put Señor Canales in as Governor instead of the other one who would have run away with it! It seems they had changed the officers. Things are rather odious at present with relations in the civil war although they say it is over. When Anselmo went away I went with him to the other end of the farm. The butcher was here today and took the ram away with him. This was his share and paid for the cow I had bought. We own the bull ourselves now. After Oliver had read we went home and the animals came into the fold and I read a poem.

Mon. 7th. Sept. A fair morning, stormy yet temperate day. Edwin and his Mother went down to the river with a sack of coal-bricks where they put them all down whole. I was making another chair in the morning. After lunch Elw and her Mother went to Mathias' house to see his wife and the new baby. Also went to see Mrs Watkins and were late getting home and there was work to be done. I went to see Gwilym shepherding while Edwin was at home with various jobs to be done.

(Errors in translation readily and graciously forgiven)

As I have said before, it had taken years of blood, sweat and bitter tears but the stubborn pioneers were now at last beginning to reap the rewards of their labours. The homesteads were thriving and there were many more immigrants pouring into the country. But for the Williams family the call of their native country grew increasingly persistent. Thus, when offered a satisfactory price for his farm Watcyn Pritchard Williams made up his mind to sell up. In 1899 he and his wife Matilda, Edwin aged 20, Gwilym Thomas aged 18 and Elw 15 years old duly sailed from Puerto Madryn. It had been agreed Watcyn Wesley would remain behind in Patagonia to give his sister Elizabeth Louise and his brother-in-law Jorge Arturo some moral and physical support until the others became settled in Wales.

Which they did, on disembarking in Swansea they stayed temporarily with relative in Port Tennant, a suburb of Swansea. Eventually they found suitable premises thirteen miles up the Swansea Valley in Ystalyfera, a sprawling but thriving centre of industry with coal-mines aplenty, iron-works, tinplate works and foundries in the lush confines of the valley. And it was here they set up an American style ice-cream soda fountain parlour and billiard-hall they named "Pelresfa" which is Welsh for "the place with rolling balls"!

Having been accustomed to the Argentine currency of 100 Centavos being equal to One Peso, a very simple metric system. Watcyn Williams found the British Currency of Pounds, Shillings and Pence cumbersome. So he made many attempts to publish a treatise on metrification to have the system adopted by the establishment and his efforts to this end are on record. He received many letters of acknowledgement from several heads of Universities in the U.K. From ex-President Roosevelt of America and from King Alfonso of Spain. It has been well-accepted that Watcyn William Pritchard Williams was mathematically years ahead of his time.

That the shop and billiard-hall in Ystalyfera became a financial success is not in doubt, but that the revenue to support a large and growing family is a matter for conjecture. Be that as it may, but when the eldest boy (Uncle Edwin) met and was courting Sarah Griffiths he wisely became ambitious to set-up a business on his own account. So, with financial help from his father he opened a similar establishment further up the valley in Commercial Road, Ystradgynlais and, for reasons best known to himself named it "The Temperance".

Edwin's marriage to Sarah was made perfect with the arrival of their first-born whom they named Edna Marie Louise. Then came the boy whom they christened 'Andes' after the famous mountain-range in South America. He was followed by their second daughter Audrey and last but not least a boy they named Watcyn Wesley after his grandad's brother who had by this time left Patagonia and had come to live with them in "The Temperance" but to avoid duplication of names the boy was thereafter always called Wesley.

With the sort of perseverance honed to a sharp razor's edge by the pioneering days in Patagonia Uncle Edwin made a huge success of his confectionary-cum-billiards business in Ystradgynlais. He won many accolades and prizes at the annual shows in Crystal Palace, London, especially with his secret recipe for ice-cream making him world-famous. In later years Wesley once confided in me that to make ice-cream from his father's recipe would make the price of a simple 'wafer' quite prohibitive. (what a sad reflection of our modern economy!).

On a lighter note, I have never in all my life seen or known a business premise change its contours as much as Uncle Edwin's, but many years later, long after his father had died, Wesley was obliged to change the nature of the premises by applying for a licence to sell alcoholic beverages. Thus the name "Temperance" became inappropriate but with what can only be described as a flash of inspiration he re-named it "MIMOSA".

Which brings us nearer home, (as it were) and to Gwilym Thomas, (destined to become my Father). While helping his parents in the running of the shop and billiard-hall named "Pelresfa" in Ystalyfera he had met Margaret Ada Evans the youngest daughter of Alderman David Evans, (better known as 'Evans the Foundry') a brilliant engineer who had inherited the experimental section of the 'Crane Ironworks' when its owner was declared bankrupt.

As his sweetheart Margaret Ada was a teacher at the local Primary School and Gwilym only spoke Welsh and Spanish it is evident she had to teach him English during their courtship. And in return he taught her the Patagonian skills with the lasso, the bolas and the 'throwing knife' which, in later years she would demonstrate, amuse and entertain her children and her children's children!!!

So, 'in the fullness of time' (as the saying goes) Margaret Ada and Gwilym Thomas were married on the 24th. February 1906 at St. Cynog's in Ystradgynlais where Ada was the church organist, the Rev. E. Glanley and the Rev. D. Teague officiating. After a blissful honeymoon on the Gower Coast they settled down to married life at his parent's home "Pelresfa" in Ystalyfera. It was here their first-born Eva Winifred Maude was christened in 1908, followed a couple of years later with the arrival of Cedric Watcyn and in 1912 by the birth of Matilda Gwenllian.

Watcyn William Pritchard Williams (Grandfather) and wife Matilda.

In that same year, (about the 12th. day of Christmas) the business premises "Pelresfa" were destroyed by fire and officially recorded "a malicious act of arson by person or persons unknown" but the perpetrators were never discovered. Although insurance compensation was duly paid-out the real tragedy was the loss of the livelihood for grandparents and parents alike compounded by the fact that Margaret Ada had given up her teaching profession to care for the children. Indeed, for all the Williams family the Winter 0f 1912-13 threatened to be a very bleak one - but all was not yet lost!

While the brothers Edwin and Gwilym were courting and wedding their respective spouses, their sister, Elizabeth Louise (Auntie Elw) had met and was wooed by Davy Rees Hopkins. A young man with a remarkable baritone voice. He had sung with the world-famous Carl-Rosa choir for many years before joining the equally-famous Morriston Male Voice Choir with the added advantage of it being much nearer home.

They were married on the 11th. September, 1906 the same year but a few months after Ada and Gwilym had wed. Their eldest child Valmai was born on the 7th. August 1908 and her brother Harding on 5th. July 1912. Then their second daughter May (or Maisie) on 24th. September 1914 a few weeks after the outbreak of the First World War.

Unable to continue his singing career during those bleak and uncertain war years Uncle Davy Hopkins and Aunty Elw bought a newspaper and confectionery shop having a small billiards room extension to one side and situated in Glanrhyd between Ynyscedwyn and Ystalyfera.

In passing I might as well mention that much of the upper Swansea Valley between Ystalyfera and Ystradgynlais belonged to Colonel and Mrs Gough. They were wealthy landowners who lived in "Ynyscedwyn House" almost entirely surrounded by landscaped lawns and gardens bordered by exotic varieties of Rhododendron. The colonel had made a career in the Army having served with gallantry and distinction with the South Wales Borderers and fought at the historic stand against the Zulus at Rorke's Drift, where no less than eleven Victoria Crosses had been awarded. And it was his sergeant-major, John Clee who eventually became his

Manager of the Ynyscedwyn Tin-Plate works a stone's throw from Grandad's foundry.

From the 'fire-insurance' compensation and other assets my grandparents, Gwilym Pritchard and Matilda Williams were able to buy a small but lucrative little sweet-shop in Penrhos, a half-mile above Ystradgynlais. And with some assistance from Ada's father (my maternal grandfather) 'Evans the Foundry' she and Gwilym were able to buy a small semi detached villa on the Ynyscedwyn Road midway between Ystradgynlais and Ystalyfera and not far from the 'Foundry' where Gwilym was found work.

At some time thereafter Ada's brother-in-law Tom Jones arrived home on leave from West Africa where he was employed as a carpenter by the Ashanti Gold-Fields Company. Gwilym and Tom had always been the closest of friends having earlier enjoyed cycling together. And it was Tom's lurid tales of salaries fit for a King and native servants to wait upon 'hand and foot' he finally persuaded Gwilym to apply for the post as 'Assayer' calculating the quantity of gold in the quartz they mined.

Surprised and delighted by a prompt and satisfactory response from the London Headquarters of the Ashanti Gold-Fields Company Gwilym lost no time applying for a passport and with Tom's help to purchase the necessary tropical kit. With everything falling neatly into place Gwilym was thus able to accompany his brother-in-law (Uncle Tom Jones) to Liverpool where they boarded the Elder-Dempster passenger ship "Apapa" for the three week passage to West Africa where they disembarked at Takoradi.

From Takoradi they travelled up-country by train to Kumasi, the capital of the Gold Coast (now called Ghana) thence by the Company car to the Gold Mine near the village of Obuasi. The terms of his contract with the Company required him to complete a first tour of eighteen months to earn a furlough of three months including ship passages. This meant that from the time of their arrival at the Mine in April 1913 he would not be seeing his family again until September 1914 which, at that moment, seemed nothing short of eternity.

Eventually Gwilym's first tour of eighteen-months at the Gold Mine near Obuasi came to an end and he was duly advised he could proceed home on leave. He took passage on the Elder-Dempster liner "Abinsi" which was making her maiden voyage and during the passage back to the U.K. he was presented with a silver pen-knife which I still have in my possession. He arrived home in "Glanffrwd" late one evening in September 1914 to find his wife Ada nursing their youngest daughter Matilda Gwenllian who was slowly recovering from a bout of chicken-pox. The other two, Cedric and Winifred, were asleep in their beds.

Mattie has always vowed she knew this was the night I was conceived. - Who am I to argue or deny feminine intuition? Be that as it may, I was born nine months later on the 7th. May 1915. A date which could never be described as earth-shaking if it were not for the fact that it was also the day in which the Cunard liner "Lusitania" was torpedoed by a German submarine and sank with the horrifying loss of 1198 lives - of men, women and children. Soon after, I was christened Gwilym, after my Father, and Dennis after the doctor who delivered me.

In November 1915, having completed the shorter tour of duty, my Father again returned home to the warmth and comfort of his little family and to see for the first (and last) time his newborn baby Gwilym Dennis. It was in the latter part of his third tour in West Africa that Gwilym was bitten by a mosquito and soon contracted malaria which in its most virulent form of black-water fever caused his death on 18th. November 1916. He was buried in the European section of the cemetery attached to the Gold Mine near Obuasi.

The mosquito is a tiny insect no bigger than our own gnat or midge, but where the gnat is relatively harmless the mosquito carries a parasite micro-organism called 'Anopheles'. And one bite of the mosquito, especially the pregnant female, can prove fatal - little wonder the Gold Coast earned for itself the title of "white mans' grave", but today is called 'Ghana'.

The reader will, hopefully, appreciate I was only six months old when Dad came home to Wales and the bosom of his family for the last time, so, unlike my brother Cedric and my two sisters, I have no memories of him. But as I grew older, the photograph of his grave in that gilt frame on the piano acted like a magnet to my young inquisitive eyes.

On the 31st. March 1936 my apprentice's indentures to the Hain Steamship Company expired while loading cargo for home on the Japanese coast. A few days later I was rushed into hospital in Kobe with multiple injuries when a large wooden crate fell out of the cargo-net and I was on the receiving end! In fact I spent my 21st. birthday there, thoroughly spoiled by all the hospital staff!

Thus delayed, being hospitalized and the long passage home I was late being enrolled at the Sir John Cass Nautical College in London to begin my studies to sit for the Board of Trade examination for their Certificate of Competency as a 'Second Mate Foreign Going Steamship'. I was spared having to find lodgings being able to stay instead with Aunty Nan and Uncle Tom Jones in Shepherd's Bush.

Late one night when Aunty Nan had gone to bed, Uncle Tom and I were seated on either side of the fireplace. Apropos of something said, I asked Uncle Tom about my Father's death in West Africa. He related how my Father had been delirious during the height of the fever and how suddenly, becoming calm and fully conscious he had recognised his brother-in-law (Uncle Tom) seated outside the mosquito-netting and in a whisper "begged me to look after Ada and the children", then he expired.

As Uncle Tom was telling me this I heard his voice break and tears began coursing down his furrowed cheeks. Then, with considerable effort he described how he had forced himself to make a coffin out of stout West-African teak, and afterwards arranged for the photograph to be taken of the grave!

I had come thus far in my sketchy history of the Williams family and the 'Patagonia Connection' when it dawned on me that, although there was much to add about the family who returned to Wales, there was so little about those who remained in Patagonia. It seemed the 'Patagonia Connection' was gradually losing its impetus.

For several days I had dabbled by way of a change with other literary adventures I had neglected for some time. And I even turned my attention to collecting millions of autumn-leaves that sap my energy every year. The price of a woodland habitat averaging sixteen or more plastic bags and enough compost to supply Sainsbury's with organic products forever!

Which is probably when I received that flash of inspiration. Those of you who have read my book "From the Captain's Table" will have noted I occasionally enjoy these 'flashes'. But, to be perfectly truthful 'inspiration' has little or nothing to do with the supernatural. The older one becomes the accumulation of experiences are carefully tucked away in the mental filing-cabinet to be used in stubborn problems. Unconsciously or subconsciously those little grey cells the famous Belgian detective Hercule Poirrot insists keep working day and night on one's behalf.

And once the idea entered my head it began germinating rapidly to this effect. From the factual account of the 'Patagonia Connection' to date, I conjured-up a scenario with purely fictitious characters on both sides of the family on both sides of the Atlantic. What follows is a synopsis of the script for film or television.

"THE PATAGONIA CONNECTION"
(Synopsis of Screen and/or TV Play)

Circa 1970, locality, a small village near Gaiman, Patagonia.

Teenagers Ricardo Aldao and young sister Felicia are orphaned when their parents die in an air-crash. They are now cared for by their paternal grandmother, Hilda Aldao - (neé Humble).

They are attending a Secondary School. Above the door is inscribed in Welsh, "Nyd Byd byd Heb Wybodaeth". Translated "There would be no World without Knowledge".

From Grandma they learn about Wales and the Welsh language. But Spanish is the official language of their adopted country. They are told about their forebears. Of the two brothers, Watcyn Pritchard Williams, Watcyn Wesley and their sister Elizabeth Louise who were among the group of Welsh emigrants who sailed from Liverpool on the "Mimosa" on the 23rd May 1865 bound for Puerto Madryn, Patagonia.

On leaving school Ricardo finds employment with the local newspaper "Ein Breiniad" which is printed in both Welsh and Spanish.

Circa 1979 Ricardo is called-up for National Service and joins the Argentine Army for a term of two years. (Perhaps short film clip can be obtained of early training in Army Barracks.)

Discharge from National Service is deferred by the Argentine invasion of the Falkland Islands (the Malvinas) - (Perhaps newsreel clips can be obtained from Argentine film library).

Circa 1980, Scene switches to the Officers' Mess, South Wales Borderers in Brecon.

2nd. Lieut. Richard Watcyn Williams arrives from Sandhurst and is taken on a tour of the Officers' Mess by the Adjutant. He is shown all the memorabilia of the Regiment's Historical past.

Memorabilia of Medals etc. The courageous stand at Rorke's Drift, South Africa. Eleven Victoria Crosses. He is also told about the murals adorning the walls in the Officers' Club in Caracas, Venezuela. When the peasant revolt, led by Simon Bolivar and aided by the South Wales Borderers fought the Federales of the tyrannical government. The South Wales Borderers hold the Freedom of the City of Caracas to the present day.

January 1982, the Argentine invasion of the Falkland Islands, (Malvinas). Explore the possibility of obtaining newsreel film clips to give added realism to the scene. Possibility of advice from Argentine and British service veterans.

Short newsreel clips - Troopship "Canberra" sailing from Southampton etc.

1982 latter-half. British troops advancing on Port Stanley but meeting stubborn resistance on 'Tumbledown Hill'.

Lieut. Richard Williams and private with 'walkie-talkie' take cover behind a large boulder from withering machine-gun fire, call up mortar fire on machine-gun position.

Meanwhile - Richard is suddenly aware of a voice from the other side of his boulder babbling deliriously in Spanish: -

"Padre nuestro, que estas en ef cielo, santificado se tu nombre oh! ooh! agua, agua Padre Nuestros, agua por favor, agua.

(translated - "Our Father which art in heaven, Hallowed be thy name, oh! ooh! Water, water Father, please water, water....)

Richard is further surprised even shocked, when he hears the same voice babbling in Welsh! "Ein tad yr hwn wyt y Nefoedd, Sancteiddier dy enw... Oh! ooh! dwr, dwr ooh! Iesu Grist....).
Translated) - "Our Father which art in heaven, Hallowed be thy name .. oh!, ooh! water, water, Jesus Christ please water....".

Richard moves cautiously around the boulder and finds a young Argentine soldier severely wounded with loss of blood etc. He comforts the young man first in English. Then remembering what he had cried in his delirium he spoke comforting words in Welsh. He gives the boy a drink of water, then finding the wound and applies a field-dressing to it. He then tells his private to call for the medic on his 'walkie-talkie'.

Minutes later the wounded boy is carried away by stretcher to a field hospital.

Much later Port Stanley is recaptured by British Forces. The Argentine flag replaced by the Union Flag.

1982-1983. Falkland Islands recaptured. British Troops consolidating. Argentine Forces evacuated.

A week later, when his unit is about to embark for Home Richard pays one last visit to Port Stanley Hospital and is advised the young Argentine soldier is semi-paralysed and when fit enough to travel will be flown to the UK for neuro-surgery.

Brecon, six months later: -

Lieut. Richard Pritchard Williams visits Ricardo Aldao in hospital to find the young lad slowly recovering from his wounds. Explaining the probability of their relationship he persuades the British and Argentine Authorities to allow the boy to convalesce at his home in Talybont near Brecon.

Ricardo now in a wheelchair is well cared-for by Richard's parents and his sister Marie who frequently pushes him around their attractive rose-garden..

(methinks love is also in bloom).

Spring 1983. Off-duty for the day from the South Wales Borderers in Brecon, Richard arrives home for early lunch and thereafter takes sister Marie and Ricardo by car on what he tells them is a 'mystery our'.

From Talybont and Brecon they take the 'A10' road toward Sennybridge. At the road-sign 'Ystradgynlais' he then takes the 'A4067' road down the Swansea Valley where Richard points out places of interest, such as 'Tavern-o-Gareg', so called for the huge boulder alongside the front door which marks 'one thousand feet above sea-level'.

A few miles further along Richard points out the world-famous 'Dan-yr-Ogof' cave complex,. He describes the marvels of the stalagmites and stalactites to be found in the labyrinth of chambers which stretch for miles into the foothills at the Brecon Beacons.

A mile or so further down they come to 'Graig-y-Nos Castle', which Richard explains was once the home of Adelina Patti. Both Richard and Marie are astonished when their young companion told them he had heard she had been a famous opera-singer who had once performed in all the major capitals of the world, including Buenos Aires.

Their journey then took them through the sprawling villages of Abercrave and Penrhos, down Jeffrey's Hill into Ystradgynlais crossroads beyond which Richard stops the car. They were at the entrance to St. Cynog's Church where they are met by the Rector, David Parry who escorts them to a quiet corner of the churchyard and the grave of their forebears.

The late April sun hangs briefly over the narrow valley between Allt-y-Grug and the grim cliff below the Varteg mountains. Richard leans forward and reads aloud the poignant inscription on the headstone: -

IN LOVING MEMORY OF

WATCYN WILLIAM PRITCHARD WILLIAMS
Who Died April 20th. 1912 Aged 80 Years

Also MATILDA His Widow
Died June 22nd. 1921 Aged 62 Years

Also GWILYM THOMAS WILLIAMS Their Son
Died and Buried in Ashanti, West Africa
November 18th. 1916 Aged 36 Years

Also WATCYN WESLEY WILLIAMS Brother of
The First Named. Died April 30th. 1915
Aged 77 Years

"Each Call Was Short & Shock Severe,
To Part From Those We Loved So Dear,
Our Loss is Great, We Won't Complain,
We Hope, Through Christ, To Meet Again."

The Above Brothers & Their Sister Formed Part of
153 Welsh Settlers in the Chubut Valley, Patagonia
1865

The Churchyard, Ystradgynlais.

When Richard had finished reading the inscription on the headstone there followed a thoughtful silence. The Rector then gave a little cough and began to recite the Lord's Prayer: -

>Our Father, which art in Heaven,
>Hallowed be thy name, thy Kingdom Come,
>Thy will be done on Earth, as it is in Heaven,
>Give us this day our daily bread,
>And forgive us our trespasses, as we forgive
>them that trespass against us,
>Lead us not into temptation, But deliver us from evil.
>For thine is the Kingdom, the Power and the Glory,
>For ever and ever. AMEN

Then all three repeated it in Welsh hoping their young companion would understand it better: -

>Ein Tad, yr hwn wyt yn y Nefoeth,
>Sancteiddier dy enw, deued dy dtrnas,
>Gwneler dy ewyllys, megis y y nef,
>Felly ar y ddaear hyfed,
>Dyro in o ddyddI ddydd ein bara beunyddiol,
>A maddeu I ni ein pechoddau,
>Nynnau yr maddau I bwb sydd yn ein dyled,
>Ac nac arwain y brofedigaeth, eithr, geared ni rhag drwg.
>Canys eiddot yn y deyrnas a'r nerth a'r gogoniant,
>yn oes, oesedd. AMEN

While Marie held his hand firmly in hers, young Ricardo in his wheelchair repeated the prayer in Spanish: -

>Padre nuestro, que estas en el cielos,
>Santificado sew tu nombre, venga a nosotros,
>Tu reino, hagase tu voluntad asi en la tierra,
>Como en el cielo, El pan nuestro de cada dia,
>Danosle hoy y perdonanos nuestras deudas,
>Asi como nosotros perdonamos a nuestras,
>Deudores, y no nos dejas caer en la tentacion,
>Mas libranos del mal. AMEN

There is and has been for many years a nautical magazine called "Sea Breezes". It has many interesting articles and photographs about ships and shipping, loaded with 'nostalgia' and, of course letters from readers. I wrote to the editor appealing for information about the 'Mimosa' and the intrepid band of Welsh people who sailed in her to Puerto Madryn, Patagonia.

Within a matter of weeks I was delighted to receive dozens of letters in response to mine in 'Sea Breezes'. Unfortunately most of them drew my attention to the article in the February 1966 issue of the magazine written by E.W. Argyle about the Argentine centenary 8 Peso stamp featuring the 'Mimosa'. Some even gave the dimensions and other details of the ship but little or nothing about Patagonia itself.

There were letters from the magazine readers from many parts of the country such as - John Rapier, of Cosby in Leicester, Fred Gilmour from Colwyn Bay, Clwyd, North Wales, Ian Fisher from Brightlingsea, and Robert Pollard from Glasgow. A second letter from John Rapier included a photocopy of the pertinent pages in 'Sea Breezes'.

But there was one letter that both interested and amused me: -

Dear Captain,

We have two ladies here in our Welsh Chapel in Penny Lane, (Liverpool). One of them's Mother is still alive in Patagonia. The lady herself was born there but is now living in Liverpool.

The other lady's brother, Bryn Williams is an ex-Archdruid of the Welsh Gorsedd of the National Eisteddfod. He was born in Patagonia but I don't think his sister Glenys was. The lady whose Mother is still in Patagonia has written her for further information.

Best Wishes

Signed - Eufryn Davies

As I've said, the letters all dealt with the commemorative stamps article in 'Sea Breezes' and or details about 'Mimosa' but nothing about Patagonia, I fear the trail is going cold.

For two consecutive years I was invited to adjudicate in a competition called "Youth Speaks" sponsored by the local lodge of 'Rotary International'. Another adjudicator, Harold Jones now also living in West Mersea had been for many years employed by Midland Bank in Swansea and we have since become firm friends.

This event somehow led to my being invited by Rotary to give a 'talk' on my seagoing experiences which was quite a surprising success so much so I became inundated with similar invitations. At all these 'talks' I waived my 'speaker's fee' in favour of a donation to the local St. Helena Hospice. And when invited to become the first President of the 'Colne Committee for the 'King George's Fund for Sailors' I would alternate the donations between the two charities.

At many of my 'talks' I found myself being advised to write about my experiences at sea in peace and during the Second World War. After careful consideration I purchased a brand-new Amstrad word-processor and settled down to master its many advantages over the common or garden typewriter. My role of 'author' had begun.

Over the months that followed I typed hundreds of pages recording experiences and incidents that had occurred during the fifty years of my seagoing career. Sundry 'Voyage ''Reports', even 'Master's Cash Accounts' came in useful in establishing certain dates and places I had almost forgotten.

The more I wrote the greater became my enthusiasm until I had amassed a considerable collection of what I chose to call 'Short But True Stories'. From my local library I obtained a disused copy of the 'Writers' and Artists' Yearbook' in which was listed the names and addresses of book publishers. That was when I discovered it is much easier to write stories than it is to have them published. I received enough 'rejection-slips' with which to paper our 'Loo'.

Among other tit-bits of information in the 'Yearbook' I discovered there were different kinds of 'publishers' listed. Those who pay the would-be author for his work and the other who expect to be paid for their services.

To my dismay and chagrin I also discovered to find a publisher prepared to pay for publishing, the author has a better chance if he or she is a celebrity of one kind or another. Actors and actresses or 'pop-stars' stand a very good chance of being accepted as are serial-killers or paedophiles. But first-time unknown writers don't stand the snowball's chance in hell, which leaves us with the other kind.

The 'Vanity Publisher' requires payment for their service and there are many of them. And it is about these that the "Yearbook' sounds a very clear warning of deceit and deception to the unwary first-time writer. Thousands of pounds can easily be lost down the drain with little or nothing returned but other than the attic or garage littered with unsold books.

But here I was very lucky indeed. I was put in touch with Bernard Durnford who was then based at Bramber, Sussex. And although a 'Vanity Publisher' I soon found him to be extremely honest and a very good friend indeed. In our early relationship he admitted that my manuscript of 'Short But True Stories' had potential so much so he was prepared to pay half the publishing costs for half the royalties received, details of which are of no consequence here.

Since then our friendship ripened and he still phones me several times a week just for a chat. Initially I suggested the title of my book to be "Tales of a Reluctant Sailor - Or the Boy Who Ran Away From Sea'. Bernard retorted, "You look after your ships and I'll look after the title"!! In June 1999 'From the Captain's Table - Tales of a Master Mariner' appeared in bookshops and in Public Libraries.

So much for my first book, sadly and reluctantly I am obliged to bring this somewhat 'splintered' narrative to a close. There is very little I can add to the 'The Patagonia Connection' which is part of another collection of 'Short But True Stories' to be published from beyond the grave!

My marriage to Joan has been blessed with three lovely daughters but it means the end of my contribution to the Williams Dynasty.

However, my first-cousin Wesley's son Huw's marriage to Beatrice produced a boy, Alun and daughter Marie. It now falls on Alun and his progeny that the destiny of the Williams family hangs in the balance. The unthinkable alternative would be complete and utter oblivion.

Meanwhile, and I am delighted to record, second-cousin Huw has realised a life-long ambition. He and Beatrice have toured the Argentine following in the footsteps of their son Alun and where they have met members of the family both in Buenos Aires and in Viedma, Patagonia.

Huw has spent a lot of time and effort tracing and recording the Williams 'Family Tree' beginning with Captain Watcyn Williams the sailor from Barmouth through to the two brothers Watcyn William Pritchard and Watcyn Wesley and their sister Elizabeth Louise. It is of her marriage with Doctor Jorge Homble and their progeny that is the essence of the tale I have chosen to call "The Patagonia Connection'.

In one of his letters to me Huw insisted he is committed to writing his version of the same history which I hope and pray he will one day have published. Young Alun has made an even grander tour of South America and I hope one day to hear, and if possible read of his exploits. Was it fate that led me to make so many voyages to the Argentine in those days long before civil airlines were commonplace and where I too might have met some of the 'Patagonia Connection'?

"Adios"

In his letter to me, dated 2nd. August 1999, Huw wrote as follows:-

> "Alun is still in South America, (back-packing), somewhere in the Amazon at present. One of the highlights of our Argentina trip was to meet the family both in Buenos Aires and in Viedma.
>
> Alun met them first in January then Beat and I in March. An important event is photographed. I enclose a precious one of Alun with Juan Carlos (our cousin).

The portrait on the wall of the flat is of Captain Watcyn Williams (approx. 1800). He had the portrait professionally restored. He is great-great-grandfather to Juan Carlos and myself and great-grandfather to you. I see a similarity to Tudor (your brother Cedric's boy).

And the portrait beneath is that of Elizabeth Louise sister to Watcyn Williams Pritchard and Watcyn Wesley Williams.

I'm sure you will find this as fascinating as I have. And Elizabeth Louise looks very similar to our Marie."

Signed Huw & Beat.

My nephew Alun and cousin Juan Carlos

On reverse of

VIEDMAN - PROVINCIA de RIO NEGRO

Vista parcial del Casino "El Faro".

Vista parcial del Rio Negro y de la ciudad

Dear Den & Joan,

Here in "Wladfa" - Tracing our roots. Have met many of the family in Buenos Aires & Viedman. What a welcome following Alun's 'back-packing exploits as he arrived here in December.

We even traced an outpost where W.W.P.W. and W.W.W. traded with Indians in approx. 1870. A lifelong ambition achieved

Hwyl a Patagonia
Huw, Beat. and Alun.

'EPILOGUE'

At the beginning of this story I described how my wife Joan and I had settled-down in our respective arm-chairs Sunday 1st. March 1980 (St. David's Day) to watch a programme on BBC television entitled 'A Valley in the Desert', produced by Selwyn Roderick and with a commentary by the late Sir Huw Weldon.

It was this programme together with so much material already in my possession given me years before by my second-cousin Huw that inspired me to write this story. Of how my grandfather, Watcyn William Pritchard Williams and his brother Watcyn Wesley and their sister Elizabeth Louise sailed from Liverpool on the 'Mimosa' to pioneer a new life in Patagonia.

While writing my attention was drawn to an article in the popular magazine 'Sea Breezes' which dealt with the issue of a set of stamps by the Argentine Government commemorating the one hundredth anniversary of that epic voyage of the 'Mimosa' and the party of Welsh emigrants to Patagonia.

I received dozens of letters from people I didn't even know, but many of whom had relatives with Patagonia connections reminding me again and again of how small the world has become. These letters triggered by the article in 'Sea Breezes' are of great interest to me but not sufficiently so to be included in this narrative.

However, the letters dealing more effectively with my story are included in the pages following. I hope the reader will find them of added interest. And with that final sentiment I will one more say; -

"Adios"

Tel.(01206) 38 3980

"MEADOW END",
14 Broomhills Road;
West Mersea;
ESSEX, CO5 8AS

7th.January, 1998.

The Public Relations Officer;
"ARGENTINE EMBASSY";
65 Brook Street;
LONDON, W1.

Dear Sir;

I am currently engaged in writing my family history which I believe may be of some interest to the peoples of both our countries.

For the chapter which I call 'The Patagonia Connection' I would be most grateful if you could advise me which department in your government, or other alternative contact, could trace those members of my family who chose to stay in Patagonia.

Of the family who sailed from Liverpool in the 'Mimosa' in 1865 there were two brothers, Watkin William Pritchard Williams and Watkin Wesley Williams both of whom eventually returned to Wales at the turn of the century. But their sister, Elizabeth Louise married a general-practitioner, Doctor Jorge A.Humble. And it is in the details of Their descendants in which I am keenly interested in order to complete the 'Williams Saga'.

Hoping this request does not greatly inconvenience you;

I remain, Yours faithfully;

(Captain) Gwilym D.Williams

Embassy of the
Argentine Republic

London, January 8, 1997

Captain Gwilym D. Williams
Meadow End
14 Broomhills Road
West Mersea
Essex

Dear Captain,

Thank you very much for your letter of January 7th. I certainly agree that the work you are doing is extremely interesting, and concerns a very important link between our two countries.

I think that the best person to help you in this matter is Ms Tegai Roberts, director of the museum of the city of Gaiman, in Chubut. Tegai, whom I met in London two years ago, is a distinguished member of the Welsh community in Patagonia and an expert on its history. She is a retired teacher, and is fluent in English and Welsh.

Her address is: Ms Tegai Roberts
Directora
Museo Regional de Gaiman
Gaiman
(9105) Provincia de Chubut
República Argentina

I hope you find this information useful, and please do not hesitate to contact me if you need further assistance.

Yours sincerely,

Samuel Ortiz-Basualdo
Head of the Cultural Department

65 Brook Street, London W1Y 1YE *Tel: 0171 318 1300 Fax: 0171 318 1301*

```
                                        "MEADOW END",
                                     14 Broomhills Road;
Tel.(01206) 38 3980                     West Mersea;
                                      ESSEX, CO5 8AS

                                     9th. January,1998.
```

Ms Tegai Roberts;
Directora
Museo Regional de Gaiman;
(9105) Provincia de Chubut,
REPUBLICA ARGENTINA.

Dear Ms Roberts, (Cariad)

    May I first wish you a very Happy and Prosperous New Year. To my everasting shame I am unable to say it in the language of our common heritage. !

    I am currently engaged in writing my family history in which there is a chapter I choose to call "The Patagonia Connection".

    Of the family who sailed from Liverpool in the 'Mimosa' in 1865 there were two brothers, Watkin William Pritchard and Watkin Wesley Williams. They eventually returned to Wales at the turn of the century and settled-down in the Swansea Valley.

    But their sister, Elizabeth Louise married a local general-practitioner Doctor Jorge A.Humble. (or was it Aumble) ? And it is THEIR descendants in which I am keenly interested to complete the Williams saga which now depends entirely in the loins of my young nephew Alun, (or else) !

    Enclosed herewith please find a copy of what we believe is a branch of the Family Tree in Patagonia but errors and omissions may be in evidence. If you know of any relatives still in existence I shall be most grateful.

    Yours sincerely;

(Captain) Gwilym D.Williams

```
                                            "MEADOW END",
                                            14 Broomhills Road;
Tel.(01206) 38 3980                         West Mersea;
                                            ESSEX, CO5 8AS

                                            10th. June, 1998.
```

Senor Samuel Ortiz-Basualdo,
Head of the Cultural Dept.
EMBASSY OF THE ARGENTINE REPUBLIC:
65 Brook Street;
LONDON, WIY 1YE

Dear Senor Ortiz-Basualdo.

Thanks to your assistance, many pieces of the jig-saw are slowly coming together giving me a picture of my family-tree and the "Patagonia Connection".

Very much delayed I received a letter from Ms Tegai Roberts in which she gave me the address of a Mr.Griff Roberts in Brecon, Soth Wales, who would have more information.

Griff Roberts replied to my letter saying he and his wife had spent sometime in Patagonia teaching the Welsh language. He furthewr mentioned they are friendly with Tegai Roberts and her sister Luned who is Headmistress of the local school.

Griff and his Wife also met a young man named Carlos Homble who could very well be a descendant of Elizabeth Williams who married Doctor George Homble and I intend writing him in the very near future.

So, you see, Senor Samuel, my grateful thanks to you for pointing me in the right direction to complete my story of the "Patagonia Connection". Muchas Gracias Senor.

Yours sincerely;

Captain Gwilym D.Williams.

Gaiman, April 25, 1998.

Mr. Gwilym Dennis Williams
Meadow End
14 Broomhills Road
West Mersea
ESSEX CO5 8AS

Dear Mr. Williams:

    Thank you very much for your letter. I've read it and the story of your life with great interest, really more than once. I am also interested in the history of the Williams brothers and sister, as there is a little desk belonging to one of them in exhibition in this museum. We also have a book written by Arnoldo Canclini on Jorge A. Humble, titled "Jorge A. Humble, médico y misionero patagónico".

    Unfortunately, I know very little about the descendants of Dr. and Mrs. Humble, as Patagones is very far from Gaiman, but I can give you the address of a Welsh teacher from Aberhonddu, who has a daughter living very near Patagones, and who recently was in touch with one of them. He also knows some descendants of the brothers in Wales. This is the address

    Griff Roberts   Tel (01874) 623302
    Glanyrafon
    Promenade, Kensington
    Aberhonddu (Brecon)   Powys, Wales LD3 9AY

I am sure Mr. Roberts will be able to help you.

    yours sincerely,

    Tegai Roberts

Tel. (01206) 38 3980

"MEADOW END",
14 Broomhills Road;
West Mersea;
ESSEX, CO5 8AS

27th.May 1998.

Cariad Tegai Roberts;

Many thanks for your letter dated 25th.April from Gaiman and the address of Griff Roberts in Brecon. And, although I am most pleased you found my letter and contents interesting I have to admit being disappointed there is no information available about the descendants of Doctor Jorge Humble & Louise nee Williams other than the small section of the 'Family Tree' I sent you.

As you know, the British Isles is a fraction the size of the Argentine and, as you say, Gaiman is a long way from Patagones. When I was a very young apprentice in a British tramp-steamer we made several voyages to South America including Bahia Blanca, Injinero-White & Galvan. Buenos Aires & Rosario carrying coal to these ports and grain homeward either to the U.K or European ports.

But little did I realize then how near I had been to where my grandparents had worked their fingers to the bone trying to cultivate the wastelands of Patagonia. I developed a taste for jerva the mate' and bomilla especially with a spoonful of marmalade. !. The rope-soled boscos were very popular for working on deck as they were much cheaper than British shoes and boots. And I became very proficient with the tango and ranchera dancing with the Anglo-Argentine girls in the Seamens' Mission in Buenos Aires. (Happy Days)

Tel.(01206) 38 3980

"MEADOW END",
14 Broomhills Road;
West Mersea;
ESSEX, CO5 8AS

Wed. 27th. May 1998.

Dear Mr. Roberts,

Or, having recently celebrated my 83rd. birthday and claiming the privelege of age, perhaps I may call you Griff. ?

My paternal grandparents were among the 156 Welsh pioneers who sailed from Liverpool in the "Mimosa" expecting to find some sort of a El-Dorado in South America. Instead, as we all know now, they found a bleak, windswept tundra in Patagonia. !

That they managed to wrest some sort of a livelyhood from the prairie, and against terrible odds of weather and native Indians has been well documented so we can justly take all that as read.

On retiring in 1978 after fifty years of a seagoing career I soon settled down to writing my memoirs and a detailed account of when my ship "Nariva" was torpedoed in March 1943. I have also written something like thirty 'Short But True Stories' none of which has yet found a publisher. (Hope springs eternal in the human breast and my breast is no exception). !!! ***

Having nothing better to do I began a story which I chose to call "The Patagonia Connection" and was well under-way when I discovered how little I knew about their ordeal and especially about my grandfather's sister Elizabeth Louise Williams who married a general-practitioner Doctor Jorge A Humble.

So I wrote to Senor Samuel Ortiz-Basualdo in the Argentine Embassy from whom I received a very courteous reply and the address of Tegai Roberts in the Museum at Gaiman. A few days ago I received a reply from her also who gave me your address bringing my enquiries almost full-circle. ! (See photo-copies enclosed herewith).

If there is anything you may care to add to what I have already written I would be most grateful. Failing which my story "The Patagonia Connection" comes suddenly and jarringly to a dead-halt.

Yours sincerely

(Captain) Gwilym D.Williams,
    Master Mariner

Glanyrafon, The Promenade, Brecon, Powys, Wales. LD3 9AY
Junes 5th, 1998

Dear Gwilym Williams,

Thank you for your very interesting letter. Incidentally, my name is "Griff" which is short for Gruffydd, as you may well know! I have chosen to reply to your letter in English, as I don't know whether or not you speak Welsh.
We have visited Patagonia three times and by now we have very many friends and acquaintances living there. I have known about your family for quite some time, as you will soon find out. Let me first of all start at Ystradgynlais in the Swansea valley. There, you have a nephew, I suppose, called Huw Williams, proprietor of the Mimosa Cafe. His grandfather was possibly the Watkin Wesley Williams you mention. If you are not aleady in communication with Huw, he would be delighted to hear from you, as he is very interested in the Patagonian connection, and cannot wait to retire and be off to explore this very distant land that many of us love so much. This year, our Argentinian connection has increased owing to the fact that one of our daughters has married an Argentinian farmer in the province of Buenos Aires, and is now living about twenty five miles from the town of Carmen de Patagones and Viedma. Our most recent visit to the Chubut Valley and Patagones was between November and Mid January, 1998 during which time we met a number of our son-in-law's friends One evening, at quite a large gathering in a party, I met a young student who quite by accident told me that his surname was "Homble"...Carlos Homble! I was immediately interested and told him that I knew of his family connections with Wales. I already knew of Elizabeth Louise Williams's marriage to a Dr Jorge Homble. Carlos then, is the great grandson of your great Aunt. Immediately upon our return, I wrote to Huw Williams to tell him and enclosed the address of young Carlos. I have not heard from Huw since but I believe that he and Carlos have since been in correspondence. Having given Huw the address, I have to admit that I cannot lay my hands on it now to give to you. I apologise for that. We shall be going to Patagonia again in October and afterwards, to Patagones. Therefore, we are quite likely to meet Carlos again. Doesn't this old world of ours get smaller and smaller?
Oddly enough, my "Argentinian Daughter" has just called in my study and having browsed through your letter, commented, that she knew the name "Ortiz-Basualdo"....one very wealthy lady living in the foothills of the Andes!
My wife and I began our Patagonian connection in July 1994. We went over there as teachers of Welsh, on a voluntary basis, for one year. It is by now our second home. I feel certain that Huw Williams can take you on from here and Carlos Homble even further. I wish you every luck and success with your research and hope that I have been of some little help.
To answer your final question...No, I am not related to Tegai Roberts, but we are very good friends with her and her sister, Luned, who is the Headmistress of the local secondary school, Coleg Camwy.
I have taken the liberty of making copies of your scripts and I am sending them on to Huw Williams at Ystradgynlais. I hope you don't mind!
This will be all for the present. Diolch yn fawr a phob bendith.

Cofion cynnes....Best regards,

Griff.

Griff. Roberts

Tel.(01206) 38 3980

"MEADOW END",
14 Broomhills Road;
West Mersea;
ESSEX, CO5 8AS

10th. June, 1998.

Senor Samuel Ortiz-Basualdo,
Head of the Cultural Dept.
EMBASSY OF THE ARGENTINE REPUBLIC:
65 Brook Street;
LONDON, WIY 1YE

Dear Senor Ortiz-Basualdo.

Thanks to your assistance, many pieces of the jig-saw are slowly coming together giving me a picture of my family-tree and the "Patagonia Connection".

Very much delayed I received a letter from Ms Tegai Roberts in which she gave me the address of a Mr.Griff Roberts in Brecon, Soth Wales, who would have more information.

Griff Roberts replied to my letter saying he and his wife had spent sometime in Patagonia teaching the Welsh language. He furthewr mentioned they are friendly with Tegai Roberts and her sister Luned who is Headmistress of the local school.

Griff and his Wife also met a young man named Carlos Homble who could very well be a descendant of Elizabeth Williams who married Doctor George Homble and I intend writing him in the very near future.

So, you see, Senor Samuel, my grateful thanks to you for pointing me in the right direction to complete my story of the "Patagonia Connection". Muchas Gracias Senor.

Yours sincerely;

Captain Gwilym D.Williams.

Tel.(01206) 38 3980

"MEADOW END",
14 Broomhills Road;
West Mersea;
ESSEX,CO5 8AS

6th. July, 1998.

Dear Huw and Beatt,

Please excuse my typing this letter. It is consideration for your eyesight that I do so because due to my arthritic hands my handwriting closely resembles an inebriated spider. !

Its a long and somewhat complicated story but some years ago to occupy my spare time I began writing what I choose to call "Short But True Stories". To date I have written 29 of these in addition to a full-length account of Convoy HX 229 from New York to the U.K. in which my ship "Nariva" was torpedoed during what the Germans later described as the greatest convoy battle of all time. Thirteen ships were lost out of the 32 ships that sailed from N.Y.

With the aid of the notes and copies you gave me some years ago, including the 'Family Tree' I began writing a story which I have called "The Patagonia Connection". Lacking more detailed information I shelved the project for a couple of years while writing my autobiography called "The Reluctant Sailor" !!!

Picking up the threads once more I wrote to the Argentine Embassy in London and received a reply from the Head of the Cultural Department, Senor Samuel Ortiz-Basualdo who gave me the address of Tegai Roberts. (see copy enclosed). Three months later, (having given up all hopes of a reply) there came her letter also with the address of Griff Roberts, Brecon. (its a small world ai'nt it ?)

Griff tells me he had been in touch with you at the 'MIMOSA' and had given you the address of one Carlos Homble in Patagonia but that he had since lost it. As you will see by his letter, (copy enclosed) it would appear you have hopes of visiting Patagonia when you retire. Your grandfather was the last member of our family to do so while the nearest I ever got to it was Buenos Aires in 1978 my last voyage before retiring.

If you are well advanced in writing your own version of the Patagonia Connection I will give you my manuscript rather than have a duplicated version. So long as one of us finishes what is a vital link for our children to know about. Alyn is our only hope for continuity of the Family Tree.

Our Love to you all;

J. J D.

Tel.(01206) 38 3980

"MEADOW END",
14 Broomhills Road;
West Mersea,
ESSEX CO5 8AS

Wed. 4th.August '99

Dear Huw and Beat;

When I received your letter and contents this morning, to say I was thrilled and delighted would be the understatement of the year. Frankly I had feared I was out of the popularity league. And when I phoned your Mum a few weeks ago she told me you were in Patagonia I went all green with envy. A letter from Griff Roberts in Brecon told me you were 'thinking' of going there. Now you are back home leaves me with a list of questions I can only hope you are able to answer, such as, what other relatives did you meet in Patagonoa and in Buenos Aires.???

I am not exaggerating when I say there was a lump the size of a golf-ball when I studied the photgraph of Alun and Juan Carlos. Would he be the son of Beatriz Humble who married Raul Fernandez. ? and if so, he would have a sister Jorgette and a brother Raul Eduardo. But what excited me most were the pictures on the wall you describe as one of Captain Watcyn Williams and a portrait of Elizabeth Louise. My mind is seething with curiosity. According to the information you so kindly gave me years ago, Capt.Watcyn was master of the sloop "Valiant" when captured and held prisoner-of-war during the Napoleonic Wars.

The calender 2000 with scenes of the Swansea Valley only served to make that damned lump even bigger. ! Not content with putting the knife in but did you HAVE to twist it. ? If you only knew what hiraeth does to a chap when his heart and roots are deep in our beloved valley. But there, I must'nt allow myself to become maudlin. When giving 'talks' to various Societiesm, Clubs and institutions, I was often asked if I missed the sea. - my reply was invariably - "it sometimes comes over me in WAVES". !!!***!!!

I sent a copy of my book to the head-teacher of Ynyscedwyn School, Ystradgynlais. I dedicated it in memory of Johnny Thomas, hadmaster, and LLew Morgan with affection. But, to date I have never received an acknowledgment of receipt. !!!

Before I close, please give you Mum my Love, Regards and Best Wishes, and of course the same to you both. How long is Alun staying in South America and what's new with Marie. ?

Affectionately, yours,

Gwilym & Joan
x   x

Tel.(01206) 383980

'MEADOW END'
14 Broomhills Road;
West Mersea,
ESSEX,CO5 8AS

3rd.December,'99.

Robert Forrester Esq.;
Editor - "ROYAL MAIL NEWS"
21 Poyntell Crescent;
CHISLEHURST, KENT, BR7 6PJ

Dear Bob,

In my current copy of "Royal Mail News" I found the article written by Michael Mortimer of particular interest. He went on to say - "when shifting ship to Puerto Deseado I found the local pilot spoke perfect English but with a very marked Welsh accent"..........

My paternal grandfather, Watcyn Pritchard Williams, his brother Watcyn Wesley, and sister Elizabeth Louise were among the 153 Welsh people who sailed from Liverpool on the 25th. May 1865 in the clipper-ship "Mimosa" bound for Puerto Madryn in Patagonia where they established the first Welsh settlement in and around the Chubut River valley.

In 1877 grandfather returned to Wales to marry his childhood sweetheart Matild Fisher and their union eventually blest with two boys and a girl. In later years the younger boy Gwilym Thomas was destined to become my father. In 1888 the family returned to Patagonia and helped turn a bleak widerness into the thriving granary it now has become.

In 1899 the family again returned to Wales but leaving behind Elizabeth Louise who had married Doctor Jorge Humble a local general-practitioner. The rest of the family then settled permanently in the upper-reaches of the Swansea Valley which is where, eventually I arrived on the scene the same day as the "Lusitania" was torpedoed by a German 'U-Boat' on 7th.May 1915.

When I resigned from Royal Mail to join Cunard Line in 1946 I little realized the opportunities I would miss of meeting and cultivating that branch of the Williams family who I now choose to call "The Patagonia Connection".

Yours sincerely;

(Captain) Gwilym D.Williams

SQUARE SAIL

8th March 2000

Captain G. Williams,
"Meadow End",
14 Broomhills Road,
West Mersea,
CO5 8AS

Charlestown Harbour, St. Austell
Cornwall PL25 3NJ
Tel: (01726) 67526 / 70241
Fax: (01726) 61839
email: info@square-sail.com
www.square-sail.com

Dear Captain Williams,

John Bates has passed me a copy of your letter of 29th February which is most interesting and it would be a great achievement to get this project off the ground.

I have pleasure in enclosing a Company brochure from which you will see that whilst we do not have a true 'Clipper' in our fleet we do have 2 three-masted Barques that may well suit your purpose for the 'Mimosa' re-enactment.

John has done some calculations and it would appear that we are looking at a voyage of some 6,700 miles each way, which, if our ships were to be involved, would be planned at a speed of 4 knots. We would therefore be looking at a potential passage of 67 days each way and add to this two weeks filming and we are looking at a charter period in the region of 150 days. To give you an idea of costings, and at the same time not wishing to cause undue alarm, we would be looking to achieve a charter fee for this voyage and time period of £320,000. This may put the project into perspective but, when broken down - if one were able to offer berths (for what is after all a truly one-off voyage) at a rate of £10,000 per head for each passage we could accommodate 12 passengers on either of the two ships and this would allow you to reimburse a sum of £240,000. Additionally, if one were able to obtain funding from the BBC or other film company then the whole project might well be approaching a break-even situation.

We would be very pleased to talk to you about this in depth and should you require any assistance in developing the project please feel free to contact me.

Kind regards,

Chris Wilson
Marketing Manager

cc: Capt. John Bates

Square Sail Shipyard Ltd   Registered in England No. 2701512   VAT No: 406 9669 21

'E.S.P.'
(Extra Sensory Perception)

The letter from Cardiff required me to attend an interview with Captain Uren, Marine Superintendent for the Hain Steamship Company at their offices in Salvage Buildings. I found him an extremely kindly man who smiled at my enthusiasm for a seagoing career. The interview over I was as excited as relieved when he told me I would be accepted as a bridge apprentice subject to passing the Board of Trade medical and eyesight tests. He then directed me to the Mercantile Marine Offices adjacent to the main gate into Cardiff Docks.

The Board of Trade doctor greeted me warmly explaining that Captain Uren had telephoned him to expect me and, without further ado began his medical examination. This was a very brief affair but the eyesight test was much more rigorous beginning with my having to read a series of letters on a card diminishing in size downwards. This was followed with my having to distinguish coloured lights smaller than a pin-head. Then, having passed all tests to the doctor's satisfaction he told me I could go straight home, that he would notify Captain Uren I had passed the medical.

There followed a week of acute suspense until the arrival of a large parcel from Cardiff. It contained three copies of their Apprentices'

Indentures which had to be signed and returned forthwith with our cheque for twenty pounds being my 'Premium' which would be returned at the end of the four year term. There was also an assortment of gilt-brass buttons on which were the letters 'E.H.' for Edward Hain embossed thereon. A cap-badge was included having a red flag on which the letters 'E.H.' were woven. Last, but not least, they had included a recommended list of uniforms, blue and white, working clothes and footwear together with sea-boots and oil-skins, etc.

My brother Cedric, home on leave from the Royal Air Force and cousin David accompanied me by train to Swansea and the tiresome ordeal of being measured for uniforms. For much of journey they were determined to dissuade me from my chosen career by elaborating maritime disasters, storms and shipwreck. This had very little effect on me. My mind was focussed on dealing with mutinous crews, pirates and buccaneers somewhere on the Spanish Main.

It was quite some time later, and much too late to do anything about it that I realized my Indentures were signed, sealed and delivered on 31st. March 1932. From this my reader will appreciate much more quickly than I, that when I joined my first ship the next day was the 1st. April!!!

Mum was very quiet on the double-decker bus to Swansea and it was with a determined effort that she held back her tears when I boarded the train at High Street Station late that evening. Luckily I was alone in the compartment so was able to give-in, at last, to a flood of stinging tears. For the remainder of the long train journey to Falmouth via Cardiff and Bristol Temple Meads, I have never felt so miserable or so guilty realising I had left poor mum all alone in the world. With Cedric in the Royal Air Force, my eldest sister Mattie also nursing in London my poor dearest Mum was now all alone in that great big house that once belonged to Grandad, David Evans the Foundry.

My feeling of guilt was all the more acute for not having given any of this a single thought busy and excited at the prospect of becoming a 'bridge apprentice' in a real foreign-going steamship. The Hain Steamship Company at this time was a subsidiary of the P & O Group. A very poor relation, but one that operated no less than forty-two tramp-steamers many of which carried coal to South America and grain back to the U.K. or other European Ports.

My train from Temple Meads ground slowly to a halt in Truro Station where I had been told I would catch the connection to Falmouth. As I stepped out onto the platform feeling cold and stiff, I glanced at my wrist-watch. It was a minute past 06.30 and I realized the date was 1st. April 1932. (April Fool's Day).

Further along the platform I caught sight of two other boys wearing uniforms similar to mine. It was evident they too were waiting for the train to Falmouth. Strolling up to them in as casual manner as I could muster, I asked if they were about to join the "Treloske' and when they nodded agreement I introduced myself. They returned my greeting and the taller of the two said his name was Jim Keddie and nodding in the direction of his companion said "And this is Robertson". We shook hands and found our instructions were identical. We were to report to the Company's agents 'Cox & Kings in Falmouth from where we would be taken by duty-boat up-river to the 'SS Treloske'.

Our animated conversation was interrupted by the arrival of our connecting train and we found an empty compartment where we continued our chat. Jim Keddie hailed from Hull where he had attended the 'Boulevard Nautical School'. I noticed his uniform was far from being as new as mine and his cap had a jaunty well-worn tilt to it while mine obviously kept its neat appearance with the wire grommet inside the crown. Robertson lived in Darlington and he proudly explained he had made several voyages with his uncle who was Master of a ship named 'Dalewood' owned my Messrs. France-Fenwick. I noticed his uniform also looked beautifully well-worn which made me feel very self-conscious because mine was obviously new.

We were still busily chatting and comparing notes when our train juddered and wheezed into Falmouth Station. With a fruity Cornish accent the ticket-collector said "You boys'll be for Cox and Kings I declare". And with that he proceeded to give us instructions how and where to find the Agent's offices. Jim Keddie remarked that as it was yet to early for offices to open we all agreed our next move would be to find a café and a bite to eat.

Feeling considerably more human after a breakfast of bacon and eggs followed by mugs of scalding hot tea and a cigarette we three 'hard-case' sailors strolled through the streets of Falmouth. Making our way towards the offices of Messrs. Cox & Kings, we were fully conscious of admiring glances from pretty young girls hurrying to work in shops and offices. I couldn't resist a few admiring glances at myself either; reflected in a variety of shop windows.

Arrived at the Agent's office we were told to collect several huge brown-paper parcels of bedding, each label bearing our individual names. For each apprentice there was a brand-new mattress, two pillows with four pillow-cases, four blankets, four cotton-sheets and two counterpanes. While identifying and selecting our bedding there entered into the office a dozen or more middle-aged gentlemen. Although they were wearing civilian suits they all carried the indefinable air of authority and were treated with obvious respect by the manager and staff in the Agent's office.

One of the clerks came towards where we were standing and with evident deference introduced us to Captain Devereaux who lost no time in telling us to carry our bedding down to the duty-boat and there to wait his return. The elderly coxwain touched the peak of his cap and asked to which ship we were bound. Jim Keddie replied we were all for the 'Treloske' then the old coxswain added, "Aye, she'll be in the tier with 'Trecarne', 'Trevorian' and 'Trefusis' above Tollverne.

We hadn't very long to wait before all the Captains, having completed their business with the Agent, returned to board the duty-boat and within minutes we were chugging out of the harbour and headed up river. Passing an old sailing ship at anchor in the Roads, the old coxwain seeing my interest spoke in a low voice, "That'll be the old 'Cutty Sark' young'un". I was amazed to see so many ships moored in the river. For mile after mile ships of all shapes and sizes. Seeing my amazed look the old man growled, "Aye, it's this blasted depression y'see, no work for 'undreds of ships, all laid up". I began feeling a bit depressed myself. Or was it the first pangs of homesickness?

Rounding a bend in the river near Tollverne I saw a tier of four ships moored alongside each other and just beyond another tier of four. The old coxswain gave me a nudge and nodding towards them he whispered, "Them's the 'Treloske's' tier where you'll be 'eading young'un".

And as the launch drew nearer I could see their names. One was moored heading downstream and on her bows I could see the name 'Treloske'. The three others were moored heading upstream. 'Trecarne with the Port of Registry beneath, St. Ives. Next to her 'Trevorian' of St. Ives and a fourth ship 'Trefusis' also of St. Ives.

As the launch drew alongside the 'Treloske' gangway, I looked up to see three faces staring down at us. Faces black with coal-dust except for white teeth when they grinned, which was often. Captain Devereaux leapt onto the platform and as he began to climb the gangway I heard him shout to the boys above, "Send down a heaving-line for all the baggage and bedding". A few minutes later we three were on deck shaking hands with the other apprentices and exchanging names. "I'm Eddy Sandle the senior apprentice", said the chap with a wide grin and a friendly face, "Come along and I'll show you to your berths". With that he led the way while we all followed carrying luggage and bedding.

The apprentices cabin was amidships on the starboard side of the ship. There were four bunk-berths, two up and two down. The two upper berths both had a porthole. At the after end of the cabin, to the right of the entrance, was a row of lockers. A mess table and two benches were inboard and opposite the bunks while on the forward bulkhead I could see a four-drawer chest, to the right of which was a doorway leading to the apprentices' bathroom and lavatory. Looking askance at Eddy Sandle he anticipated my question and nodding to a lower bunk said "That's yours Taffy". Then added, "With your arrival today making six of us, me and the next senior will be occupying two engineer's single berth cabins.

Perhaps it was my diminutive size compared to the others I shall never know but the senior apprentice, Eddy Sandle from the moment I arrived on board 'Treloske' taught me a lot. Not that the 'lot' of an apprentice was much to go by anyway! He showed me which drawers were mine, helped me unpack the brand-new mattress and bedding before leaving us to get showered. I learned that Saturday mornings' apprentices were required to restock the galley with coal from the ship's main bunkers hence their blackened faces. It so dawned on me that the next Saturday and all subsequent Saturdays I would be equally as blackened by coal-dust.

We three newcomers were introduced to the Chief Steward and his very pleasant white-haired wife who between them prepared all the meals on board. For Captain and Mrs. Devereaux, the Chief Engineer and his wife and six apprentices. We were required to carry our meals from the galley to where we would eat 'temporarily' in the engineers' mess and to wash-up all our dishes and utensils afterwards.

Eventually, with the midday meal over, the washing-up and dishes stowed away, my new-found friend, Eddy Sandle and some of the others took us on a tour of inspection of the 'Treloske' from stem to stern including the bridge and engine room. Eddy made a very good tour-guide describing and explaining every part or parts of the ship and showed great patience dealing with our questions. Of course, thanks to their previous backgrounds, Jim Keddie and Robertson already knew a great deal, but to me, it was all very very new indeed.

By the time we returned to our quarters my head was reeling with all the information I had absorbed. At four o'clock in the afternoon I was delighted with the arrival of tea and a generous slab of fruit cake. How was I to know then that the food prepared down on the River Fal bore little or no resemblance to what we would be eating at sea, later on! We were also told week-ends were 'theoretically free' but that we were expected to devote some of the time to study.

We turned-in soon after eight o'clock that night. My new mattress was well sprung and the cotton sheets beautifully cool. Jim Keddie and Robbie were still plying George Mallory with questions, George the fourth occupant of our cabin was the third senior apprentice having arrived on board 'Treloske' in early February. He had been a cadet with Ben Line for two years before joining the Hain Steamship Company.

Soon I became unconscious of their droning voices and my mind went back twenty-four hours, to when Mum and I had left home by bus to Swansea High Street Station. Then I began thinking of poor dear Mum travelling back home alone, to an empty house. A lump formed in my throat and with it a flood of tears. How could

I have been so acutely selfish? It was with effort that I choked off my sobs rather that have my cabin-mates hear me. Why oh why had I been such a fool to leave my poor defenceless Mum all alone in the world?.

And that dear reader, is how I began my seagoing career. With the prospect of four years apprenticeship ahead of me. Four years that seemed an eternity. When sleep finally overtook me I think the last conscious thought was what those four years were to bring me. The years beyond that would remain a mystery because sleep finally eclipsed all further speculation.

In the weeks and months that followed, first Eddy Sandle received instructions to join one of the seagoing ships of the Hain fleet. The another until by August I awoke to find myself senior apprentice with the questionable pleasure of introducing new boys to the 'Treloske'. And many were the nights when I would be awakened by stifled sobbing and I would climb out of my top bunk to comfort some poor homesick kid in one of the lower bunks. Then, at last came my instructions to join the 'Tremorvah' in Cardiff and my first voyage to sea!

The 'Tremorvah' was a three-island type of cargo ship known as 'standard'. Built with dozens like her during the First World War. They were far superior to the 'flush-deck' ships built immediately after the war. Where the 'flush-deckers' had a primitive rod and chain method of steering the 'standard' ships, like 'Tremorvah' had telemotor-steering. While on the subject of 'steering' I joined 'Tremorvah' when, by International agreement, helm orders were changed. When the tiller was superseded by the wheel the helm orders remained the same, that is to say, if the Master or ship's officer wished to turn the ship to port the helmsman turned the wheel to starboard as he would have put the tiller to starboard. But this was now all changed. To turn the ship to port the wheel was also turned to port as one would do with a car or any other road vehicle. And similarly, if the ship was to be turned to starboard the wheel was also turned to starboard.

Captain Evans, the Master of the 'Tremorvah' lived in Cardiganshire while the Mate, Mr. Matthews was a lean, hard faced Cornishman. The senior apprentice James, from Swansea, whose four year apprenticeship would expire during the forthcoming voyage. The other apprentice, Flint, was the most taciturn and morose person I had ever met. The third apprentice, George Mallory had left the Fal some months before me. All the seamen were ex-apprentices who had obtained their Certificates of Competency but were offered employment as Able-Seamen by the Company rather than to remain on the 'dole' during the 'depression'.

Abe Harry, the Bosun, was a fiery little Cornishman with an irascible temper who made no effort to conceal his dislike of apprentices and especially 'ex-apprentices' who, he knew, would one day be his superior officers. 'Chippy' the ship's carpenter was a cheery Welshman who chewed plug-tobacco incessantly and wasn't particular about the direction in which he squirted the brown-stained spittle. Little did I know it, but I was destined to be his labourer for the rest of the voyage.

We four apprentices were called at 06.30 the next day and were 'turned-to' by the Mate promptly at 07.00. Two derricks were rigged for'ard at number two hatch and cargo nets attached to the hook of a 'union-purchase'. Within a few minutes a large lorry arrived alongside with a large selection of ships' stores which we hoisted onboard and stowed for'ard under the foc'sle-head. I learned we would be sailing the next day, light-ship, (without cargo) and bound for Vancouver, British Columbia where we were to load a full cargo of grain. 'Jimmy' James estimated the voyage would be of about three months duration.

When the first lorry-load of stores had been stowed away the Bosun yelled out 'smoko' and all hands drifted away to enjoy a mug of tea or coffee, either of which brew bore a closer resemblance to stockholm-tar than its namesake and in which a teaspoon could stand at a forty-five degree angle. I remained behind under the foc'sle-head sitting on a coil of sisal-rope and feeling miserably homesick.

If my reader, or anyone else for that matter, doubts the power of prayer I can assure them, it works. Feeling sorry for myself I gave way to a bout of weeping and began to pray. I can't remember the exact words but I prayed, and prayed. After a while, feeling a bit ashamed of my weakness, and scared of being seen in such a state,

I dried my eyes. I could hear the lorry with another load of stores backing up against the ship's side.

We were eating our midday meal in the apprentices' mess when Mr. Matthews, the Mate arrived in the doorway. "Williams, your mother and aunt are climbing the gangway, you'd better go and meet them". In my excitement I very nearly tipped my mug of tea as I hurriedly left the table and, with a blurted "Thank you Sir", brushed past him and made for the gangway. My dear Mum and Aunty Ivy had just arrived at the top of the gangway...... So now I can reassure my reader of the power of prayer!!!!

Of my first voyage to sea in the tramp-steamer 'Tremorvah' I remember almost every detail. It is what may interest my reader most, is what really concerns me. Steaming down the Bristol Channel in the teeth of a south-westerly gale in a 'light-ship' condition I was ordered to stay in the shelter of the foc'sle-head sorting out various sizes of nails and screws. The violent motion of the ship and the all-pervading smell of tarred-rope, paint and tarpaulin canvas is a vivid today as it was all those years ago. For hours on end I wanted and wished to die and I would have welcomed death with open arms.

But by the time we steamed through the Mona Passage into the Caribbean I was back to my old cheerful self even inclined to whistle until ordered to "belt up!". The transit of the Panama Canal kept me awake when I should have been asleep during my four hours 'watch below'. Thrilled with seeing flying-fish skitting across the bows and porpoises escorting us while riding the bow-wave ahead of the ship kept me continuously entranced.

For much of the time steaming northwards from the Canal to British Columbia we worked in the holds preparing shifting boards for the grain cargo we were to load. Eventually we were moored alongside in New Westminster under the grain silos until for five whole days the 'Tremorvah' looked like a ghost-ship under the blanket of grain-dust. To a young and impressionable boy from Wales, Vancouver presented itself as a city of pure magic with its tall skyscrapers and very wide streets. Our radio-officer, 'Sparks' took George Mallory and myself through Stanley Park and its two-hundred feet Douglas Fir trees and bridle paths. But, five days later, fully-loaded and all hatches battened-down and grain-dust hosed-down we prepared to sail. The most magical and emotive word in a sailor's vocabulary is "homeward-bound". And the word was soon around the ship like wildfire that Glasgow was our port of discharge.

In December 1932 we left the Panama Canal astern and the warm waters of the Caribbean, and, to use the vernacular, we 'rolled our guts out' crossing two thousand miles of the Winter North Atlantic. But, bad things as well as good things come to an end and we eventually approached Greenock near the 'Tail of the Bank' where we embarked the River Clyde Pilot. It was cold, wet and miserable with a fine drizzle and much of the surrounding countryside hidden by mist and we were too wet and cold to pay much attention to our surroundings.

Until, slowly rounding a bend in the river we could see the lofty cranes and slipways of shipyards on either side. Then suddenly on the port hand we saw the most enormous skeleton of a passenger liner. As we drew abreast of this monster we could see and read the board hanging over the stern. And the notice read 'JOHN BROWN'S SHIPYARD NUMBER 534'. Suddenly the men standing around on stations all began talking at once. Charlie Tucker, one of the certificated able-seaman, spoke authority. "That's the new Cunarder on which work was halted for lack of funds, damn and blast this depression".

As the huge skeleton slowly dropped astern fading into the mist I could swear I heard a mysterious, hidden voice saying, "One day my son you will be the Senior First Officer of this truly regal leviathan". This imaginary soliloquy was suddenly shattered by the voice of the Second Mate shouting, "Come on you dozy lot, stand by to make tugs fast!'.

When finally the 'Tremorvah' was moored alongside her berth under the grain elevators on Meadowside Quay I was ordered to turn-in as I would be 'nightwatchman' for the duration of the ship's stay in port. Crew mail arrived with the Company's agent in Glasgow and I was delighted to receive a letter from Mum in which she had enclosed a very welcome ten-shilling-note. Thus ended my first voyage to sea. Memorable for a variety of reasons not least having seen that enormous ship on the slipway, 'JOHN BROWN'S SHIPYARD NUMBER 534'.

As I have just said, thus ended my first voyage to sea. The first voyage of the 'April Fool'. There were to be many many more voyages after that, and in many ships.Equally so, there were to be many experiences, incidents and accidents. Many books have been written about boys who run away to sea. Mine is the story of the boy who ran away FROM sea. But the April Fool was persuaded to return to his ship, and lived to regret it for the rest of his life!

The four years apprenticeship included voyages in 'Treneglos' with a sadistic Master who later had his comeuppance when he flogged the log-book (altered entries). Then came the sister ship 'Trevose' which was involved in collision with the Swedish tanker 'Castor' which all but destroyed the apprentices' accommodation while I was asleep in it! Temporary repairs were effected in Las Palmas thence to the Tyne for dry-dock. We were then sent home on leave and while at home I heard the launching ceremony on our wireless and Her Majesty Queen Mary naming ship number 534 "Queen Mary'!!

My next appointment excited me tremendously, it was to the P & O fast cargo ship 'Bangalore' manned by a Lascar crew but with Hain Steamship Company Master, officers and apprentices trading from the U.K. and Continent to the Far East. A year later I was admitted to Colombo Hospital with a painful 'slipped disc'. Then, on 31st March 1936 my indentures expired while in Japan and I was promoted 4th Officer but not for very long. While supervising the loading of cargo a large crate fell from a dizzy height and I stood in its way. I regained consciousness two days later in Kobe Hospital having sustained multiple injuries. And it was in Kobe Hospital that I celebrated my 21st. birthday, 7th. May. 1936.

Ten weeks later I took passage on 'Behar' sister ship to 'Bangalore'. Dear brother Cedric motored down to the docks and drove me to our new home 'Normandy', Old Heath, Colchester, Essex. A week later I enrolled in the Sir John Cass Nautical College to study for the Board of Trade examination for my first Certificate of Competency as Second Mate.

The ink was barely dry on my newly-acquired Certificate of Competency when I was required to join the Company's 'Tregenna' as Third Mate in Leghorn, Italy. During the next two years I began to realise I had no 'stomach' for tramping around the world. By 1939 I had earned sufficient 'sea-time' to qualify for my next Board of Trade examination and returned to Sir John Cass Nautical College.

At 11.00 a m Sunday, 3rd. September 1939 the Prime Minister Neville Chamberlain spoke on the wireless to say we were now at war with Nazi Germany. A week later I passed the Board of Trade exam for the next higher certificate of Competency and joined Royal Mail Line's 'Loch Katrine' as Third Officer and my 'tramping' days were over. Instead, I had to learn how to keep 'station' in convoy and improve my signalling skills. For over a year the 'Loch Katrine' maintained her peacetime itinerary from the U.K. to the West Coast of North America via the Panama Canal. And when 'Spud' Middleton left the ship to sit for his Master's Certificate I was promoted Second Officer.

In 1942 I also left 'Loch Katrine' to sit for my Master's 'ticket' and thereafter joined the 'Nariva' for what was to become a very long journey culminating in being torpedoed while homeward-bound in the fateful convoy 'HX 229' afterwards described as the fiercest convoy battle of all time. All hands from 'Nariva' were rescued by the corvette 'HMS Anemone' together with survivors from other ships. Eventually we were safely landed in Gourock to proceed home on leave pending further appointment.

In July 1943 when Second Officer of 'Empire Confidence' we landed troops on the invasion of Sicily and a few months later on the invasion of Salerno. A year later we were in Bombay when the 'Fort Stikine' caught fire and disintegrated. Much of the harbour installations and eleven other merchant ships were destroyed either by fire or further violent explosions. In this holocaust 'Empire Confidence' sustained some superficial damage but this was later repaired in dry-dock in Baltimore, USA.

My fellow officers and I had been celebrating my 30th. birthday on 7th. May 1945 on board the company's troopship 'Alcantara'. We were in Alexandria when news came through the Germans had signed the instrument of unconditional surrender and the next day was officially declared 'V.E. Day'. All I remember now is that my eyes were bloodshot for 48 hours!!!

When the Board of Trade re-introduced the examination for Extra-Master, (which had been suspended during the war years) I wrote to the Company asking for extended leave but Royal Mail Line refused my application. In a fit of pique and forever the April Fool I resigned and enrolled once again in Sir John Cass Nautical College for the obligatory eight month course.

In August 1946 I joined The Cunard Steamship Company and was appointed Junior Third Officer in their 'Mauretania'. The years immediately following the Second World War saw the flood-gates of travel open across the North Atlantic. As a complete change from the war years at sea I now enjoyed seeing and meeting many interesting people. Aristocrats, people from commerce and politicians. Stars of stage, screen and radio. Television was still in its infancy. They were all passengers travelling between Europe and the United States of America.

The three years I served in the 'Mauretania' were significant for several reasons. I began as Junior Third Officer, then promoted to Inter. Third and eventually served as Senior Third. Then came the excitement of making five fortnightly cruises from New York to the West Indies and a welcome change from the North Atlantic. Last, but by no means least, I married a beautiful girl who also lived near Colchester.

In the Cunard Steamship Company promotion on seniority often meant a change of ship which is how I next found myself First Officer of 'Scythia'. In the four years in this stately old ship two were spent carrying Displaced Persons who had suffered years of deprivation in the hideous concentration-camps of Auschwitz, Belsen, Dachau and dozens of others. I still vividly remember them staggering up the gangway at Cuxhaven, all half-starved, pale and frightened. But ten days later, thanks to the tender care of the whole ship's complement, they tripped ashore in Quebec bright-eyed and pink-cheeked, ready to face new lives in Canada.

Now came periods when I was required to serve ashore as Temporary Assistant Superintendent in the London Dock Offices.

Although this was a pleasant change from sea duties, and a more regular home life, the mal-practices of London stevedores and dockers often irritated me. So much so there came a time when I received the customary green envelope from Liverpool with instructions to take short leave before joining one of the Company's ships at Southampton.

I shall never forget that morning when I climbed out of the taxi that had brought me from Southampton Central Station. As the driver unloaded my luggage I glanced up at this enormous but graceful Leviathan alongside Ocean Terminal. Her gleaming black hull rising to pristine white passenger accommodation. I counted fourteen lifeboats snugged into the davits and higher still three enormous red funnels with black tops and two slender masts raking slightly backwards. There came a lump in my throat as I looked at the white apron around the port bow and in letters three feet high, stretching fifty-two feet aft I saw the magical name 'QUEEN MARY'. My memory took me back to that cold, wet afternoon in December 1932 when I had first seen this graceful ship on the slipways of John Brown's Shipyard. When I imagined hearing a mysterious voice say "One day, my son, you will be First Officer of the truly magnificent ship!!!".

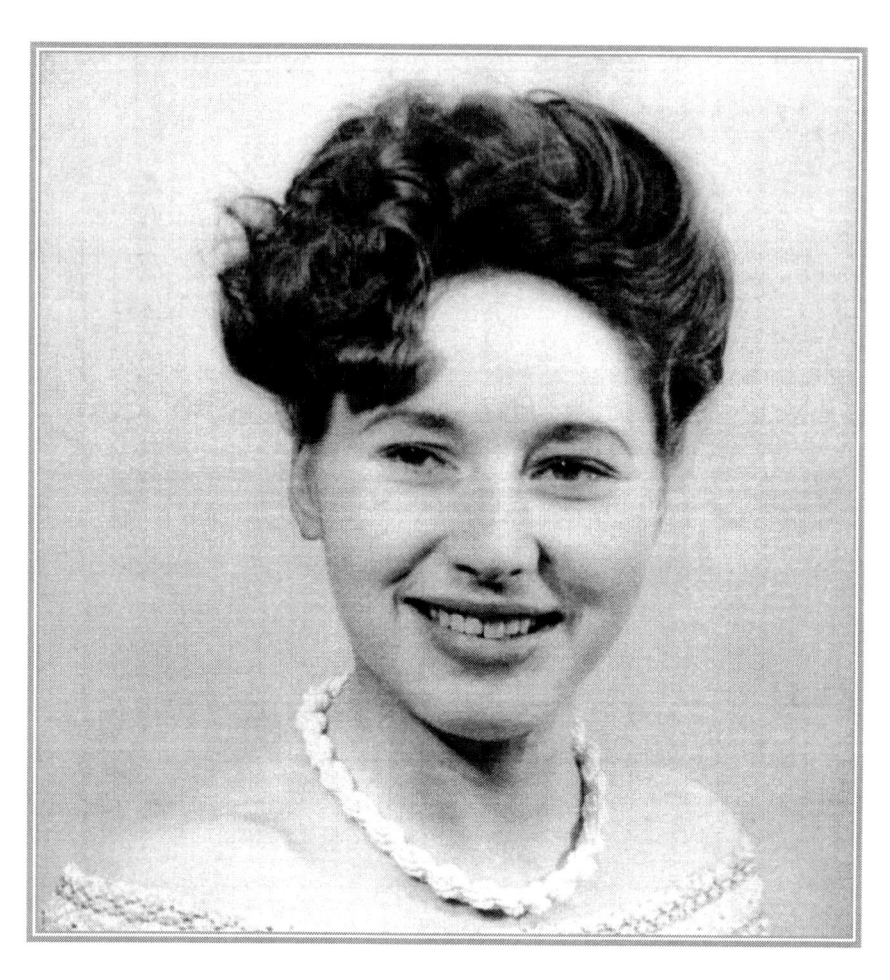

Joan Novello

Queen Mary

THE BRIEFEST ENCOUNTER

Since the troopship 'Alcantara had arrived back in Liverpool towards the end of March 1944, dockyard workmen had been busy removing all the ship's armaments from the gun-positions while others had been painting large Union Flags on the ship's sides. At the same time gangs of stevedores had been loading thousands of Red-Cross parcels into her cavernous cargo-holds. Meanwhile I had been included on the list for the second leave party.

Although it had not been officially confirmed it was generally understood 'Alcantara' was due to sail for Gothenburg Sweden in an exchange of medically-unfit prisoners-of-war, when the negotiations were eventually finalised. It had been six months since I had last seen my Mother and two sisters and I was looking forward to the week's leave.

After having been at home five days I had again enjoyed a few hours in the company of friends at 'The Anchor' in Rowhedge but long before 'time' was called I bade 'goodnight' to all and sundry and left the noisy smoke-filled bar. As I weaved my way slowly homeward I succumbed to a fit of giggles as I compared myself with the 'lowing herd' in Grey's 'Ellergy'.

On arrival home I found my Mum bright-eyed and cheeks flushed with excitement. It appeared that while I had been slurping pints of bitter she had taken a telephone-call from John Swallow the Chief Officer of 'Alcantara'. He had 'phoned to say there had been a fire in the troop canteen which, although not serious, meant some delay in sailing and I was to remain on leave until further notice. When she had finished telling me the good news I said. "Mum, this calls for a special celebration, where's the Port?" And I slept better that night than had for months, even years.

Unfortunately even extended leave comes to an end, and soon it was kisses, hugs, handshakes and goodbyes before climbing into the taxi that was to take me to Colchester North Station. The familiar feeling of acute indigestion had all but gone until my train was delayed by an air-raid over Chelmsford and it was with only a few seconds to spare that I made the connection at Euston.

As expected in wartime Britain the train to Liverpool was crowded and it was only by a stroke of luck I was able to find a centre seat in a first-class carriage. No sooner had I placed my suitcase on the luggage-rack when a shrill whistle from the guard, echoed by the 140 ton locomotive, and with a few preliminary jolts we began to crawl out of the station. Clumsily I fell rather than sat in my seat much to the amusement of the other occupants in the compartment.

With nothing to read and nothing better to do I began a furtive study of my fellow-travellers. Directly opposite sat a young fair-haired pink-cheeked naval midshipman. I soon became aware that he couldn't take his eyes off the ravishingly beautiful blonde girl seated on his right. To his left sat a senior army officer, who, by the red tabs, I took to be a staff officer but much of his face was hidden behind a copy of 'The Times'.

On my right sat a Royal Canadian Air Force officer wearing the two rings of a flight-lieutenant and on his left breast a half-wing and the letter 'N' identifying him as a navigator. Seated to my left was a mature but the most beautiful woman I had ever seen. Wearing an obviously expensive fur coat, I noticed she was reading a small green-covered book and on her lap an open exercise book in which she was frequently making notes. Quite suddenly she looked directly at me and, to cover my embarrassment, I blurted "It looks very much like Greek to me".

The lady gave me a bright smile, showing even white teeth, then, with a little laugh she replied, "No as a matter of fact it's Russian". Noting the look of surprise on my face she then added, "Languages are a hobby of mine - this is the fifth I am attempting to learn", she paused for a second then, with a little self-concious deprecating laugh she added, "It's almost as difficult as Japanese". I told her my Japanese was limited to the few words of greeting such as, "oayogosaiimus", "conichiwa" and "conbanwa" and the trite expression for goodbye, "syanara". I concluded with embarrassment. Giving me another bright smile she said, "Well. at least that's a start". And we both laughed.

And as our train thundered northwards and the minutes slipped by, this very attractive lady and I chatted away as though we'd known each other for years. At first her hobby for languages remained the topic of conversation but gradually I became aware how cleverly and subtly she was encouraging me to talk about myself. How, for instance, had I learned those few Japanese expressions? Rather self-consciously I went on to explain how, in 1936 I had been badly injured on board my ship and rushed to hospital in Kobe. In reply to further questioning, and with another self-concious laugh I went on to describe how the little Japanese nurses had thoroughly spoiled me.

During this time I had been aware of other attractive young ladies passing to and fro along the corridor who had lightly tapped the window of our compartment. I had also noticed how my companion had acknowledged their tap with a wave of her hand. At last I couldn't contain my curiosity and remarked she appeared to have many friends on the train. My companion then explained that they were all members of her band. At the very mention of 'band' I then realized who my beautiful companion really was - none other than the celebrated and world-famous ladies band leader 'Ivy Benson'!

Seeing the look of utter incredulity on my face Miss Benson nodded towards the pretty girl seated opposite and said, "That is my tenor-sax player who has been with me the longest". She paused then added, "Sandra takes charge whenever I'm absent for one reason or another", and with that she leaned forward and tapped the girl playfully on the knee.

Miss Benson then went on to say they would be playing that evening at the 'Grafton Rooms' in Liverpool and that they would be 'on the air' with the BBC between nine and ten o'clock. Suddenly she patted my hand and said, "Why don't you come along?", there was a slight pause then she went on, "By the way, what is you name?" For a few seconds I hesitated, then replied, "Williams - Gwilym Williams", then added apologetically, "From West of the Severn", at which she gave a little chuckle.

At that moment our conversation was interrupted by the screech of brakes being applied as the train approached the outskirts of Crewe and eventually, as it came to a grinding halt I saw we had stopped immediately opposite the station buffet. Few of my readers will now recollect that during the Second World War the weary travellers seldom enjoyed the luxury of 'Buffet or Restaurant Cars' on the railways. So, on a sudden impulse I turned to Miss Benson and my questioning lips framed the magic word "tea?"

With a beaming smile of gratitude Miss Benson nodded and I gave the young midshipman opposite a wink as I said, "Come on Snotty it's teatime". Then, opening the carriage-door leapt on to the platform with the youngster close on my heels, burst through the door of the Buffet demanding of the women behind the counter, "Six teas please". Within a matter of minutes we were back in the compartment with six steaming beakers of fragrant tea, much to everyone's delight. Even the grizzled old Colonel gave me a broad smile as he growled, "Good show old boy, good show - what!".

As much as I could have wished this journey could have gone on indefinitely, all too soon the train slowed as it entered the soot-grimed tunnel approach to Lime Street Station and ground to a halt. Without uttering a word I leapt onto the platform to the sound of doors slamming behind me. I made a beeline for the taxi-rank and with luck and friendly persuasion commandeered the first three having confided to the cabbies who their fares were about to be.

With the help from a couple of lady porters we managed to squeeze the twelve ladies and their musical instruments into the taxis much to the amusement and advice of the drivers. As I turned to assist Miss Benson into the leading cab she gently held my arm and said, "Thank you Gwilym West of the Severn you've been a great help to us all". And, as I was about to mumble something about it being a pleasure she added, "Please try to come to our show tonight, I'll leave word at the door". With that she gave my arm a gentle squeeze before climbing into the taxi where she wound down the window to repeat, "Please try".

Just as the driver started the engine I managed to say, "If I can't make it tonight, would you, could you play a request number for me?" She nodded and said "Of course dear boy what would you like?" so I said, " Somewhere Over The Rainbow", to which she replied, Yes of course, it's a lovely number from 'The Wizard of Oz' sung by Judy Garland". And as the taxis moved away my memory slipped back to that evening in San Francisco! And as her taxi passed under the arched station exit I saw a tiny white-gloved hand still waving. I took the tram to Pier Head and the overhead railway, (now long since gone) to Sandhills Station, Gladstone Dock and the officers' quarters in the troopship 'Alcantara'. And all the way back to my ship the one thought uppermost in may mind, "Would I ever see or meet that very attractive, celebrated Ivy Benson again or was it fated to be just a 'Brief Encounter' ? ".

When I arrived on board 'Alcantara' it was to learn there had been some changes of personnel. First of all, and to my satisfaction, 'Bogey' Knight had been superseded by Captain W.J. Carr and a junior officer, 'Polly' Perkins who was to become my new watch-mate. Both Captain Carr and Perkins, had been taken prisoners-of-war when their ship 'Natia' had fought a losing battle with the German surface raider 'Thor'. The self-same enemy raider that had previously fought 'HMS Alcantara' earlier in the war when she had been an armed merchant cruiser. I was to learn much more of their misadventures when together in the watches ahead.

Meanwhile, after dinner that evening I joined some of the officers in the wardroom for a few beers and a chat. It must have been several minutes after nine o'clock when over the wireless I heard a familiar voice saying, "Ladies and Gentlemen, please take your partners for the next dance - this is a special request number from a very special sailor-friend of mine". My heart gave a few extra thumps and I held up my hand admonishing my fellow officers for silence as the refrain 'Somewhere Over The Rainbow' came over the air. Needless to say I had to suffer the torment of leg-pulling and innuendo after having confided how I had met Miss Ivy Benson on the train.

A few days later 'Alcantara' sailed from Liverpool on the short run to Belfast Lough where we lay at anchor to await the outcome of negotiations between the Red-Cross Commission, the German and British Governments on the exchange of these medically-unfit prisoners-of-war. While at anchor 'Polly' Perkins and I calculated and plotted courses on the charts between Belfast and Gothenburg. While doing so he told me all about events from the time he and Captain Carr had been taken prisoner when the 'Natia' sank and eventually ending up in a German prisoner-of-war camp.

The days and weeks slipped by while 'Alcantara' remained at anchor in Belfast Lough. Evidently negotiations had come up against something insurmountable. Meanwhile I had heard more of 'Polly' Perkins' misadventures at the hands of his German captors. He told me life at the 'Marlag' P.O.W. camp not far from Bremen was not as hard as he had at first feared. They were allowed to play all kinds of games both outdoor and indoor and the Red-Cross parcels were fairly regular. He told me they had quite a good library including text books to enable them to study for the written parts of the Board-of-Trade examinations. Leaving only 'signals' and the oral part of the examination to be sat on eventual return to the U.K.

When my watchmate mentioned the library I told him that when I had passed the examination for my 'Master's Certificate Competency' in 1942 I and many of my fellow-students had readily obeyed the call from the Red-Cross to hand in text-books, if no longer required, to be sent to P.O.W. camps. I had barely finished saying this when 'Polly' let out an excited exclamation, dug a sharp elbow into my ribs and almost shouted "G. D. Williams, 'Normandy', Old Heath, Colchester, Essex!" Angrily massaging my ribs I snapped, "So what, that's my home address you fool". Flushed of face he retorted, "Don't you get it Sir, from the camp library I borrowed 'Brown's Deviation and the Deviascope', and in the fly-leaf of the book of the book you had written your name and address".

For a matter of seconds we stared at each other while I was still massaging my bruised ribs, then suddenly I exploded with the words, "Well I'm damned" and we both burst out laughing. When we regained a semblance of composure all I could think of saying was, "That's the long arm of coincidence 'Polly'". His reply to that was to say, when repatriated from Germany on health grounds and on arrival home he'd received a letter from the Board of Trade saying he'd passed their written examination for 'Second-Mate - Foreign Going Steamship'.

A few days later it appears all negotiations had broken down and we were recalled to Liverpool. Our navigational calculations and chart-plotting a sheer waste of time, but then, worse things can often happen at sea. We duly weighed anchor and returned to Liverpool where stevedore gangs unloaded those thousands of Red-Cross parcels. Shipyard workers returned all the ship's guns to their rightful positions and the beautiful Union-Flags in 'Technicolour' erased with dull grey paint.

A week later we moored the ship alongside Princes Landing Stage to martial music and within minutes we were embarking hundreds of military personnel. Throughout most of the morning The Royal Marine Band played blood-stirring tunes while the troops were embarking, some in Air Force blue, some in Navy blue but most of them wore Khaki. Meanwhile, my watchmate and I busied ourselves putting away some of the unwanted charts and replacing them with those required for the Mediterranean,

For the next several months we delivered troops to various theatres of war and returned with German and Italian prisoners-of-war to POW camps in North Africa. For much of the time we carried Nigerian troops as permanent guards over the prisoners. At first we found it pretty disconcerting to come face to face around the bridge on a dark night with a Nigerian soldier not seeing him until a wide smile uncovered two rows of enormous white teeth!!!

We only returned once to the U.K. for dry-dock repairs, the removal of barnacles and fresh coats of red boot-topping and antifouling paint. Christmas 1944 came and went and the New Year ushered-in. We were in Alexandria Harbour celebrating my 30th birthday, 7th. May 1945 at the same time as General Jodl was signing the instrument of unconditional surrender of all German forces. The next day was officially designated 'V.E. Day' and our celebrations went on a while longer, (I think)!!!!

Perhaps dear reader, I could call this a 'Sequel' to what has gone before. I'm not a professional writer so how should I know? Anyhow, the years have rolled away, the Second World War is all but forgotten, except by those who were deeply traumatised by it. Peace to a war weary world. In 1946 I resigned from Royal Mail Lines to enjoy much shorter voyages with the Cunard Steamship Company serving in the second 'Mauretania' of that name.

By 1948 I had also met, courted and become betrothed to the girl of my dreams, Joan Novello Matthew with plans for our nuptials in October. After war service in the Womens' Auxiliary Air Force Joan had been seconded to the Air Ministry in London where she had a little flat in Maida Vale.

Each voyage was to New York and on return to Southampton I would invariably, (when off duty) nip up to London and spend a few hours with my fiance. There was another girl, a musician, whose flat was on the same floor as Joan, and although I had never met her, I'd often hear her practising her scales on her Oboe.

On one of my periodic visits I happened to hear this girl sobbing and I asked Joan if she knew what was the matter. Yes she knew alright, and I was told that the girl had been out of work for some time and was five weeks behind with her rent. A few hours later when following the fond rituals of saying goodbye I suddenly remembered the plight of the girl next door. I told Joan to tell her neighbour to go and see Ivy Benson and to say that "Her young sailor friend had sent her".

A few weeks later, on the next visit to my fiance, I was met with a very cool reception. In spite of it being mid-July the atmosphere in the flat was positively chilly. It didn't need a Sherlock Holmes to deduce something was up. Puzzled out of my scalp I tried every little trick in the book to wheedle out the reason for her coolness until, eventually, she blurted out, "How well do you know Ivy Benson?". So that was it!!!

Joan resisted my first attempts to embrace her but with the help of a few soothing words she eventually thawed and sat beside me with my arm around her waist and I began - "Now I'm going to tell you exactly how well I know Ivy Benson - and I'll tell you the whole story if you promise not to interrupt." She was about to say something but I placed my forefinger against her lips and said "Promise?" and after a slight pause she nodded her head.

Starting with my returning home from 'The Anchor' and finding my Mum excited with the news that my leave had been extended due to a fire, I told her the whole story from beginning to end. Well, at least up to the point where I had helped Miss Benson and her band into their taxis - omitting my request to play 'Somewhere Over The Rainbow'! I was afraid my darling would then have been suspicious about 'that evening in San Francisco'.

When I had finished my story her only remark was, "and that's all?" I gave her tiny waist a squeeze and, nodding my head replied, "and that my darling is the truth, the whole truth and nothing but the truth - so help me Gawd". At that she gave a little giggle but then in serious mood again she said, "and on the strength of that you told me to send that poor girl for a job with Ivy Benson?" Again I nodded and said "well I admit that was just a bit of bravado to impress you" - I paused, then innocently asked, "by the way, did she get a job?" Joan turned and almost hissed, "yes, she did". And she got to her feet and began doing things with kettle and teapot.

When Joan had poured the tea into the willow-pattern cups she brought out the tin of biscuits and held it out for me to take one. They were my favourite 'Garibaldi' (the ones we always said had dead flies in them), I knew right there and then I was back in favour with my darling and all was right with the world.

Phew!

EPILOGUE

As I write, it is thirty years since Joan and I were married in Saint Mary's Church, Lawford, Essex on Saturday 2nd. October, 1948. This beautiful old church, part of which dates back to Norman times, had been decorated for the Harvest Thanksgiving Services next day. Ex-Army Chaplain Lt. Colonel Strover officiated and gave us his blessing.

We now have three daughters and they too are married providing us with seven grandchildren to whom we are ridiculously indulgent - and why not? During much of these years my wife has had to wear many caps in my absence at sea. As gardener, painter/decorator, chauffeuse and much else besides, and who I appreciate and am eternally grateful.

Since retirement I became 'founder member' of Mersea Island Probus Club and more recently President of the Colne Committee of the 'King George's Fund for Sailors'. Often invited to give 'talks' to various Clubs, Societies and Institutions I have waived a 'speaker's fee' in favour of donations to the 'Saint Helena' Hospice' or the 'K.G.F.S' charities.

It was while returning home late one evening from Manningtree where I gad given one of my 'talks' when, on my car radio, I listened to Miss Ivy Benson being interviewed. Almost immediately my memory took me back to that wartime train journey from Euston Station in London to Lime Street Station in Liverpool - hence this narrative, 'THE BRIEFEST ENCOUNTER".

Ivy Benson

THE MILLS OF GOD

For once the North Atlantic was in a benevolent mood. The weather as near perfect as anyone could wish. My young watchmate Harry Dormer and I returned to the bridge of the passenger ship 'Franconia' having been relieved for lunch as was the custom. Although it was bitterly cold outside the wheelhouse the sun shone in a cloudless sky and the sea as calm as the proverbial 'mill-pond'.

We were outward bound on what was to be our last voyage to Montreal in 1961. Our next crossing would be to New York and the beginning of Winter cruises to the Caribbean. At this late time of the year we were taking the shortest route to the River St. Lawrence via the Straits of Belle Isle. And a period when icebergs are (theoretically) few and far between.

As already stated, although bitterly cold, it was still a pleasure pacing up and down the bridge in the sunshine while chatting to my watchmate. Suddenly I spotted a dark shape on the horizon and a few degrees on our port bow. Through binoculars I identified it as a lone fishing-boat and by radar just over seven miles away.

As most sailors are aware there is a high incidence of fog around the Grand Banks of Newfoundland. A rough rule of thumb is when the 'dew-point' between the wet and dry thermometers falls below the sea-water temperature one can assume fog is imminent. It was with this knowledge I thought it prudent to call the fisherman on our VHF (Very High Frequency) radio-telephone. "Ahoy fishing-boat on my port bow, this is the 'Franconia' - 'Franconia' how do you read - over" I didn't have to wait more than a couple of seconds when a marked Welsh accent replied. "Hello 'Franconia' this is 'Rose Valiant' replying - good afternoon Sir, how can I help you?" I then said. "Good afternoon 'Rose Valiant' how long have you been fishing these waters, and have you sighted any icebergs? over".

Again within seconds came the reply, " Hello 'Franconia' - we've been five weeks out here, haven't sighted one iceberg and what is more, we haven't seen much bloody fish either but we'll be heading for home at the end of the week, over" I then asked, "Where is home skipper, over" and he replied "we're hoping to be home for Christmas 'Franconia' what about you - over" I replied, "this is our last trip to Montreal this year skipper but we'll be cruising in the West Indies during Christmas, over" and with that we exchanged the usual seasonal sentiments before 'signing-off'.

But that wasn't the end of our brief encounter by which time the fishing-boat was now well abaft our beam and I still hadn't switched-off the radio telephone. I became aware of a faint voice which turned out to be the 'mate' in a dory a couple of miles further away. So faint I had to turn-up the volume control as we listened to the conversation between the skipper in the larger fishing-boat and his 'mate' in the dory. To call the conversation 'ripe' with bad language would be the understatement of the year! The skipper's 'mate' was not only cold but totally fed-up with a disappointing fish-catch.

I called 'Rose Valiant' again and told the skipper how we had enjoyed the 'fruity' language between himself and his 'mate' we had put the conversation over the 'Tannoy' and all our passengers were rolling on the decks with helpless laughter. His last retort was a laughing "Bon Voyage you saucy sods!!!"

The years rolled away, or to coin the phrase, 'much water had passed beneath the bridge, (or bridges)'. And with it came my promotion, based purely on seniority, until appointed Master of my own ship and the courtesy title of Captain.

During much of those years we - that is to say, my family and I, lived in London. But with retiring age fast approaching we finally bought a modest but attractive bungalow on Mersea Island nine miles from Colchester in Essex. In the last twelve-months of my service with Cunard Line I had seven weeks accrued leave which took me up to my 63rd. birthday on 7th. May, 1978 and my official retirement.

Be all that as it may, my reader will readily appreciate the memory of that chance encounter with 'Rose Valiant on the approaches to Belle Island Strait had faded considerably from my memory. It was not only the passage of time but a very sad period entered into my life with the terminal illness of my older sister Win. For the last several months of her life my wife and I made countless journeys by car to and from my sister's home in the Swansea Valley. As is so often the case, it was as much relief as it was heartbreaking when she died.

But there was a certain amount of compensation to my frequent visits to my birthplace in that I was able to see dozens of my relatives whom I hadn't seen for many years. Among them my first-cousin Wesley Williams and his wife Margaret. I was particularly interested to learn their son Huw was researching the Williams family-tree with considerable help from Aberystwyth University. So much so that on the final visit to attend my sister's funeral Huw presented me with a copy of our family-tree together with much associated information. When time permitted a leisurely study of these papers a spark of interest and enthusiasm blossomed in my mind.

I have frequently been asked why I had chosen a seagoing career and were there no other sailors in the family who may have influenced my choice. To the first question I have given the terrible years of depression that followed the First World War as being responsible. Because there were so few options of employment open to a young school-leaver. To the second question I confessed not knowing of anyone in my family daft enough to choose a seagoing-career.

But there I was hopelessly and helplessly very wrong indeed, for the earliest inspection of the 'Family Tree' given me by Wesley's son Huw indicated that my great-great-grandfather Watcyn Williams had also been a seaman. He had served his apprenticeship, and later as 'mate' on board ships sailing out of Barmouth when the slate-quarries of North Wales provided the civilised world with their product.

It appears that from s very early age Watcyn had followed in his father's footsteps of being a keen gardener and in much of his spare time away from ships he had cultivated and grown a variety of standard and climbing roses. Unfortunately for his hobby and passion his ship was captured by the French at some time during the Napoleonic War 1803 - 1815. With others of the crew he was landed in Lorient and for many weeks incarcerated in the dungeons beneath the fortress.

A week or so later in company with other prisoners-of-war he was marched under escort for many miles inland until they arrived at an old army barracks on the outskirts of Pontivy in Brittany. They found the accommodation and their treatment by French army personnel a big improvement. Much of their food was grown by themselves within the precincts of the barrack grounds with chicken-runs and a piggery cared-for by the inmates.

As a young schoolboy I had known of Breton farmers arriving in Swansea Docks loaded with onions. They would cycle up the valleys with ropes of onions slung from poles across their shoulders. Their Breton patois was so similar to the Welsh language they could communicate fully with the valley-folk.

Not surprisingly therefore, our intrepid Welsh sailor Watcyn Williams found it comparatively easy to converse with some of his French guards. Day after day as they laboured in the barrack gardens under the watchful eye of the guards Watcyn became quite friendly with a corporal named Phillipe. Until one evening in late autumn he was sent for by the elderly commandant whom, he found, spoke fairly good English.

It appears his friendly corporal had reported to his superiors something of Watcyn's gardening skills which had come to the notice of

Colonel Vercher the commandant. Satisfied about his knowledge of horticulture the retired old soldier then led Watcyn out into a secluded rose-garden adjacent to the commandant's residence.

Looking around the garden Watcyn immediately recognised all the symptoms of 'rust', 'canker' and the powdery-white evidence of 'mildew'. Closer examination showed the rose-bushes to be suffering from soil depleted of the vital elements such as 'potash', 'nitrogen' and 'phosphates. Pointing out these deficiencies to Colonel Vercher young Watcyn made the obvious recommendations and was given a free hand to set about restoring the garden to its former glory.

While he and the commandant were discussing the provision of various manures they were joined by the Colonel's teen-age daughter Estelle. She was in a wicker bath-chair pushed along by her middle-aged 'nanny' she looked pale and very frail suffering a persistent cough. Although she spoke to her 'Papa' in French she kept glancing at Watcyn from time to time so he was able to get the gist of what they were saying.

Perhaps, at this stage, the reader should be reminded that in those far-off days there was none of your 'Geneva Convention' conditions to protect prisoners-of-war. (not that any so-called protection has been strictly adhered to since). But letters to and from loved-ones were unheard of during the Napoleonic Wars. It is to be appreciated therefore that huge gaps appear in Watcyn's account of his incarceration for three years as a POW in France. What scraps of information we have is what was told to his parents when released from the barracks in Pontivy and subsequent return to Wales and, in later years, what was told his wife and children.

That he devoted much of his energy and expertise to the commandant's rose-garden is not denied. And while he laboured at enriching the soil and nurturing the sickly bushes he was often watched critically by the commandant's daughter Estelle. What is well know is that by the following summer there were dozens of healthy bushes and a crop of beautiful roses.

It was in his third year as a POW in Pontivy that he awoke one morning to hear the chapel bell ringing continuously and was later told by the friendly corporal that the commandant's daughter had died. Outside, when paraded for roll-call in the old barrack square he saw the French tricolour flag at half-mast. Later in the afternoon he knocked at the door of the commandant's residence and handed the old colonel a flower-pot with a young tea-rose he had secretly cultivated. The stem bore a single rose with petals of pure white to resemble his daughter's pale features and edged a pale yellow to match her pale yellow hair. To the grief stricken old man he explained he had called this newly cultivated rose 'Valiant d'Estelle'. Without a single word spoken between them it was the warm hand-clasp that said everything.

It is not known why or when Watcyn was released from the prisoner-of-war camp in France and returned home to Wales. It could have been at some time after Napoleon's retreat from Moscow in 1812 and his exile on the Isle of Elba on 11th. April, 1814. Or later still, having escaped from Elba to raise another conquering army he was finally defeated by Wellington and Blücher at Waterloo on Sunday 18th. June, 1815. And to die a very lonely prisoner six years later on the island of St. Helena.

Pure speculation leads me to believe it was the kindly old commandant of the POW barracks in Pontivy that arranged Watcyn's release or escape. He must have been grateful for the rejuvenation of the rose-garden but especially for the new bloom Watcyn had named 'Valient d'Estelle'.

That Watcyn returned to sea is well established and that he was Master of the sloop 'Valiant' when he married his childhood sweetheart Mary who had always been known locally as 'Mair Gwilym'. Records show that their union was blessed with six children all of whom were baptised by the Rev. John Jones, Rector, but only three survived to maturity and these were: -

Watcyn Pritchard Williams. Born 21st. January, 1832 (my Grandfather)
Elizabeth Louise Williams. Born 30th. April, 1835 (Aunt Elw)
Watcyn Wesley Williams. Born 11th April. 1838

The three who did not survive but died in infancy were as follows:-
Elizabeth Williams Baptised on 4th. July 1830

Mary Nancy Williams Baptised on 9th. October 1833
Charles Thomas Williams Baptised on 8th. July 1839

All six were Baptised at Llanaber Parish Church near Barmouth, Cardiganshire, West Wales.

Again it is not clear why or when Watcyn Williams' family left their home in Wales unless it had been something to do with his business as a shipmaster. But at the Baptism of his children it is recorded on their certificates as being a 'wine merchant' and living at 'Number Thirteen' Whitechapel in Liverpool. He died on the 22nd. November 1862 aged 74 and buried at St. Asaph. But his tombstone describes him as 'Captain W. Williams'. His widow 'Mair Gwilym' died two years later on the 20th. May 1864 and she was buried next to her husband at St. Asaph, Birkenhead.

It is a pity the records of the 19th. century were not as detailed (or as accurate) as they are today in the millennium of the 21st. century. It draws a curtain over the events that concerned my great-great-grandfather, Captain Watcyn Williams, on the other hand it brings into focus his three children out of six, two boys and one girl, who survived to maturity, namely, Watcyn Pritchard Williams, (my grandfather), his brother Watcyn Wesley and sister Elizabeth Louise, (Elw).

Here again little is known of their early lives. Education was in its infancy and only available to the 'well-off'. Few could read or write so records and diaries unheard of. But at about this period governments of Canada and Australia were enticing people to emigrate with promises of assisted-passages and grants of land. The Argentine government, keen to cultivate the barren provinces in the far south made similar offers of a promising future. An epidemic of migration fever swept the two boys and their sister into joining a party who sailed from Liverpool to Patagonia on the 25th May 1865 in the clipper-ship 'Mimosa'. The story of their successes is told elsewhere in 'The Patagonia Connection'.

The years have rolled inexorably on since my chance encounter with the fishing boat 'Rose Valiant' when I was First Officer in the 'Franconia' on passage from Southampton to Montreal. And how the encounter triggered the story about the adventures of my great-

great-grandfather Watcyn Williams. When he died in 1862 and was buried in the churchyard at St. Asaph and his widow 'Mair Gwilym' died two years later and buried alongside him and of their three children who survived to pioneer in Patagonia.

My reader would be excused thinking this would or should be the end of the story but strangely enough it didn't quite end there. In fact it was in June 1997 when I attended the annual reunion of the Cunard Steamship Company employees at a hotel in Warwick that the story really ends.

Over one-hundred and eighty ex-shipmates attended the reunion and, as can be imagined, a very good time had been enjoyed by all. The after-dinner speeches had been made and the diners began moving from table to table renewing old acquaintances. My wife Joan and I were chatting to Glyn Parry and his wife when a tall young man approached our table.

"Excuse me, Captain Williams isn't it?" said this good-looking young chap, "I don't know if you remember me, but I called-in at your office on the Fred Olsen Terminal and explained I was instructed to join the 'Parthia' as electrician". It was then I remembered the occasion pointing to a vacant chair invited the young man to sit.

He went on to say "Yes Sir, you told me the 'Parthia' had been delayed and wouldn't be on the berth until the next morning". I nodded, then added, "Yes I remember now, I also invited you to stay the night at my home to save you the expense and trouble of finding a hotel for the night". He laughed and replied, "Yes Sir, it was very kind of you and Mrs Williams to put me up for the night".

As we were chatting to the young ship's electrician who's name was Adrian Hughes he suddenly asked, "Were you serving as First Officer of the 'Franconia' around about 1960-61?" For a few seconds I gave it some thought, then nodded and replied "Yes, if I remember rightly I was First Officer when we made a couple of voyages on the Belle Isle route before starting a series of West Indies cruises". I stopped abruptly when I saw him grinning from ear to ear.

At first he apologised the said, "Then it must have been you who spoke to my father on the VHF radio/telephone" he paused for a second then went on, "Dad was skipper of the fishing-boat 'Rose Valiant' at the time and I can't count the number of times he's told us kids while laughing his head off!"

While Adrian was telling us this story I had unconsciously been holding my breath. Now, I let it all out with a low whistling sound. I simply couldn't believe my ears. I have experienced many coincidences in my life, dozens of them, but this really took the biscuit. I turned to look at Joan to find her eyes and mouth wide open with astonishment and all I could say was "Bloody 'ell".

When I next found the opportunity to say something I said with a smile, "You know, Adrian, 'Rose Valiant' is a pretty posh name for a fishing-boat" - his reply shook me rigid. "I can't remember when my mum and dad bought our house in Whitechapel, Liverpool but my older brother and I were born there". As I felt a sudden chilling premonition, I interrupted him with "What was the number of your house Adrian?" And without hesitation he replied, "It was Number Thirteen". I felt another cold shiver run down my spine.

In spite of the thoughts racing through my mind I apologised to Adrian for interrupting and pouring out a glass of wine to wet his lips, he went on, "As I was saying about dad's boat, there was a beautiful rose-bush under the kitchen window". He took a sip of wine, "The petals were almost totally white but the edges were a pale gold colour - I remember dad once telling us - "the Rector told your mum and me, it was called 'Valient d'Estelle'" and he'd said "if I remember rightly Mr. Hughes there's another one like it somewhere in France" . Again I couldn't help interrupting with, "Yes, there is - it's in a place called Pontivy somewhere in Brittany". And again I apologised for my interruption.

Adrian looked surprised but went on to say, "When dad became senior skipper of the Widdecombe fishing fleet they bought a brand-new boat and invited mum to name it and without hesitation she called it 'Rose Valiant'". He took another sip of his wine then said, "What did you mean when you said there was another rose like it in France Cap'n?" I then gave him a brief resumé of my great-great-grandfather's experience when taken prisoner-of-war, after which, he was silent while allowing this information to sink in. Even then, all he could say was "Good God" and I replied, "Amen to that".

I understand many, if not most landlubbers believe sailors are very superstitious. I don't think I am. I will leave it to my reader to decide if my story is fact, fiction or plain superstition. I can only hope my reader remembers Psalm 107.

"They who go down to the sea in ships and occupy their business in great waters. These men sea the works of the Lord, and his Wonders in the Deep"

A LITTLE OLD LADY

It was mid-July 1958 when I received the letter from Liverpool appointing me Junior First Officer of the Cunard luxury cruise-liner 'Caronia' in Southampton. She was in the dry-dock as I climbed out of the taxi that had brought me from Central Station and I immediately noticed something quite strange about the shape of her forefoot. That is the area where the stem meets and is welded to the 'coffin-plate' part of the keel. Later in the day I was told that when 'Caronia' was leaving Yokohama earlier in the year she had struck the harbour breakwater causing considerable damage to herself and the little lighthouse. Dry-docked in Yokohama to effect repairs a much shorter piece had been welded in its place, hence the strange-looking section I had first noticed.

A week after I had joined the ship we sailed for New York via Cherbourg and six days later arrived in New York much the worse for having encountered severe weather conditions on passage. The topmast yard-arm had broken loose and crashed to the deck but luckily there were no passengers around at the time due to the inclement weather. So, in the three days prior to sailing on the 'North Cape Cruise' not only were fresh stores taken on board - freshly-laundered linen, fresh water and fuel-oil - a new yard-arm was fitted too.

But right on time and amid the customary razzmatazz of balloons, bunting, colourful streamers and the band playing 'Auld Lang Syne' the 'Caronia' slipped her moorings to sail down the Hudson River on passage to her first port of call, Reykjavik in Iceland. Thence via the Arctic Circle to the land of the midnight sun to Hammerfest in Norway and North Cape.

The officers' table in the 'Sandringham Restaurant' was over on the port side adjacent to the ornate and heavy glass doors. At another table nearby sat a middle-aged couple, Mr. and Mrs. Gammy and their pretty little daughter Vicky, the only child among the passengers. At the insistence of his brother, a taxi driver in Chicago, they had emigrated from Birmingham to join him and within ten years they now owned a fleet of cabs and were millionaires, hence being able to afford a 52-day cruise in the 'Caronia' the 'Millionaires' Yacht'. More affectionately called by her millionaire passengers and her crew 'The Green Goddess'.

And at another table nearby sat a very elderly but sprightly lady whom I came to know as Miss Clara Macbeth and whom, I was told, had recently celebrated her 88th. birthday. There was a light drizzly rain the whole day spent in Reykjavik, bringing an air of gloom and despondency over the whole town. And it rained for much of the time between Hammerfest and the North Cape. So only a few of the hardiest passengers even bothered to make the climb to the top of the Cape itself.

Through and south of the Islands the weather improved somewhat and by the time we arrived in Trondheim the sun came out to apologise for its absence. One of our nursing sisters and I took a stroll ashore to see something of the town and in particular the very quaint old church there. The 'Caronia' steamed slowly around the little island in the fjord to give passengers a close view of the 'Svartisen Glacier' the biggest in Europe, thence down the Norwegian coast to Ytterdahl, Merok and Bergen where two 'Caronia' restaurants; 'Sandringham' and 'Balmoral' played local teams at football after the annual carnival there.

From Bergen the 'Caronia' continued her itinerary southwards to Oslo where the Chief Officer, Ginger Irvine and I went to visit the Maritime Museum. Of all the magnificent exhibits there I think the best was an exact replica of a 'Viking Longboat' in a beautiful state of preservation. And alongside it Thor Heyadahl's balsa-log raft 'Kon-Tiki'.

It was a warm balmy evening in Stockholm when Ginger and I decided to take a stroll ashore after dinner. The sun had just set a few minutes earlier but Stockholm enjoyed a fairly long period of twilight. We entered a park where we found a kiosk selling the most delicious, large black cherries and we each bought a bag. Then we came across a large gathering of young people chanting some Swedish slogans, which of course we couldn't understand a word of. Suddenly we could hear the sirens of police cars approaching and from out of which came dozens of police. Evidently they were determined to break-up this demonstration using the flats of their swords. Initially, Ginger and I were anxious in case we too would be set upon by the police, until, it seemed, every time a policeman dashed past he would halt in mid-stride tear-off a smart salute which we returned just as smartly - and soberly!

It rained almost continuously in Helsinki but during a dry spell Ginger and I took a stroll ashore and what we found remarkable was how every person we saw looked so gloomy. The town looked grey and the people looked just as grey. So we cut short our walk and returned to the ship to seek more congenial company over a pint or three.

And in Visby, on the island of Gotland, although it didn't actually rain the sky remained heavily overcast. The cobbled streets and houses were quaint and Ginger managed to get some interesting transparencies with his expensive camera. Yet again I was glad to be back onboard 'Caronia'. When we arrived in Copenhagen we were informed by the pilot the ship's draft forbade our entering the harbour so we were obliged to anchor and use our special cruise-launches to ferry our passengers to and fro. By midnight everyone was back on board, the launches snugged under their davits and we headed out into the North Sea on our way to Queensferry near Edinburgh in bonny Scotland.

The weeks had slipped by and now, as we crossed the North Sea towards Queensferry it was more a matter of days. We anchored in the Firth of Forth a few hundred yards downstream from the famous bridge. And again our six special launches were being used to take our passengers ashore from where dozens of coaches were waiting to whisk them away on tour to the many exciting parts of Scotland. I took some time off to run ashore and telephone my wife at our flat in London.

To arrive at our next port of call, Oban, we timed our departure from Queensferry in order to catch a favourable tide through the Pentland Firth giving us an extra five knots of speed for the better part of five hours. I was glad to accompany the Chief Officer in a stroll ashore in Oban if only to stretch our legs and again took the opportunity to telephone Joan and have a brief chat with two of our three daughters, the eldest having gone to a cinema with a couple of school chums.

From Oban we steamed through the 'Minches'; bringing back memories of so many wartime convoys which invariably used this route to avoid enemy 'U-Boats'. Once again it was our deep draft that prevented our entering the port of Dublin so we were obliged to anchor off the smaller port of Dun Laoghaire and use the cruise-launches. This procedure was repeated at the exotic little port of Glengariff in Southern Ireland where palm-trees grow in such an abundance one could imagine being in one of the West Indies.

Where, not long ago it had been a matter of weeks, then days but now, on leaving Glengariff the cruise was measured in hours to Le Havre and finally Southampton. Some of the passengers left at Le Havre to tour the continent while others chose to tour the U.K. with the choice of returning to New York in either of the 'Queens' or within the week in the 'Caronia' which was now due to make two Atlantic 'round-voyages' to New York via Cherbourg. As for your author, I was given leave for the first voyage and rejoin 'Caronia' for the second in two weeks time.

As many of us know only too well, those of us who find employment away from home and loved ones, the time away drags by on boots of lead while the time at home flies on winged feet. And so it happened I found myself unpacking suitcases in my cabin back on board 'Caronia' again. But there was one consolation, in just over two weeks we'd be back for the Winter dry-dock and overhaul period with the prospect of having either Christmas at home or the New Year.

But then again, the time slipped by so quickly it was January 2nd. 1959 and we were outward-bound to New York from where the supreme Cunard itinerary would bring us to the 108-day 'Around the World' cruise. Although I was not entirely surprised, it was a pleasure to see Miss Clara Macbeth and her Irish companion seated at their customary table a matter of a few feet from ours in the 'Sandringham Restaurant' again. And to see them waited upon by the same steward John Carter who fussed over them like an old mother-hen.

The itinerary of this cruise from New York would be taking in such places as, Trinidad, Pernambuco (Recife), Rio de Janeiro, and the lone outpost of Empire, Tristan da Cunha. Capetown, Durban, Zanzibar, Mombasa, the Seychelles, Bombay, Colombo, Singapore and Bangkok thence to Manila in the Philippines, followed by Hong Kong, Okinawa, Nagasaki, Kobe, Yokohama, Honolulu, San Francisco and Acapulco thence through the Panama Canal and finally the return to New York.

In some of the major ports the Company's Agent would bring me a parcel containing anything up to a dozen 'Admiralty Notices to Mariners'. The receipt of which would entail my spending hours in the chartroom correcting hundreds of charts. At times like these luckier mortals (like my fellow-officers) would be relaxing on a sun-drenched beach or enjoying the night-life. Believe me, the lot of the Jnr. 1st. Officer in Cunard ships was never-ever intended to be a happy one!!

If by chance I have created the impression I had a miserable 'Around the World' cruise in the 'Caronia' I should apologise, but I'm blowed if I will! On the other hand there were moments when I actually did enjoy myself. For instance, Mr and Mrs Pinchin whom I had known for several years, took me to dinner on one of the floating restaurants in Hong Kong. They also took me out to dinner in Yokohama and to the famous revolving restaurant at 'The Mark', in San Francisco. When Jim Pinchin had been a young man he'd been a radio officer at sea until emigrating to Canada where he ended up being President of the Canadian Wheat-Growers Association and a millionaire several times over.

Then again, at some port or another when Miss Macbeth had no desire to romp ashore I would escort her to the ship's cinema and watch a movie. As a piece of useless information the 'Caronia' screened only the latest releases and they were regularly exchanged at certain specified ports of call. The Purser was required by the Company to report passenger comments on each film. On other occasions if Miss Macbeth's companion wished to spend some time with some Irish stewardess who also hailed from Limerick I would volunteer to stay with Clara and play her favourite game of 'Scrabble'. But she was an inveterate cheat and in a fit of giggles admit it!

There were four or five elderly women who, like Miss Macbeth lived almost permanently on the 'Caronia' to avoid keeping huge domestic staffs to run their large and expensive homes. The only time they left the ship was during the dry-dock and overhaul periods. Mrs Dodge, widow of the founder of the Dodge Motors Company was another. She once confided she kept the large 280 foot steam-yacht simply because her husband had loved it so much, but its upkeep was a King's Ransom. Another lady whose name I've forgotten, because she was always known as 'Itsy-Bitsy' and she also lived on the 'Caronia' for cruise after cruise.

Our sailing from Yokohama was certainly something of an event. Remembering that in the previous year (1958) she had collided with the outer breakwater destroying the little lighthouse and in doing so had damaged her stem right down to the forefoot. On this occasion (1959) no sooner had we left the berth and headed for the gap between the two breakwaters, from the bridge I could hear the sounds of a hundred voices. On looking over the the top of the bridge-dodger I saw most of the crew mustered on the foredeck - and they were all wearing their life jackets! I drew the Captain's attention to the spectacle, but before he could utter a word the 'Caronia' steamed majestically through the gap and at the same time a roar of cheering approval welled upwards from the foredeck!!!

I suppose it was about now that the vague idea in my head began to crystallise and I found the opportunity to enlist the help of Esme O'Driscoll. Sworn to secrecy I asked her to list the number of cruises her employer had made in the 'Caronia'. I also coaxed the ship's joiner to make a picture frame to my design with the promise of a bottle of 'Scotch'. When I had all the information I required from Esme O'Driscoll I then asked the ship's printer to set it all out on parchment. Then, when all efforts were brought together we held a party in the wardroom to which Miss Macbeth and other passengers were invited. Staff-Captain Nicholas gave a speech then presented Miss Macbeth with the framed certificate which read as follows.

"TO OUR WELL-BELOVED CLARA MACBETH"

HAVING MADE SEVEN WORLD-CRUISES - FIVE NORTH CAPE CRUISES

SIX MEDITERRANEAN CRUISES and EIGHT WEST INDIES CRUISES

IN RMS 'CARONIA'

IS HEREBY MADE AN HONORARY MEMBER OF THE OFFICERS' WARDROOM

GOD BLESS HER

In Honolulu a couple of fellow-officers and I took the afternoon off to explore the island. There were still a few signs of the Japanese raid on Pearl Harbour. We opted for a swim off the world famous Waikiki Beach and found a disappointingly narrow beach where the sand has to be brought around from another part of the island. And from the water's edge razor-sharp lumps of coral that could cut your feet to ribbons so we returned on board very disillusioned.

Between Honolulu and San Francisco, Mrs Dodge wanted to return the hospitality shown her by the officers of all departments and held a party in one of the lesser used public rooms. With gin and tonics in hand, Robin Wadsworth and I were chatting to her lawyer and I couldn't hold back my curiosity. "Tell me Carl, with yourself, her private doctor and a nurse-companion what sort of income does she have?" He thought for a moment while stirring his drink, "It's very difficult to give an exact figure, Willie, but I would guess it to be in the region of $168,000 a day"!! As Jnr. 1st. Officer in the luxury cruise liner 'Caronia' at that time my salary was just under $300 a month!!

As I have already mentioned, in San Francisco I was taken out to dinner by Mr and Mrs Pinchin in the revolving restaurant at 'The Mark'. And a few days later some of us went ashore in Acapulco to see the devout young catholic boys kneeling in prayer before diving into the surf 180 feet below. Then came the transit through the Panama Canal from Balboa on the Pacific side to Cristobal on the Atlantic side. And six days later the 'Caronia' was steaming up the River Hudson and back into her berth alongside Pier 90 in New York. At long last it marked the end of her 108-day 'Around the World Cruise'. But, wait for it, in three days time we were due to make the 52-day 'Spring Mediterranean Cruise' where I would enjoy the company of my wife for three days in Venice. But that dear reader is another story!!!

The 'Spring Mediterranean Cruise' rather like the 'North Cape Cruise' ended in Southampton with passengers having the option to return to New York at leisure in either of the 'Queens' or in the 'Caronia' a week later. Be that as it may, in the Company's 'docking letter' I was withdrawn pending reporting for shore duty in London as Assistant Marine Superintendent. So it was quite some time before I was told the story that follows about our "well beloved" Miss Clara Macbeth. -

While the 'Caronia' was undergoing Winter overhaul in the Winter months of 1960-61 Miss Macbeth was sitting in the lounge of her luxurious penthouse apartment overlooking Washington Square, Lower Manhattan, feeling rather uneasy and disconsolate. She had just received a letter from John Carter, her favourite waiter of many years in the 'Sandringham Restaurant'. It seems his wife, due to some pique and jealousy, had forbidden him to sail in the 'Caronia'. He would have to apply for a post in either one of the 'Queens' or the 'Mauretania' - period!!!

John Carter had been her waiter for many more years than she cared to remember. He knew her every like and dislike of food and to nurse her delicate digestive system he always cut her food into small manageable pieces. And if she were, for one reason or another, a little off her food, he would coax and cajole her into eating. From the officers' table nearby I had often heard him bully her, but in the gentlest way, to eat.

The more she thought about it the more vexed she became. "Drat that stupid jealous woman" - she stamped her little foot - "And drat that stupid man as well". In her petulance she walked to the huge picture-window that gave her a magnificent view of the waterfront as far as Piers 90 and 92, the Cunard Piers. And there she saw the floodlit funnels of the 'Queen Mary' and her mind was suddenly made up, which made her feel much better.

She telephoned high-ranking Cunard officials in their head-office at 25 Broadway to book her a return passage on the 'Queen Mary' sailing for Southampton the next day. And as usual a request from 90 year-old Miss Macbeth was their command. Early the next day she took the private elevator from her luxurious apartment down to ground floor where she climbed into the waiting taxi to take her up-town to Pier 90 where she boarded the 'Queen Mary'

On her arrival at Southampton she took a taxi to the Carter's address opposite the Polygon Hotel. And without mincing words she told Mrs Carter not to be such a stupid woman. From a reliable source I was told she then accepted a cup of coffee then climbed back into the waiting taxi which returned her to the Ocean Terminal and the 'Queen Mary'.

A week later, when the 'Queen Mary' berthed alongside Pier 90 Miss Macbeth took another taxi downtown to Washington Square and her private elevator sixteen floors up to her penthouse. Pausing only to kick off her shoes she flung herself into her favourite armchair with a quiet smile on her pale lips and a feeling of satisfaction of having achieved what she had set out to do.

Three weeks later, in mid-January 1961 the overhauled and freshly painted millionaires' yacht, 'Caronia' steamed slowly and majestically up the River Hudson and North River to her berth alongside Pier 90 in Manhattan, New York City, NY, USA. And among her crew none other than John Carter, 1st. Class waiter. Prepared and willing to wait upon Miss Clara Macbeth in the 'Sandringham Restaurant' of RMS 'Caronia' (the Green Goddess).

There must be a moral to this story, although for the moment I cannot think of one - perhaps my reader can???

PARTICULARS OF RMS 'CARONIA'

Signal Letters: GYKS   Summer Freeboard: 21ft 9in
Builders: John Brown, Clydebank   Fresh Water Allowance: 7½in
Official Number: 182453   Engines: Impulse Steam Turbine
Port of Registry: Liverpool   Service Horsepower: 28,000
Length Overall: 715 ft   Breadth: 91ft 4in
Gross Tons: 34,172   Nett Tons: 18,633
Draft Summer: 31ft 7in   Boilers: 6 Yarrow   Propellors: 2   Pitch 18.42in   Diameter: 18ft 9in
Anchors: 3 180cwt each   Cables: 165 fthm
Fresh Water Capacity: 4,710 tons   Fuel Oil: 3,350 tons
Service Speed: 22.5 knots   Maximum Speed: 24 knots

Heights Above Keel: Mainmast Truck: 222ft
Crowsnest: 178ft

Lifeboats: 16 (1,614 Persons)   Rafts: 20(400) Persons

"THE MASTER AND HIS SHIP"

by

Charles H. Cotter, BSc, Extra Master.
(Foreign Going Steamship)

INTRODUCTION

A labourer is one who works with his hands,
A craftsman is one who works with his hands and his head,
An artist is one who works with his hands
and his head and his heart.

In relation to a shipmaster's function, ideally, he should become an artist in his profession, embracing the various aspects of his responsibilities. That is to say, good shipboard husbandry, dealing efficiently with changing meteorological conditions; the exercise of prudent and precision navigation; to insist upon exemplary safety procedures; to know the legal aspects of business and insurance.

The shipmaster should be well-versed in the Merchant Shipping Acts to prepare himself for marine and medical emergencies; to exercise discipline firmly and fairly. Above all to be a wise judge, to be independently-minded and kind to all that sail under him.

A ship's master should be a man of many parts with a wide scope of interests. Further, he should be well-versed in several branches of knowledge in order to work his ship intelligently. And finally he should be a well-informed ambassador of his country.

In fact, the ship's commander is 'Master Under God' invested with almost absolute power.

A burden of responsibility indeed.

A CHARISMATIC SKIPPER

I doubt if management of the Cunard Steam-ship Company ever realised, much less appreciated, that Captain Donald Sorrell, Extra-Master Square-Rigged Sailing Ships, had the kind of charisma that inspired all who sailed under him into a state of euphoria and hero-worship.

It was not only his superb skill as a shipmaster, of which there was no doubt, but it was his quiet, unassuming friendliness and charm that won him respect, loyalty and an abiding affection.

After a spell ashore in London as Temporary Assistant Superintendent I was delighted to be appointed to the Company's world-famous 'Queen Mary'. Especially as I would be serving under the command of this legendary Captain.

On meeting him for the first time I was astonished to find this 'giant among men' to be merely five feet tall. But during those two years I was privileged to serve under him he became, to me, just as he was to the other 1153 members of the ship's total complement, nearer to ten feet tall!

I shall never forget my first voyage on the 'Queen Mary' during 1963. We had sailed from Southampton with over a thousand passengers - First, Cabin and Tourist Class. Down in her capacious cargo holds there were many 'freight' cars and almost as many 'baggage' cars belonging to passengers on board. And as usual there was a considerable amount of passengers' baggage, Mail and 'high freight' cargo. And stowed in special security lockers a quantity of gold and silver bullion.

The cross-channel passage to Cherbourg was made in good time and in fine weather. With a breeze of under 25 knots we were able to berth alongside the Gare Maritime. Winds of over 25 knots would have obliged us to anchor in the outer harbour. And passengers, baggage and Mail would then have to come out in a 'tender' a much more expensive and time-consuming operation.

During that first voyage I came to know and admire Captain Sorrell a great deal. He would frequently appear on the bridge to enquire about the ship's position, speed and weather prospects. But I began to suspect it was just as much for a chat. On one such visit to the bridge he asked why I had left Royal Mail Line to join Cunard, adding that he realised by doing so at 31 years of age I had lost a considerable amount of seniority.

Feeling a bit self-concious I had explained how I had applied for extended leave to study for my 'Extra Master's Certificate' which had been refused, so, in a fit if pique, I had resigned. Captain Sorrell gave a grunt of sympathy and had then asked, "And did you obtain your 'Extra Master's Ticket'?" Feeling even more self-concious and not a little foolish, I explained that the course of studies took eight months. I had miscalculated my financial resources and had become heavily overdrawn at the bank and had applied to Cunard for a berth forthwith. With a wry smile I had then explained how I had hoped to have become an instructor at the Sir John Cass Nautical College. His only reply was "What a bloody shame Willie".

For the remainder of the voyage, and for that matter, for the two years I was privileged to sail with Captain Sorrell there grew quite a bond of liking and a great deal of respect between us. I soon discovered he kept remarkably fit at sea by taking a swim every morning at 6.30 and a regular pummelling and massage by the ship's physio-therapist. He also had a puckish sense of humour as will be illustrated by the following anecdote: -

On one particular voyage the itinerary of the 'Queen Mary' westbound included a call at Cobh Harbour in Southern Ireland. The reason for this was that the two Cunarders that normally called there were cruising in the West Indies. But the size and draft of 'QM' forbade our taking her into the inner harbour so we were obliged to anchor out in the 'Roads' not far from the "Daunt Rock' lightship. This also meant all passengers, baggage and mail being brought out in the tender 'Killarney'

It just so happened on this occasion the skipper of the 'Killarney' was on holiday and the 'Mate' left in charge. Captain Sorrell and I were still on the bridge, having just anchored the ship, when we sighted the tender steaming out of the harbour and heading in out direction. Making quite a normal approach at first the 'Killarney' came within eight or ten feet of the 'Queen Mary' when, for no apparent reason, she veered off to some distance away, dropped astern and then manoeuvred to make a fresh approach. And again when within a few feet of being alongside she veered off the second time to drop astern and another attempt.

Somewhat puzzled by these strange manoeuvres Captain Sorrell snorted and said, "Pass me the megaphone Willie". I did what I was told then listened open-mouthed as the 'old man' hailed the tender with "Ahoy skipper, stay where you are and I'll bring the 'Queen Mary' alongside you". I suppose it was due to my vivid imagination and the very thought of Donny Sorrell carrying out such a ridiculous manoeuvre that tickled me so much and I burst out laughing. The 'old man' looked over his shoulder at me with a frown of astonishment and then with a snort, he too began to laugh and we both collapsed in a fit of the giggles. Then, with tears streaming down his face he managed to blurt, "Come on Pilot, let's have a gin."

I had been in the 'Queen Mary' about a year when one day during my forenoon watch I was plotting the ship's position, on the chart when the 'old man' came onto the bridge and with a 'Good morning Willie" he threw a radio-signal in front of me with, "What do you think of that?" Looking up I replied, "Good morning Sir, I think we will have a good day's run today." Picking up the radiogram I read its contents: -

> With a threatened tug-strike in New York called to coincide with your arrival, suggest you proceed Halifax to disembark passengers and mail. All cargo to remain onboard until next voyage.
>
> Signed CUNARDSTAR

I called called out to my junior-officer Keith Garrard, Work out a Course and Distance to Halifax Keith." Captain Sorrell interrupted me with, "Belay that order Garrard." Then, turning to me said, "Willie these passengers have paid their fares to New York and it is to New York we shall go." My reply was, "Then you'll be docking without tugs Sir." Captain Sorrell gave a crisp, "Sod the tugs."

Three days later we arrived in New York with no sign of a tug anywhere in the harbour. Slowly we inched our way into the narrow gap between the Cunard Piers 90 and 92. Captain Sorrell stood in a corner of the wheelhouse frequently peering at his now famous semi-circular block of wood. He gave every order to the quartermaster at the helm and the others at the engine room telegraphs without raising his voice once.

Fifteen minutes later we were snugly moored alongside Pier 92 and the gangways lifted into position. I doubt if we would have cracked an egg during the whole operation. Needless to say almost every newspaper in the world carried headlines of this achievement. What is more to the point, all the New York tugs were back at work next day. (What one Master can do today - others can do tomorrow).

That Captain Sorrell was unquestionably confident in his own skill and ability there is not the shadow of doubt. And that he had the same confidence in his officers followed as night follows day. To me this was vividly illustrated by this simple anecdote: -

Homeward-bound from New York one voyage I arrived on the bridge to relieve the Chief Officer's watch. At this moment we were steaming up the English Channel on a fine summer's day and faintly on the starboard bow the outlines of 'The Casquets' the westernmost part of the Channel Islands group. Checking our position I calculated we were much to early to make our estimated time at the Cherbourg Fairway Buoy, 'C.1' where we would embark the harbour pilot M. Frelaut. I telephoned the engine room and asked the engineer on watch to reduce speed to 85 revolutions.

A few minutes later the bridge telephone rang and was answered by the standby quartermaster who held out the 'phone to me saying, "It's the Captain Sir." Taking hold of the handset I said "Good morning Sir' - "Good morning Willie, how are we doing?" I replied with, "We are almost abeam of The Casquets Sir, and I've reduced to 85 revs." "Right ho", said Donny Sorrell, "Keep her close to give the passengers something to look at, I'm with the PMO (Principal Medical Officer) at the moment, let me know when the Pilot is on board." And with that he rang off.

Never before in all my life as a watchkeeping officer had any Captain entrusted his ship to my sole care. I felt a surge of pride few have enjoyed as much as I did right then. Captain Donald Sorrell was leaving everything to me, bringing one of the world's fastest and largest ships to the Pilot station on the approaches to Cherbourg harbour. With the French Pilot on board we were passing Fort l'Quest and entering the outer harbour when Donny Sorrell ambled casually on to the bridge.

On another occasion, we had sailed from Cherbourg shortly after lunch one day and were steaming down-channel with the Channel Islands to port. Our speed was gradually increasing as the engineers coaxed the superheated steam into the turbines. It took the better part of six hours to bring the 'Queen Mary's' revolutions up to the required 176 to give her her service speed of $28\frac{1}{2}$ knots.

Suddenly the 'lookout' in the crowsnest reported "Ship on the starboard bow". With the aid of my binoculars I was able to identify the stranger as one of our own aircraft-carriers with two destroyers escorting her in the opposite direction to ours. With years of experience I anticipated the aircraft-carrier would flash a signal at any moment so I warned my junior to switch-on our signalling-lamp in readiness.

He had barely done so when the 'carriers' ten-inch projector began flashing the 'calling' signal of a series of 'A's', (dot-dash, dot-dash, dot-dash) and when Keith gave the acknowledging 'T' (one long dash), the aircraft-carrier continued flashing the signal "What ship?". With his mouth opened wider than usual, Keith, looking over his shoulder said, "He's asking what ship Sir". Rather irritably I snapped, "I can read too!"

Stepping out of the wheelhouse I looked aft along the Sport's and Sun Decks and there I was reassured were the 'Queen Mary's" three enormous red funnels with black tops. My junior gave a cough and said, "What shall I send Sir?" I replied, send "WE are not amused." Almost immediately came the reply, "Sorry Ma'am - Bon Voyage!"

We were still laughing our heads off as, when the 'carrier' and escorts were abeam the quartermaster 'dipped' our Red Ensign and I gave three long blasts on our sirens, the sound of which could be heard for twelve miles! The aircraft-carrier did likewise and with her escorts was soon lost to sight.

My two and a half years service in the 'Queen Mary' slipped by all too quickly. More than at any time in my seagoing career, I had thoroughly enjoyed being in a ship every schoolboy in the world knew. In particular I had enjoyed, even treasured serving under the command of Captain Donald Sorrell. I had enjoyed the friendship and companionship of my fellow-officers also. In short, from mast-truck to keel, from stem to stern the 'Queen Mary' had been a very happy ship indeed.

Alas, as sayeth the old cliché, all good things must come to an end. And this was no exception, one day on arrival in Southampton I was handed that all-too-familiar green envelope from Liverpool with instructions to "Proceed on leave pending further appointment". A week later I was again instructed to report for temporary shore duties in London as Assistant Marine Superintendent. This was one occasion when I would have preferred to remain in the 'Queen Mary'.

This spell in the Surrey Dock office in London lasted for over a year with its usual irritations at work but the bliss of being at home every night and seeing so much more of my family. Then came my appointment to the 'Queen Elizabeth' and to serve under the command of the Commodore of the Cunard Fleet, Sir Ivan Thompson who turned out to be as different from Donny Sorrell as chalk is to cheese. As a matter of fact the moment I joined her in Southampton I was told, "The Commodore eats First Officers!"

Where the 'Queen Mary' had made her 'maiden voyage' on 6th. May 1936 and was now over twenty years old, the 'Queen Elizabeth' had made her maiden voyage under great secrecy in 1940 to New York when both ships served their country well throughout the Second World War carrying thousands of Allied Troops to every theatre of war. In fact it has been claimed both 'Queen Mary' and 'Queen Elizabeth' probably shortened the war by over a year!.

I'm not at all sure about the Commodore's penchant for 'eating' his First Officers, but outward-bound on my first voyage in 'Queen Elizabeth' I got the distinct impression he was completely unaware of even my presence in the ship. After a most uneventful passage across the Atlantic we arrived at the 'Ambrose Lightship' in dense fog with the ship's siren making one long blast every three minutes. As I arrived on the bridge I heard the Commodore give the order "Stop all engines" and in the silence I could hear the 'put-put-put' of the pilot boat's engines approaching the ship's side.

Taking advantage of waiting for the pilot to embark and taking the lift to the bridge, I nipped into the chartroom to begin the various calculations of passage distances and speeds etc. This data is always required by the Purser's Office for processing and thereafter sent down to the Printer for the Log-Cards which were distributed to the passengers before disembarking. A beautiful artist's impression of the 'Queen Elizabeth' on one side and the voyage data on the reverse.

My calculations were well advanced when I heard the Commodore yell my name in no uncertain fashion. In spite of my protestations that the passage details had to be completed he scolded me rather rudely reminding me my place was with the pilot and in a way to which I took great deal of exception.

On the way up the Hudson River to New York the Purser's Office rang several times requesting the passage information. And each time they rang I told them in no uncertain terms they would have to wait until we were alongside. Needless to say the passengers disembarked that voyage without their Log-Cards. But while we were in New York the Chief Officer had orders from the Commodore that, in future at the end of a passage I was to be relieved from the wheelhouse to complete my calculations, by the day-officer or the night-officer depending on the time of arrival!!!

And so it was that during the eighteen months I served under the command of Commodore Sir Ivan Thompson there became, what I can only describe as a 'truce' between us. But that I exploded the myth the he 'ate' First Officers, I'll not deny. On the other hand, remembering he was also a director of Liverpool Football Club, woe betide everyone if Liverpool lost their match on Saturdays! Even I kept well out of his way. But if his team won its Saturday fixture then his 'vestry-meetings' after Church Service on Sunday he would be a most genial host.

Then it came to pass that a 'terminal illness; in the London Marine Department brought me ashore there once again and this time it was for a much longer period than previously. It was yet another opportunity to see more of my wife and children. But, as this story has nothing to do with my duties, trials and tribulations ashore I will skate rapidly through it and bring my narrative up to 1958 and my return to sea when appointed to the Company's 'Caronia'.

Built specifically for cruising, this 35,000 ton 'Caronia' can only be described as 'a thing of beauty and a joy forever'. Known as 'the millionaires' yacht' and 'the green Goddess' her hull livery was a complete departure from traditional Cunard colours, with seven varying shades of green. But her huge single funnel was typical Cunard red with narrow black bands and black top and was big enough for three double-decker buses to pass through!

Named 'Caronia' and launched by Princess Elizabeth on 16th. October 1947 her building in all its stages was supervised by Captain Donald Sorrell who became her first Master for several years until being given command of the "Queen Mary'. But from the moment I joined her in Southampton, I could tell she still bore that all-pervading atmosphere created by Donny Sorrell, that charismatic Captain.

Before sailing from Southampton I was kept busy sorting hundreds of charts in preparation for the voyage to New York and from thence on the North Cape Cruise with wealthy American passengers. This itinerary included Reykjavik in Iceland and the Arctic Circle to Hammerfest in Norway and North Cape. There followed calls at the Lofoten Islands and Trondheim, to the Svartisen Glacier, Ytardellm, Merok, thence to Bergen, where the ship's football team played the locals every year. Thence to Oslo and through the Great Belt into the Baltic Sea to Stockholm, Helsinki and the quaint little town of Visvy on the island of Gotland.

The next port of call would be Copenhagen thence to Queensferry in the Firth of Forth near Edinburgh and from there through the swift tidal waters of the Pentland Firth to Cape Wrath and Oban. Through the narrow channels of the 'Minches' to Belfast, Dun Laoghaire and the south-west corner of Ireland to Glengariff in Bantry Bay to l'Havre and finally Southampton! As my reader will appreciate, I had quite a lot of preparation to make for the forthcoming voyage.

Queen Elizabeth

'THE CHRISTMAS SPIRIT'

To the best of my knowledge it had always been a rule of the Cunard Steam-Ship Company that officers' wives were permitted, albeit begrudgingly, to visit their husbands on board while their ship was in port, but they were to be 'off the ship' by 20.00 hours (8.00 pm). It would appear that dalliance, and amorous adventures, would have to be enjoyed before that 'witching-hour'. Naturally the age of the devoted couple would play an important part in this scheme of things 'eight bells' notwithstanding!

But when Cunard was acquired by the entrepreneur Trafalgar House Investments Limited this rule was abandoned in favour of allowing senior officers to have their wives accompany them on a limited number of voyages in the year. Later this was amended to include the wives of junior officers.

But to get back to those darker days when the Cunard Steam-Ship Company were begrudging towards their officers. My wife Joan and I lived in a little flat on New King's Road in Fulham, London where our lives were enriched by our four-year-old daughter Carol-Anne. Joan being pregnant for the second time, we were

Julie, Joan, Carol-Anne, Gwilym, Jane.

expecting further additions to the family. Our happiness was now complete because at this time in our lives I was 'relief' First Officer in the Company's cargo ships having London as their terminal port.

A few days before Christmas 1952 our London Marine Superintendent, Captain John Woods telephoned me at home asking if I had received instructions from Liverpool regarding my next appointment to which I replied in the negative. Captain Woods told me the Company's 'Asia' was due in port the next day 23rd. December and was concerned there were no reliefs for the three officers during the Christmas period.

Before he rang-off I asked Captain Woods if he intended being on board after she had docked, to which he replied, he expected to be on board about eleven o'clock. I then said I would meet him there. After saying, "Thank you Williams, you've taken quite a load off my mind" he rang-off.

I gave Joan the gist of what we had discussed on the 'phone and she agreed with doing what I proposed, adding a few very uncomplimentary comments about the 'couldn't care less' attitude of bigwigs in Liverpool and Cunard in particular.

After a delicious breakfast prepared by my lovely wife, a quick kiss and a cuddle, I set off for the ten minute walk to the District Line station at Parsons Green. The sky was overcast and dry but with the threat of rain and the easterly wind bitter cold. With a grimace I thought we could be in for the rare white Christmas. I gave a little shiver of anticipation.

For anyone with a rudimentary knowledge of London's underground railway system a quick reference will reveal there are twenty-two stations between Parsons Green and East Ham stations. And the time taken by the District Line train allows one to read the Daily Telegraph from front to back page. At East Ham it often happens one has to wait a good ten to fifteen minutes in a queue in all weathers to board the 101 bus to the King George V Dock Gate. Provided there is no waterbound traffic between the King George V and the Royal Albert Docks the swing bridge is open to vehicles and pedestrians alike.

On this particular morning the road was clear and my walk from the dock-gate to the 'Asia' at Number 7 Shed uninterrupted so it was but a few minutes after 10.00 am when I climbed the gangway. My arrival at the First Officer's door was greeted by a mixture of jeers and cheers from Chief Officer, Alan Bull and his two fellow-officers as I shook hands with each in turn.

On arrival at its terminal port, whether Liverpool, Southampton or London and be it cargo or passenger ship, all Cunarders received information via the 'green envelope' indicating which officer would be sent on short leave during the ship's stay in port, or, for a longer 'voyage-off' period. Occasionally an officer would be sent on leave 'pending further appointment.'

Waving the 'docking letter' in my face and in his inimitable 'Scouse' accent Alan Bull said, "If there's no reliefs available Willie, like it says in this letter, what the hell are you doing here?" The Second and Third Officers had something similar to say but were waved to silence by the Chief Officer. Thus given the opportunity to reply I said, "Captain Woods 'phoned me yesterday to ask if I'd received instructions from Liverpool - and when I told him I hadn't, I suggested we meet here this morning - he said he'd be on board at about eleven o'clock."

I gave a quick glance at my wrist-watch and said, "That gives us half-an-hour, Alan, to go through the repairs and stores lists together while you get changed into civvies ready to buzz-off, I'm relieving you." The look of astonishment on his face made me want to burst out laughing but the looks on the other officers' faces discouraged it. Rather lamely I said, "As for you two, I think we had better wait to hear what Captain Woods has to say.

Alan poured-out two glasses of 'Scotch', then, as I went through the repair-list and other 'Voyage Returns' he began changing into his civvies while answering any queries I had and adding detail as and when necessary. Then, just as we were nearly through with all the paper-work Captain Woods arrived and for a few minutes there followed the customary greetings.

Knowing Alan Bull would also have some gin in the 'booze locker' and while he and Captain Woods were discussing the 'Voyage

Returns' I anticipated his wishes and poured him a glass of G & T, then waited until they were through.

Having satisfied himself with all the paper-work Captain Woods produced his pipe and tobacco-pouch then, having filled the bowl he proceeded to light it and when the coals were glowing to his satisfaction exhaled an aromatic cloud of blue smoke. Looking directly at Alan he said, "I'm sorry there seems to to have been a slip-up in the relief arrangements, Bull, but I 'phoned Liverpool before leaving the office and was told by Captain Pollitt there has been something of a 'flu epidemic up there and there are no reliefs available at the moment."

Alan empties his glass before replying, "Yes Sir, we know all about that, it's called Christmas 'flu up north." He put his glass down before adding, "But Willie here says, subject to your approval, he's ready to let me get off." Captain Woods looked at me before saying, "That's very generous of you Williams, but I'll have to clear it with Liverpool first in case they have other plans for you." I replied, "The shore-gang have already put the 'phone on board Sir, if you would care to ring them before lunch then Alan could catch an early train from Euston."

The 'Old Man' nearly knocked his glass over as he hastily got to his feet making for the door and the telephone downstairs. Alan looked at me, "I'm alright Jack with the ladder up, but what about the Second and Third Mates?" I shrugged, "Top up his glass Alan and we'll wait until he comes back". I paused then added a warning, "Don't make it too strong, he knows exactly how much gin there should be." And while we awaited Captain Woods return he took down his bottle of 'Scotch' and topped-up our glasses as well.

I have to admit, that when Captain Woods returned to the Chief Officer's cabin he was positively beaming. And I knew it had nothing to do with the half-glass of gin and tonic he'd imbibed. So it had to be good news. When reseated he removed the pipe from his teeth, took a long swig from his glass and said. "Well I've spoken to Liverpool", he paused to take another appreciative sip, "I spoke to Captain Letty, and, it seems Captain Pollitt is also down with this 'flu thing". He looked hard at Alan Bull as though defying him to repeat his joke.

Anyway, the upshot of it all was that owing to a complete misunderstanding in the Marine Department it had been the intention I should relieve the Chief Officer of the 'Asia' for the duration of the ship's time in London. After Captain Woods had finished imparting this piece of information I asked, "And what about the other two officers Sir?" Poor old John Woods looked uncomfortable, "I don't know, Letty told me they would have to decide among themselves how to arrange the watch-list."

For several minutes there was a complete silence in the Chief Officer's cabin, then I spoke of the idea that had buzzed around in my head. "Excuse me Sir" I began, "Supposing I were to volunteer to stay on board night and day over Christmas Eve, Christmas Day and Boxing Day, could the other two officers go home?" There was a long pause, Captain Woods evidently giving my suggestion some consideration, then, at last he nodded his approval. I gave a little cough then, looking him straight in the eye asked. "Would it be alright Sir if my wife and daughter could join us on board for Christmas dinner?"

Captain Woods spluttered into his gin and tonic then, in a choked voice said, "I don't see why not, I think she should be proud of you for what you're doing", he paused, looked at his watch and said, "And that reminds me, my wife is expecting me home for lunch, thanks for the gin Bull, and my compliments of the season to you all." As he left the Chief Officer's cabin we both wished him a 'Merry Christmas and a Happy New Year."

The activity around the officers' quarters for the next twenty minutes can only be described as 'frenetic'. Chief Officer Alan Bull and the Second Officer went off first sharing a taxi to Euston. Taffy Howells the diminutive Welsh Third Officer followed minutes later heading for Paddington Station and somewhere 'West of the Severn'. Having cut cards before leaving the ship, it had been agreed the Second Officer would return the day after Boxing Day.

Meanwhile I telephoned Joan to appraise her of the situation and arranged that she and Carol-Anne would come down to the ship in plenty of time for Christmas Dinner. And bringing with her a few changes of clothing to tie me over until I was able to go home when the Second Officer returned from leave. She also assured me the turkey we had bought would remain in the 'fridge' until later in the week.

It looked as though I would be lunching alone in the dining saloon until a couple of engineer officers turned up, so I immediately invited them to join me at the centre table. I learned from them that reliefs had been better organised by their superintendent so there were no complaints. I also discovered lunch was prepared and served by relief catering staff. So very few of the ship's original crew remained on board.

There had been no stevedore-gangs on board to discharge cargo but before leaving to catch his taxi Alan Bull had told me to expect a couple of gangs the next day. This I took with a pinch of salt because it is and accepted fact that priority is always given to sail ships before the Christmas holiday period. Later in the afternoon and before it became dark I made my 'Rounds' to ensure the moorings and gangway were satisfactory and to remind the watchman to call me at once should it be necessary.

The next day as I shaved I heard the usual rattle of hatch-boards being handled by stevedores preparing to discharge some of our cargo. As I stepped out onto the deck I shivered with the cold and returned to my cabin to don Alan Bull's duffle-coat. I found two gangs allocated as had been promised but after a few words with one of the foremen I learned they would be 'knocking-off' at five o'clock instead of the usual seven as a reminder this was, after all, Christmas Eve!

After breakfast and during the rest of the forenoon I received visits from various officials. Ray Williams came to collect the 'voyage papers' and stayed for a chat over coffee and later on my old friend Peter Cain, the assistant manager with the engineering and ship-repair company Messrs Green and Silley-Weir, to go through the repair list with me. Then came my old friend and ex-shipmate Ron Bryden who was now a partner with Captain Walters, 'Cargo Surveyors'. Ron had been a cadet on watch with me when our ship 'Nariva' had been torpedoed while homeward-bound on March 17th. 1943.

During the afternoon I telephoned Joan for a chat and to remind her that, on arrival at East Ham station all she had to do would be to cross the road and almost immediately opposite she would find the 'dispatcher's office' who would arrange a taxi to bring her and little Carol-Anne down to the ship. She assured me she knew and remembered all I had told her and "not to worry" etc., etc.

That done, and long before five o'clock, I heard the hatchboards being replaced over the hatches, I donned Alan Bull's duffle-coat and made my 'rounds' to make sure all was as it should be. I dropped in for a chat with the Chief Steward and was invited to a gin before the evening meal. I had the presence of mind to compliment him and his staff on the decorations in the saloon which comment earned me a second gin!

Christmas morning, 25th. December 1952. The sky overcast and bitter cold NE'ly wind with a promise, or would it be a threat of snow? I sat alone in the saloon with a couple of boiled eggs and a mountain of toast on the table in front of me. I wondered where the few engineer officers were and guessed, (rightly) they were suffering from a hangover!

When I left the saloon I stopped at the telephone and rang the number of the taxi company. A voice said "Metcalfe Motors can I help you?" I said, "Yes, this is the Chief Officer of the 'Asia' and I'm expecting my...." and that was as far as I got because the voice at the other end said, "Is that Mr Williams?" somewhat mystified I replied, "Yes but...." and again I was interrupted with the question, "Mr G.D. Williams?" and again I answered, "Yes but...." "hello Mr Williams" said the voice, "I was with you in the old Scythia' Sir - I was quartermaster in your watch - on the eight to twelve!!!"

As my reader can well imagine, there followed a lengthy conversation between myself and the 'dispatcher' who told me his name was Murray. And of course I remembered him. He told me that when he left the 'Scythia', when we were in Liverpool for the Winter overhaul he had left the sea to become 'dispatcher' in the taxi firm owned by his wife's father and he said he didn't regret swallowing the anchor in favour of a job ashore.

Eventually I managed to tell him I was expecting my wife to call in his office at about eleven o'clock and that I wanted a car to bring her down to the ship. He replied that he had been on the night-shift and would be off-duty at nine. "As a matter of fact, Mr Williams, it has now turned nine and my mate has just arrived to relieve me.

But not to worry, I'll make sure Mrs Williams will be well cared-for." A few seconds later, after wishing him a Merry Christmas etc. etc. I rang off contented Joan and Carol-Anne would soon be joining me safe and well.

Twenty years of my seagoing career had taught me to expect the unexpected. When the taxi drew up at the foot of the gangway the driver stepped out and opening the boot lifted out my hold-all. I recognised him immediately as Murray, ex-quartermaster in the 'Scythia' when we were carrying Displaced Persons from Germany to new lives and homes in Quebec, Canada. I particularly remember him for his skills in carving little wooden dolls for the children among the passengers. The poor little devils had probably never seen a doll in their lives.

I ran down the gangway to hug and kiss Joan and little Carol-Anne. Then, turning to the driver I said, "Hello Alec, it's good to see you again", and he made a similar reply. "But you told me you were 'off-duty' after nine o'clock", I said. To which with a deprecating grin he replied, "Well Sir, I couldn't resist the temptation to see you again." I shrugged then he added, "Besides, I wanted to make sure Mrs Williams and the little lass got here safely," handing me the hold-all.

Out of sheer courtesy I was about to invite Alec Murray on board for a drink but, and to my relief, he said, "Well I must be off Sir, it was marvellous seeing you again and meeting Mrs Williams and the little red-head here." As he spoke he tousled the top of her head. "I told the misses over the radio I'd been delayed she'll be well-pleased to hear I've met-up with you again - I've often talked about you and those poor beggars from the concentration camps."

We shook hands again before he climbed into the car and switched-on the ignition. Then, just as he let the clutch in he shouted, "Merry Christmas to you all and a Happy New Year." As his taxi began moving away we waved and kept waving until he turned the corner at the end of the cargo transit-shed. I escorted my wife and daughter up the gangway, into the accommodation and upstairs to my cabin where I gave them both another welcome hug and a kiss.

Joan was standing at the wash basin in the cabin doing things to her hair when I observed Carol-Anne tugging at her skirts and whispering. I failed to catch what she was saying but I did hear something like. "....... tell Daddy". I said, "Come on you two, what's the secret?" Joan gave a little self-concious laugh then said, "You remember last week I attended the pre-natal clinic?" I nodded and she went on, "Yesterday morning they 'phoned to confirm the baby was due about the second week in March," she paused, long enough for me to say, "Well?" She turned to look again in the mirror and I hardly heard the whisper, "It's going to be twins!!!!!"

For a few seconds there was a shocked silence. My heart gave a thud then I blurted out, "Twins?" Joan turned to look directly into my eyes searching to see what effect this earth-shattering news had on me and in her own eyes a hint of fear and anxiety. Swift to dispel any doubt whatsoever I jumped to my feet, grabbed her around the waist and hugged and kissed her so fiercely she cried, "Careful darling, don't hurt the little beggars." But that she was greatly relieved and happy with how I had reacted to her news there was no doubt in my mind.

We were still talking about it, even to the point of discussing their names when the 'phone rang. It was Dick Jones the Chief Steward inviting us down for drinks before Christmas Dinner was served. On our way down to Dick's cabin I felt as though I was floating on air. Twins - twins - twins. In my excitement I wanted to tell the world but Joan had begged me not to mention it, or as she had put it, "Not yet anyway." Which was going to be something of a struggle. Turning to Carol-Anne I teased her about having two brothers or two sisters to boss about, but in her quaint, self-possessed way she replied. "I will love them just as you and Mummy will!"

On entering the Chief Steward's cabin we found most of the skeleton crew left on board to 'keep-ship'. All had drinks in hand and the atmosphere of a typical Irish Parliament, (everybody talking and nobody listening). Joan had already met Dick Jones on other occasions so, after introducing her to to rest of the crowd I told them about the coincidence of the taxi-driver being an old shipmate and ex-quartermaster. It appeared none of the chaps had served in the 'Scythia', but a few of them knew someone who had.

After a while, as a subject of conversation it faded with other reminiscences being aired.

With the room so full of smoke I was relieved when the bell rang to indicate our Christmas Dinner was ready to be served. With a wide grin on his face Dick Jones placed a couple of settee-cushions in the Captain's chair and lifted Carol-Anne into it much to everyone's amusement. With bottles of red and white wine on the table Dick had very thoughtfully produced a bottle of 'Babycham' for Carol-Anne.

Needless to say, the meal as a Christmas Dinner, was a huge success and enjoyed by us all. The main meal of turkey and all the usual trimmings was followed by a chorus of carol-singers who escorted the Christmas Pudding alight with burning brandy. When the coffee, fruit and nuts were being passed around I asked the steward to call the kitchen staff into the saloon and when they were all assembled just inside the door I spoke a few words of praise and invited all hands to drink a toast in their favour. It was a small gesture for which the Chief Steward, Dick Jones later thanked me, saying it had been greatly appreciated.

As the meal had lasted well into the afternoon, and to allow the kitchen staff some time off I had agreed with Dick's suggestion that there would be no evening meal served but, instead, there would be ample supplies of cold meats etc. left on the centre-table for anyone who wished to pick and choose.

It was a quarter to four by the time Joan, Carol-Anne and I arrived back in the Chief-Officer's cabin. Not surprisingly the first thing Joan said as she sat down was, "I'm dying for a cup of tea." Obediently I retreated to the officers' pantry to brew-up and in one of the cupboards found a part tin of biscuits. While in the pantry, I made a quick check to see all the necessary ingredients were there for my purpose.

When I took the tray of tea things back to my cabin Joan asked, "At what time will you be ordering the taxi to take us up to East Ham station?" Carefully placing the tray down on the little coffee table I said "You are staying the night darling, you and Carol-Anne will be sleeping in the Captain's quarters." You should have seen the look on her face as she whispered, "Isn't that against the rules dear?" to which I replied, "Sod the rules, I have it all worked-out, no-one will be any the wiser, leave it to me."

At six o'clock there was a change of watchmen and I made my 'rounds', making sure the new man had arrived and was sipping tea from a pint-sized mug in the galley, then made my way back to the telephone opposite the Chief Steward's cabin. I could tell by the voices inside that Dick Jones had company. So, keeping the cradle depressed I dialled the taxi number, knowing it wouldn't ring, and making sure anyone within earshot would hear me ordering a taxi to take my wife and daughter to East Ham station!!!

Approximately twenty minutes later, I escorted Joan and Carol-Anne to the top of the gangway. As anticipated, the watchman was still enjoying his mug of tea in the warmth of the galley, so I urged them up a flight of stairs to the boat-deck and forward to the Captain's quarters to which I held the key. The bemused look on Carol-Anne's face was a sight I shall never forget and we made the whole escapade look as though it were a huge joke and a game of sorts - well wasn't it?

A few minutes after eight o'clock the next day - Boxing Day. I rang the inter-com telephone in the Captain's cabin and Joan answered it. I said "Good morning darling, did you sleep well?" and she replied, "Yes dear, I must say the Captain's bed is very comfortable", she paused, then added in a lower voice, "Carol-Anne is still fast asleep, she hardly moved all night." So far, so good. I went into the pantry and made a pot of tea, a few slices of toast and with a jar of marmalade made my way upstairs to the 'old man's' cabin. I told Joan to run the bath for herself and Carol-Anne, (if she thought it necessary). I said I would be back after I'd had my breakfast.

On my way into the dining saloon I popped in to wish Dick Jones a 'Happy Boxing Day', but was greeted by a series of groans. With a bit of a laugh I told the Chief Steward the best way to avoid a hangover was to stay drunk. Another series of groans told me my joke was unappreciated. Not surprisingly I was the only one in the saloon for breakfast.

On my return to the Captain's cabin I told Joan to have herself and Carol-Anne fully clothed and well wrapped-up by ten o'clock. At which time I made a similar call on the telephone making the pretence to order a taxi - even though I knew everyone on board were beyond earshot or even caring!

Taking a quick look out on deck I saw the day watchman leaning over the bulwark near the gangway so I nipped for'ard and opened the starboard mast-house door, making sure it began slamming to and fro in the wind. Then, as soon as Joan and Carol-Anne were ready I sent the watchman for'ard to close tha damned door and, as soon as he had shambled away I brought my family down the same stairs from the boat-deck past the gangway and into the accommodation loudly declaring what a beastly cold day it had turned out to be - I need hardly have bothered!

In the late evening of Boxing Day I went downstairs to phone the despatcher's office but this time without the need for subterfuge I actually requested a taxi to take Joan and little Carol-Anne up to East Ham Underground Station. Unless anything untoward were to happen Second Officer Seymour would be rejoining his ship the following day, Friday 27th December and I would return home for the weekend.

And, as luck would have it, everything turned out the way I had hoped it would. Pete Seymour arrived back on board mid-afternoon having enjoyed the few days of Christmas with his family and for which he again thanked me. I told him a couple of gangs had worked until five o'clock on Christmas Eve and that all the 'Voyage Returns' had been collected etc., etc. I also mentioned the wharfinger, John Wellings, had told me to expect four stevedore gangs Monday morning and that I would be on board soon after that.

It was dark and with a bitter N'ly wind when I said cheerio and made my way down the gangway to walk the long and lonely road to the dock-gate and the 101 bus to East Ham. At any other time, I supposed, I would have felt the cold and the journey home to Fulham but on this occasion I felt a certain contentment and satisfaction. I had been able to 'cock a snook' metaphorically speaking, at Cunard's stupid Rules. I also remembered with a grin my reply when Joan anxiously asked if I might get the sack if the Company had found out. My reply was the same as what Clark Gable had said to his leading lady Vivien Leigh "Frankly my dear, I don't give a damn."

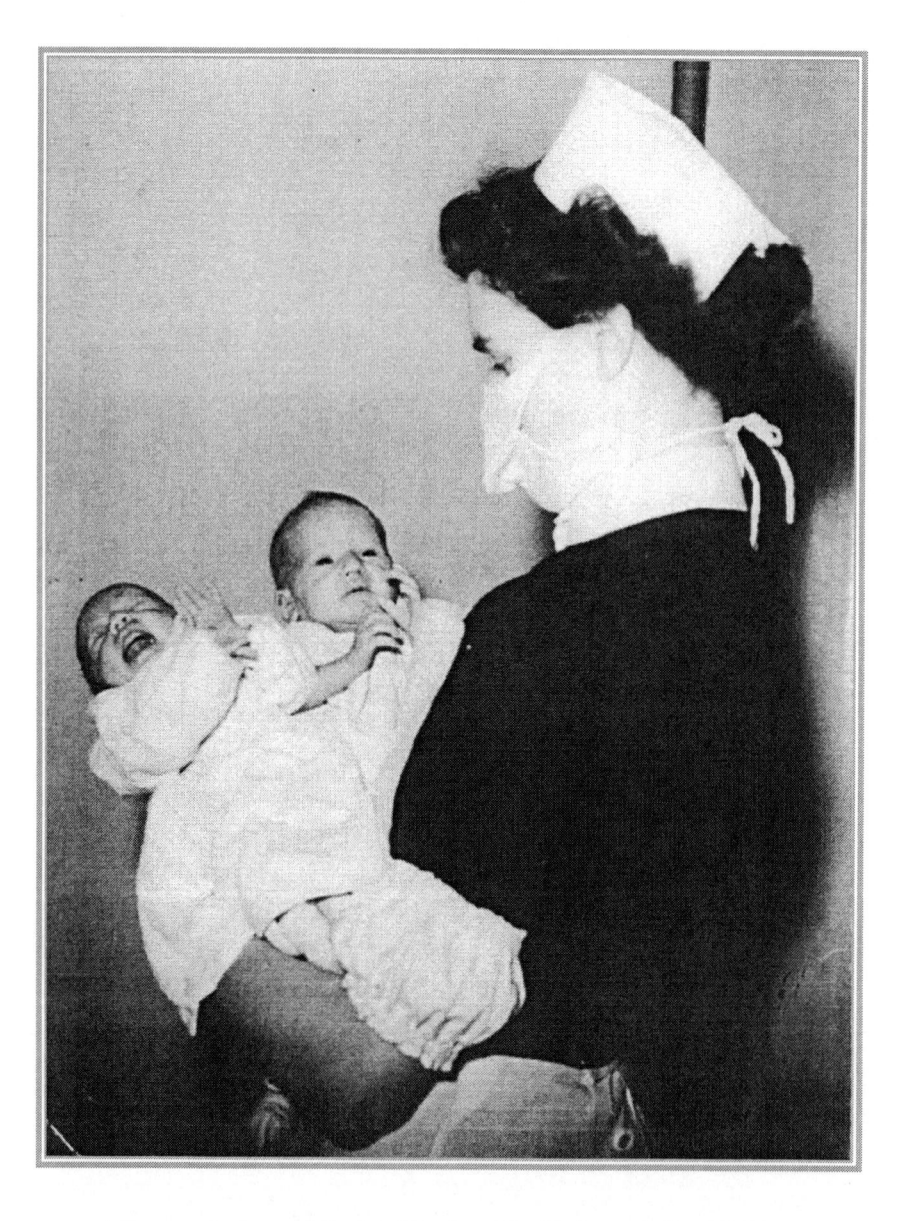

A few months later while travelling home by Underground and reading the 'Evening News' I found this picture on page 3. Twin girls born earlier that day in St. Mary's Maternity Hospital, Parsons Green, Fulham. They were later Christened as follows: -

Jane Denise   (my middle name being Dennis)
Julie Novello (my wife Joan's middle name)

UNASHAMED NAME-DROPPING

Had it been 'Providence' - 'Destiny' - 'Fate' or that other old faithful 'Coincidence' when General Jodl, representing all German Forces, signed the instrument of unconditional surrender on my birthday. 7th May 1945. Precisely thirty years after the sinking of the Cunard Liner 'Lusitania' with the tragic loss of 1198 precious lives, of men, women and children.

Three months later, in August 1945 soon after the atomic devices had been detonated over the cities of Hiroshima and Nagasaki came the Japanese surrender aboard the battleship 'USS Missouri' in Tokyo Bay.

At long last, peace and sanity were restored to a war-weary world and with it the freedom for the people to travel again, how, when or where they chose to go.

After suffering severe losses of ships owing to enemy action those units of the Cunard Fleet still afloat were hastily decommissioned from trooping service to resume their peace-time Trans-Atlantic sailings to Canada and America.

Which is precisely where I come into the picture (enter stage left), and serving as a Watchkeeping Navigating Officer in the 35,000 ton 'Mauretania' on regular sailings between Southampton and New York via Cherbourg and Cobh in Southern Ireland.

An hour or so prior to each sailing copies of the passenger-list would be delivered to the Officer's Wardroom. The list of First-Class passengers could often read like 'Burke's Peerage, 'Debrett' even 'Who's Who'. With titled people, diplomats and politicians, trade delegates and executives from industry and commerce, actors and actresses from stage, screen, radio and television, they were all there.

During a typical North Atlantic gale and having inspected the ship's lifeboats I was returning to the bridge along the boat-deck when I espied the lone figure of a young girl leaning on the teak-wood rail. She was wearing a heavy tweed overcoat and a kerchief around her head and it was when I enquired how she was feeling she turned her head and I barely recognised the well known movie star Ginger Rogers. Wearing very little make-up I couldn't help but notice her lovely face had a number of tiny freckles.

Yvonne De Carlo discovered a very ardent admirer in the ship's Doctor and wherever I happened to be making the rounds of the ship I would find them in close embrace. At that particular time I didn't know her marital status and as the Doctor was a voyage relief from one of the Liverpool Hospitals I wouldn't have known his either!

At six o'clock one evening while on passage to New York we were entertaining some passengers in the Wardroom when our Steward announced - "Mr Billy Graham". A tall well built young man came into the room. The most remarkable thing I noticed was his huge forehead, bright blue eyes and a most disarming smile.

The usual loud buzz of small-talk suddenly fell silent and from that very moment he held the monopoly of all conversation. An endearing quality of his stories were that they were almost entirely against himself and he confessed to being an avid reader of Conan-Doyle. He then proceeded to tell of the time when Sherlock Holmes and Doctor Watson went on a walking camping holiday.

"Having arrived somewhere in the Peak District they made camp and after a hot meal decided to retire to their respective sleeping-bags. At half-past two in the morning Holmes kicked the Doctor awake. "Watson, look up and tell me what you see". Churlishly Watson growled, "I see a crescent Moon, a planet that could be Jupiter, millions of stars and a few galaxies - why? For a minute or two Sherlock Holmes remained silent, then said "Watson, I think someone has stolen our tent!"

While I had been attending the Sir John Cass Nautical College in London, my cousin had taken me to Pinewood Film Studios, where he was employed as a carpenter. Over a period of half-an-hour I had watched Siobhan McKenna and her leading man do a short scene from a film they were making. The scene had to be repeated so many times, I grew bored and shortly thereafter left the studio with cousin Jack. Tea-time at Aunty Nan's was much more exciting. Some years later when she was on her way to Hollywood via New York, I was able to remind Siobhan of that botched scene in a stable and we both enjoyed a good laugh.

Homeward-bound one voyage we carried Princess Marina, Duchess of Kent and her lovely eighteen-year old daughter Princess Alexandra. Accompanied by Ladies-in-Waiting, they were duly entertained to tea in the Wardroom. The card accepting our invitation stated they would arrive at 4.00 pm and depart at 5.30, but it was nearer 6.30 pm when they finally left - which probably speaks well for the quality of our entertainment.

Ralph, now Sir Ralph Richardson, was a frequent visitor to the bridge by invitation from the Captain as was Noel Coward some voyages later. They were extremely interested in our latest Marconi Radar and all other aids to navigation. I was greatly disillusioned when Noel Coward described how many of the shipwrecked scenes of the film 'In Which we Serve' had been shot in the studio with ingenious props and clever camera work.

Returning to New York after a period in the West-End we enjoyed the company of a very talented actress as much at home on Broadway as in Hollywood. Mercedes McCambridge was once featured on the front page of 'Life' magazine after winning several specialist awards in America.

In the Winter of 1947/48 we were taken off the North-Atlantic to begin a series of five 14-day cruises from New York to the West Indies.

Three months later we arrived back in Southampton sun-tanned and with an insatiable taste for Bacardi and Coke. In the usual 'Directive' from Liverpool advising changes of officer personnel, I was required to 'Proceed on leave pending further appointment'. Having served three very happy years in the 'Mauretania' I was somewhat dismayed having to leave her but felt better when the Chief Officer reminded me a transfer to another ship invariably meant a promotion also.

And so it did, toward the end of my three-week's leave I was instructed to join the Company's 'Scythia' as First Officer in London. For the next two years we were employed carrying 'Displaced Persons' from the German port of Cuxhaven near the mouth of the River Elbe to Quebec in Canada. Voyages that gave little or no scope for an exercise in 'Name-Dropping' but an experience in human tragedy I shall never forget.

On our arrival alongside the ferry terminal in Cuxhaven we saw a train of battered old railway-carriages grind to a halt alongside the gangways from which hundreds of bedraggled old men and women tumbled out onto the quay. Exhausted and emaciated after years in the Concentration-Camps of Auschwitz, Belsen, Dachau and scores of others they looked dejected and fearful of what fate now had in store for them.

But during the ten day passage across the North Atlantic our Canteen Manager reported the ship's crew had bought his whole stock of sweets and chocolate to give these hapless creatures. Incredible as it may seem, but as they disembarked from the ship in Quebec and making their way down the gangways, many of them would pause, turn and wave to the crew who were lining the ship's side rails. And this picture was to be repeated each and every voyage broken only during the annual Winter overhaul and dry-dock periods in Liverpool. Pictures that will remain vividly in my memory for the rest of my life.

The mention of our Winter overhaul and dry-dock spells in

Liverpool brings with it the memory of a certain steward serving in the 'Scythia' at this time. Anyone with a knowledge of boxing history will probably recall the name of the British Empire Middleweight Boxing Champion, Dom Volante. In the years between mid 1920 to late 1930 Dom Volante was the boxing idol of almost every schoolboy in and around Liverpool. He had a very pronounced 'Scouse' accent, unmarried he simply worshipped his 'Mam'.

Perhaps it was because I had once been juvenile 'Indian Clubs' Champion of Wales, but whenever we met on board the 'Scythia', I always enjoyed a few minutes chat with Dom. And there were a couple of occasions when going ashore in Liverpool we would fall into step on our way to the 'Overhead Railway Station'. While standing on the platform awaiting the train I found myself basking in reflected glory as hundreds of workmen would shout and wave to their idol 'Dom Volante'.

He once told me that when his boxing days were over he was invited to join a small musical group of sporting 'has-beens' on a tour of the 'Moss Empire' circuit. There were Neil Tarleton, Dixie Dean, Dom Volante and another old ex-heavyweight champion Frank Goddard. Dom admitted ruefully they always received rapturous applause, not for their musical talent but simply for what they had once been.

I then told him Frank Goddard kept a little newspaper shop a few hundred yards from where I then lived near Colchester. There was a hint of a tear in his eyes when he said, "Well I hope he keeps a better shop than he plays a mouth organ!" On another occasion Dom confessed his one ambition was to become a Gymnasium Steward and expressed disappointment the 'Scythia' didn't possess the amenity. A few years later I was able to help him realise his ambition in the Company's 'Britannic'.

Just as J D Armstrong, Chief Officer in the 'Mauretania' had once predicted 'A transfer to another ship inevitably meant promotion' and so it proved to be when I found myself 'First Officer' in the Company's cargo-ship 'Andria'. And furthermore having London as our terminal port, which meant seeing as much of my Wife and family as before.

As the cargo-ships had no passenger accommodation, this being the sole preserve of the passenger liners, there was little or no opportunity of seeing or meeting anyone to add to my list of very important people, with one exception.

Any livestock to be carried on board was invariably left to the day of sailing. On this particular voyage there were two magnificent horses, each in its own well-padded box, being returned to New York. They were secured in a sheltered area on the afterdeck. I had been advised earlier that both horses belonged to the famous American singing-cowboy, Gene Autry. That he and his party would be arriving on board and, in the absence of the Captain I was required to entertain them.

When told of their arrival I repaired to the Officers' Wardroom and introduced myself to Gene Autry and his wife Annabelle. Their Manager Colonel Ed. Witting, and the horses' groom Frank Causter. All were wearing colourful western-style clothes, complete with high-boots and ten-gallon hats.

For want of something to say I asked, "Which of the two horses is 'Trigger'?" For a second there was a stunned silence and I have rarely seen so many eyebrows work overtime until the Colonel spluttered, "No siree, theys 'Champion' and 'Little Champion' - 'Trigger' belongs to Roy Rogers." I gave a feeble attempt at a laugh as though I had intended it as a joke!!! To my erstwhile habit of 'name-dropping now add 'brick-dropping'!

It was at about this time in my career, I discovered living in London had certain advantages. When for instance, our Marine Superintendent in London fell ill, I was directed by Liverpool to take up duties there as Temporary Assistant Superintendent. The appointment also taught me the truth in the old cliché, 'It's not what you know, it's who you know'. In the Port of London Authority I found many good friends among the Dockmasters and Traffic-Officers alike.

I also found many irritating obstacles to what I would like to call a quiet life, especially the 'hide-bound' dogma of Union Officials and the restrictive practices they encouraged among their members. So, it was with mixed feelings when I received instructions to join 'Queen Elizabeth'.

Two names taking passage with us spring to mind; on one voyage, superb British actor Wilfred Hyde-White and the novelist C S Forrester, author of the 'Hornblower' series, who confessed to knowing little about sailing-ships and even less about how to sail them!!

It may have been coincidence when the American film-actor Victor Mature took passage in the 'Queen Elizabeth' from New York to Cherbourg on his way to filming in Italy. One of the films being screened in the ship's cinema that voyage was entitled 'Samson and Delilah' in which he had the lead role. Groucho Marx commented "First picture I've seen in which the male lead has a bigger bust than the female."

While on watch one evening I received a report on the bridge that the actor was very intoxicated and an embarrassment to other passengers in the Veranda-Grill. The usual procedure was immediately put in to operation. The 'Night Officer' and Charles Mason, the Chief Master-at-Arms, were instructed to investigate the disturbance. Needless to say the drunken actor was quietly escorted to his cabin by 'friendly persuasion.

By contrast, the most likable and charming actor David Niven said very little about his real life part as a Major in the British Army during the Second World War. He was very modest about being 'Mentioned in Despatches' and his well earned decorations.

When Mr and Mrs Dickie Hamilton were invited by the Commodore to visit the bridge I knew it would be Diana Dors, to whom I would be explaining the functions of our various 'aids to navigation'. When she confessed to being terrified of the reception she would get in Hollywood, I gave her a chaste kiss on her cheek and told her, "Diana, you are going to 'Wow' them." and was rewarded with a gentle squeeze of her tiny hand.

As the saying goes, "There's no show without punch." Taking passage with us one voyage from New York back to their home in Paris were the Duke and Duchess of Windsor. The Commodore invited them on the bridge as we approached Cherbourg Harbour and I was astonished to see how small he was beside the Duchess and how very old he looked. When I handed each of them a pair of binoculars they smiled their thanks but said nothing.

Mr and Mrs James Pinchin were old friends whom I had met over the years on many of the Company's ships. I tried matchmaking between my young watchmate and their beautiful but very tall daughter Jane but to no avail, so I gave up the attempt.

It was soon after this when once again I was required ashore in London owing to the terminal illness of the Marine Superintendent there. Although I was glad of the opportunity to see more of my family again there was less chance of adding new names to this, my unashamed list of very important people.

In 1971 the Chairman of Cunard advised all sea and shore staff of the impending sale of the Company to an entrepreneurial group called 'Trafalgar House Investments'. Then came a period of 'Rationalisation' followed by that most hated word 'Redundancy', when I lost a number of friends and shipmates.

On the credit side of the takeover by 'Trafalgar House' the unpopular ruling by Cunard where officers' wives were required to be 'off the ship' by 8.00 pm was now reversed and wives of senior officers were permitted to accompany them on a voyage. Furthermore, Masters and officers were expected to serve, if necessary in any of the Group's subsidiary fleets, such as Port Line and Brocklebank Line.

What was even better news for me on my return to sea-service was being promoted to the rank of Captain, initially as relief Master of the Company's cargo-ships. And thanks to our new employers I was delighted to take my Wife with me on voyages to New York, Boston, Baltimore and Norfolk-Virginia. The greatest thrill was having her with me when our usual itinerary to Montreal was extended through the St. Lawrence Seaway into Lake Ontario to Toronto and Hamilton thence the Welland Canal to Cleveland, Detroit, Milwaukee and Chicago.

There followed even more exciting voyages abroad in the fully refrigerated vessels of the Port Line subsidiary to South Africa. To Cape Town, Port Elizabeth, Durban, Laurenço-Marques, Beira and to Hobart Tasmania. Then we were together in ships of the subsidiary company T&J Brocklebank to Port Said and a transit of the Suez Canal to the Red Sea ports of Aquaba, Port Sudan, Hodeidah and Aden. And after the sticky heat of the Red Sea to enjoy the cool breezes across the Indian Ocean to Colombo thence to Calcutta, Chalna and Chittagong.

In Calcutta we met the charming Chief of Customs, Ahmed Khan whose name can be found in the 'Guinness Book of Records' as an Olympic champion playing Hockey. We also entertained several well-known British flat-racing jockeys who annually escape to Calcutta during the steeplechasing season in the UK. In return we were invited to the 'Members Enclosure' at the Calcutta Races, where we won a few rupees and of course lost a few. But that's life.

Joan also accompanied me in the refrigerated ship 'Matangi' through the Panama Canal where what were once called electric mules are now called locomotives because the drivers objected to being called muledrivers. From the other end of the canal we faced the long haul across the Pacific to 'Bluff' which is the southernmost town in New Zealand, and where oysters cost a fraction of those sold on Mersea Island!!

By way of a complete change, I was then required to relieve Captain Ian Borland as Operations Manager in San Juan, Puerto Rico tending the needs of the two cruise-liners 'Cunard Princess' and 'Cunard Countess'. My wife flew out to join me in our comfortable air-conditioned flat and the use of the Company's car. I wouldn't dream of being blasé but for Joan it was a novel experience. And on Ian's return from a well-earned rest at his home in Petersfield, Hampshire, Joan and I flew home to Mersea.

Then came other voyages followed by an idyllic spell lasting eighteen months in charge of the two passenger liners 'Franconia' and 'Carmania', laid-up in the River Fal, near King Harry Ferry. The dispute between the Shipping Company and the Seamens' Union had become a stalemate, until the Company issued its ultimatum "You settle the dispute, or we sell the ships."

The whole sad affair ended with the Company accepting an offer it couldn't refuse from a Russian Cruise Line in Vladivostok. Captain Don Lee took the 'Franconia' around the coast to the Swan-Hunter shipyard in North Shields on the Tyne. And a week later I took the 'Carmania' to the same yard for dry dock and survey.

Unhappily it sounds very much like the tale of 'Old Soldiers - never die, they simple fade away.' I sometimes wonder what Samuel Cunard, founder of the Cunard Line, would have to say to that? But the narrative I choose to call 'Unashamed Name--Dropping would not be complete if I neglected to include two ex-shipmates, Miles Wingate and Josh Cosnett.

Miles Wingate served as Third Officer with me in the 'Empire Confidence' when we took part in the invasion of Sicily and late onto the beaches of Salerno. And the following year in Bombay when the cargo-ship 'Fort Stikine' disintegrated in two massive explosions and the 'domino effect' destroyed ten other ships and much of the port. But who then could have foreseen that same young officer would one day become 'Sir Miles Wingate' for services to Trinity House'.

Josh Cosnett, ex-shipmate and a very dear friend wisely decided to leave the sea to begin an entirely new career with a well-known rubber-tyre company, although remaining a Royal Naval Reservist. In the years that followed he launched his own very successful tyre-distribution company and for services to the RNR and RNVR Associations he was awarded the 'Order of the British Empire'.

At the monthly lunch-meeting of the Mersea Island Probus Club we were once treated to a very interesting and emotional talk by Mrs Eva Hart who, as a twelve-year-old, she and her mother survived the sinking of the 'Titanic' on 15th April 1912. Her father however was among those poor souls who were lost in that tragic disaster. She admitted to being forever grateful to Captain Rostrom and the crew of the Cunarder 'Carpathia' for rescuing them.

Port Line - T & J Brocklebank and Moss Tankers were subsidiary companies of the Cunard Steamship Company. But in their individual spheres of operation they were managed separately from the parent Company.

Port Line vessels, all of which were fully-refrigerated, operated between the UK and Europe to Australia and New Zealand, with 'cross-trade' services between Australasia, Canada and the East Coast of the United States of America.

Brocklebank ships operated between the UK and Europe to the Red Sea and the Bay of Bengal ports with 'cross-trade' services to Mexican Gulf ports.

Moss Tankers on the other hand were obliged to trade world-wide as required by fluctuations in the International spot-markets for fossil-fuel supply and demand.

In August 1971 the Cunard Steamship Company, including its subsidiaries was sold to Trafalgar House Investments Limited who introduced a considerable programme of rationalisation in which Masters and Officers were offered opportunities to serve in any of the Cunard, Port Line or Brocklebank fleets.

From the vagaries of the North Atlantic Ocean, often described as 'nine months of bad weather and three months of Winter' Or the continuous, repetitive cruises around the West Indies with early morning arrivals and late evening departures. Instead, I enjoyed visits to South Africa, Australia, Tasmania and New Zealand. I had the opportunity of visiting the hospital in Colombo where, as an apprentice, I had once been treated for a 'slipped-disc'. And in all my years at sea I had never before enjoyed the sights of Calcutta, Chalna or Chittagong. My thanks now went to Trafalgar House for making this all possible.

Table bay Cape Town - South Africa

MATANGI (ex-Port St. Lawrence)

Built by Harland & Wolff - Belfast, 1961.

Tonnage 9,040 Gross: Length 508ft: Beam 68ft.

Six Cylinder H & W Diesel Engine.

Renamed Matangi when transferred to Brocklebank Line.

THE BROOCH

Incorporating the Floods of Johnstown
Pennsylvania, USA, 1889-1936-1977

When the Company's personnel manager, Captain Braithewaite telephoned me to say I was required to take command of the 'Matangi' in Avonmouth I was at first somewhat mystified. Rather rudely I interrupted him to ask if the 'Matangi' was a recent acquisition. Tony gave a short laugh and replied, "No Gwilym, you've been Master of her before when she was the 'Port St. Lawrence'."He went on to explain that as part of their rationalisation programme she had been transferred from Port Line to the Brocklebank Line. Her name had been changed to 'Matangi' and she was now manned by an Indian crew.

The rest of our conversation was taken up with other important matters, finally ending with the remark that my railway-voucher to Bristol was in the post and that the 'Matangi' would be sailing in ballast to Bluff, New Zealand. We would be loading a full cargo of frozen lamb carcasses a part of which would be for Avonmouth discharge and the remainder for Liverpool.

The 'Matangi' - ex -'Port St. Lawrence', I knew was a fully-refrigerated motor-vessel and had always been manned hitherto by a

British crew, but I didn't mind having an Indian crew. I had sailed with them in other Brocklebank ships and had rather enjoyed the novelty of being waited-upon (hand and foot as they say) by a Goanese steward.

On joining the "Matangi' in Avonmouth I was delighted to find my Goanese steward 'Gupta' had already unpacked my gear, while I had been meeting several old friends and shipmates among the officers. A few days later, having discharged all her cargo, we left Avonmouth on 14th. May 1977 bound for Bluff, New Zealand via the Panama Canal. On passage across the Atlantic we encountered the usual mixture of good, bad and indifferent weather and noticed considerable vibration owing to the ship's 'light' condition.

During our overnight stay in Cristobal our fuel-oil and fresh-water tanks were topped-up prior to making the Canal transit the following morning. Ever since my first voyage to sea as a young apprentice in 1932 the Panama Canal has never failed to interest me. Each and every time I marvel at what can only be described as one of the greatest feats of civil engineering and enterprise. Forty miles long, it connects two mighty oceans from Cristobal on the Atlantic to Balboa on the Pacific seaboard

Probably the most amazing feat of all was excavating the channel through almost solid rock of the Culebra Mountain. Set into the face of a cliff, a traveller cannot fail to se the tablet on which is inscribed the memorial to the American Army Engineer Officer in whose honour it is justifiably named 'The Gaillard Cut'.

At the Atlantic end of the canal powerful electric locomotives haul seagoing vessels from one 'lock-chamber' to the next while lifting it up to the level of the man-made 'Gatun Lake'. Thence to another series of 'locks' where the vessel is then lowered to the level of the Pacific Ocean, the whole operation from start to finish takes, on average, nine hours. By day the heat is almost unbearable but within minutes of sunset it can become quite cold. But at all times, for the Captain, it can be somewhat exhausting.

Hopefully my reader will appreciate, from Cristobal at the Atlantic end of the Canal to Balboa at the other, I had endured a long and tiring period on the bridge. As I have already said, where others of my crew enjoyed relief from their duties the Captain has what is humorously known as a 'Chinese-watch' that is to say he 'comes on and stays on'. Be that as it may, when we eventually disembarked the pilot near Balboa and rang 'Full Ahead' on the engine-room telegraph I was glad to hand-over to the Third-Mate - and to treat myself to a shower and so to bed.

In certain circumstances I should have slept like a log, perhaps I was overtired, or was it the news brought me by the Chief Engineer that gave me such terrible dreams? When crossing the Atlantic I had spoken to him about the excessive vibration and he had voiced concern about the leaking stern-gland which he thought had been aggravated by the vibration. He had assured me the bilge-pumps would contain the leak adequately but the problem must have become lodged in my subconsciousness.

Ahead of us now the vast expanse of the Pacific Ocean and over six and a half thousand miles to Bluff, New Zealand. I asked the Chief Engineer to keep me informed daily of how the pumps were coping with the leaking stern-gland in which there are sixteen octagonal nuts of five-inch diameter. This is the gland through which the 'tail-end-shaft' penetrates the hull outwards to the propeller. Any further tightening of the nuts could possibly only end with making matters worse and would have to be attended to immediately on arrival at Bluff.

Five days out from Balboa we sighted the famous Galapagos Islands and later on, our calculations revealed we would be passing within eight miles of Pitcairn. As the time of passing would be shortly after midnight, there was no point in adjusting our course to pass even closer. Calculations also revealed our estimated time of arrival in Bluff to be 0600 on 15th. June, so I sent our Agent there a radio-message to that effect making due allowance for the 'International Date Line'.

For the benefit of my readers who may not know or understand the 'International Date Line' I will try to explain its purpose and its complexities. First of all, let it be understood that every fifteen degrees of longitude, east or west of the Greenwich Meridian is the equivalent of one hour in time. Thus, fifteen degrees longitude east of Greenwich is one hour ahead of Greenwich Mean Time and, similarly, fifteen degrees west is one hour behind GMT.

From the foregoing my reader will accept that as one travels eastward, time is advanced one hour for every fifteen degrees of longitude up to the 180th. meridian EAST. And similarly, as one travels westward time is retarded one hour every fifteen degrees of longitude up to the 180th. meridian WEST.

Somehow, I almost see my reader nodding his or her head with some satisfaction having grasped the problem thus far. But now it becomes a little more difficult to understand. If the traveller heading eastward keeps advancing his or her watch every fifteen degrees continuously all the way around the world it follows that he or she will arrive back in the UK one whole day ahead of the calendar. And similarly, if heading westward the traveller retards the watch every fifteen degrees all the way around the world he or she will arrive back in the UK one whole day behind the calendar!!

So, to avoid this irritating contretemps, the 'wise-ones' introduced the 'International Date Line' at the 180th. meridian where, if the traveller was heading east, he or she would miss that particular day, for instance, from Tuesday to Thursday missing out Wednesday. Or, if heading westward and retarding his or her watch one hour every fifteen degrees until crossing the 180th. meridian where they could enjoy the doubtful pleasure of having two Tuesdays or whatever in the week. Just to confuse my reader the Date Line is not always on the 180th. meridian. For a variety of valid reasons it 'snakes' through groups of islands on or about the 180th. for convenience of trade and commerce.

It is truly said that the darkest hour is just before dawn and it had been raining earlier, but it was now quite dry, as we finally moored the 'Matangi' safely alongside the berth at Bluff, New Zealand. The moment our gangway was secured Mr Watson himself, of J E Watson, our Agents in Invercargill came on board and as we shook hands he remarked, "Welcome to New Zealand Captain, you're a long way from your usual Cunard back-yard." I gave him a friendly grin and replied, "It's a refreshing change to have all this fine weather too." I had the immediate impression I was going to like this chap and in the days that followed, I had no reason to alter that impression.

As it was yet a few minutes to seven o'clock and much too early for anything stronger, we settled for tea and toast. And when we had settled ourselves in armchairs he came out with the news for which I had been praying. Mr Watson went on to explain there had been a major problem in the refrigeration plant ashore and it would mean some delay in our loading operations. I cut short his apologies by describing our own problem of the stern-gland packing and before he left the ship we both agreed to keep each other well-informed of progress.

Over breakfast I was able to tell the Chief Engineer and the Chief Officer my news and it was agreed to begin transferring oil and water from aft to forward tanks to bring the ship's stern up clear of sea-level. Later, I joined the Chief Officer in his calculations, when we came to the conclusion we would have to fill the forward deep-tank. To my chagrin I discovered that even by using the maximum of four hoses from the deck-service line it would take days to fill the tank to its capacity of 500 tons.

One of our junior engineers had a close friend living locally whose father was Chief Officer of Invercargill Fire-Brigade and within a couple of hours two powerful auxilary-pumps were in operation. The deep-tank filled, the propeller trimmed clear of sea-level and work on the stern-gland put in hand.

I dare say it would take ship's engineers and a few other nautical experts to appreciate the amount of effort involved in removing and renewing packing from a ship's stern-gland. In the 'Matangi' there were the sixteen nuts, each five inches in diameter. I can assure you, dear reader, it was a Herculean task, but it was accomplished in record time.

But on this occasion, time was not on our side. Even though our stern-gland problem had been resolved, there was now the transfer of fuel-oil and water to bring the ship back to an even keel. And our Agent J E Watson had brought me news they would commence loading frozen and chilled lamb the next day. I had no alternative but to ask our friends in the fire-brigade to pump out the forward deep-tank.

Much to my relief they responded immediately and a team of firefighters arrived on board with their auxilary-pumps and in a matter of hours the tank was empty. But not before a few of the men had to be rushed to hospital suffering from carbon-monoxide inhalation from the two motor-pumps. Luckily they were only detained short while for observation and were soon allowed home none the worse for it.

Loading operations commenced the next day as promised with thousands of carcasses of lamb, hoggart and ewe for the UK where, these days, one seldom hears of 'mutton'! During our stay in Bluff we enjoyed limitless supplies of oysters which, although not as famous as their Colchester and Mersea cousins, they are certainly more plentiful and a fraction of the price.

On the 6th. July, being fully loaded and ready for sea in all respects, 'Matangi' slipped her moorings and left her berth. Behind her lay many hospitable and generous friends both in Bluff and Invercargill. We set course and full speed towards Balboa, the Panama Canal and Home!

By a little manipulation that only a navigator would understand, I contrived the 'initial course' for the 'Great Circle' between New Zealand and the Isthmus of Panama to bring the "Matangi' within a couple of miles of Pitcairn Island. This time luck was with us and we sighted the island in the early afternoon passing close enough to hear the ship's whistle echo back from the cliffs and we 'dipped our ensign' when abeam of the Signal Station which responded courteously.

We were favoured by fine weather all the way, which enabled most of us to enjoy deck-tennis, deck-golf and other pursuits, as well as getting more that a fair share of sun-bathing. While in Bluff our Radio Officer had managed to exchange our six films, so we were able to enjoy a movie one night alternating with bingo or 'horse-racing' the next night. During the ten minute 'intermission' on movie night our popular Catering Officer brought round 'choc-ices' which went down a treat.

Now the 'Matangi' was loaded 'down to her marks' she was very comfortable indeed, without a single tremor, and the Chief Engineer reported being more than satisfied with the new 'packing' in the stern-gland, from which not even a dew-drop was seen. In other words our passage north-eastward towards Balboa and the Panama Canal, was as pleasant as anyone could wish.

And again we passed well within sight of the Galapagos Islands and for mile after mile with a flat calm sea we we were treated to spectacular displays by porpoises, dolphins and even by sea-lions. Five days later we made landfall near the Las Pelias Islands in the gulf of Panama. The bright sun was rising clear of distant mountains when we finally arrived in the quarantine anchorage near Balboa on 25th. July 1977. And there to await the 'visit' from Port Health and Customs officials. I hastened to my quarters for a quick shave and a shower leaving the Third Officer to call me the instant he sighted the launch approaching.

The American Pilot for the canal transit arrived on board along with the Customs and Port Health Authority doctor. Following the age-old practice of Pilots around the world he brought with him a selection of recent newspapers. His very first remark while shaking hands was. "Good morning Cap'n, the minute those other guys, (referring to the port officials) are off the ship we can get under weigh." I asked him if he'd had breakfast, "Hell no", he replied, "can your steward rustle up some bacon sandwiches and a pot of coffee?" I looked at my Goanese steward and said, "Make that for two Gupta". With his habitual "Atcha Sahib", he glided away to do my bidding.

I rang the bridge and spoke to the Third Officer, "As soon as you see the port officials appearing at the top of the gangway have the carpenter, Bosun and anchor party to station, put the engines on 'stand-by', I'll ring the Chief Engineer." As I replaced the 'phone in its cradle I turned to the Pilot to ask about the Canal traffic. He replied it had been very quiet for over a week. "If we get under weigh before eleven o'clock Cap'n there's every chance we'll make Cristobal by 20.00 hours (8.00pm). At that moment Gupta returned with a large tray of sandwiches and a steaming pot of coffee.

The Pilot and I were enjoying our second cups of coffee when the Third Officer rang to say the port officials were making their way down the gangway and that the anchor-party were 'standing-by'. Ten minutes later the anchor was aweigh and the 'Matangi' slicing her way towards the Pedro Miguel brace of lock-chambers and the beginning of our Canal transit. With the expected shimmering heat in the Canal Zone. I had Gupta provide a plentiful supply of iced-water and lime-juice in the wheelhouse, which I knew would be as welcome as it were necessary for all of us on the bridge. Thus began a second transit of the Panama Canal this voyage, but this time we were 'homeward-bound'.

Having already given a 'thumb-nail' description of the Panama Canal I might add here another piece of information, perhaps useless to some but of interest to many. Pilotage all around the world in harbours, rivers or canals may be compulsory but at all times the ship's Master is responsible. With a Pilot on the bridge the commonest entry in the ship's Log is as follows: - 'Courses and Engine movements to Pilot's Advice and Master's orders'.

But the Panama Canal is of such great strategic value to the United States of America, Pilotage is compulsory, the Pilot is in complete charge of the ship and if or when necessary can overrule the Master's orders. During the Second World War armed US Naval units boarded all ships making the canal transit. Some on the bridge, some in the engine-room while others patrolled the decks to prevent sabotage to such an important and strategic waterway.

It was a great relief to me when, at last, we were safely moored alongside Pier 2 in Cristobal a few minutes before nine o'clock that evening. A lukewarm shower followed by a chicken sandwich washed down with a glass of ice-cold milk and I was ready for bed. The ship's engineers would supervise bunkering operations and the carpenter the replenishment of our fresh-water tanks in readiness for the Atlantic crossing ahead.

I was about to climb into bed when I caught sight of the newspaper Gupta had left on my settee. A few minutes in which to read, relax and I would be asleep, after all, it had been a very long day. The newspaper was a copy of the 'Miami Herald' dated Sunday July 24th. 1977 which was the day before we'd arrived in Balboa. But it was the 'banner headline' which immediately caught my attention, 'SOBS AND SIRENS CHOKE THE AIR IN MUDDY JOHNSTOWN', I sat bolt upright, all thought of sleep utterly and completely forgotten.

From early morning when the 'Matangi' had approached the 'Quarantine Anchorage' near Balboa until the moment that night when my eyes could no longer focus on the print in the 'Miami Herald'. I had been awake, and very much alert, for eighteen hours and sleep finally overcame me. But with dozens of kaleidoscopic pictures conjured-up by the newspaper article on the Johnstown Floods it became a troubled and restless sleep indeed.

All too soon, it seemed, I was awakened by my steward with tea and toast. By all the sounds emanating from below my quarters I could tell the ship was 'coming alive' with the preparations for leaving the berth at Cristobal. With barely enough time for a quick shave and a shower there came a knock on my door and a young man, not unlike Errol Flynn entered with a cheery "Good morning Captain," - "Good morning Pilot," I replied, "If you'd care to go on to the bridge, I'll organise some coffee for you."

An hour later and just inside the harbour breakwater the Pilot was scrambling down the pilot-ladder into his launch, and with a quick wave dropped astern as I gave the order, "Full Ahead." The 'Matangi' surged ahead as though she was just as eager to be on her way home as we were. Then, when we had set course for the 'Mona Passage' between Santo Domingo and Puerto Rico, I handed-over to the Third Officer with the customary reminder to, "Call me if in doubt."

For a change I found time to join the other officers for breakfast in the dining-saloon. It was not only the titillating smell of 'bacon and eggs' that lifted my spirits, it was the realisation of being on the last leg of our voyage home. Given reasonable weather I calculated we should arrive in Avonmouth on or about the 7th August. There would follow a few days while discharging a part of our cargo before proceeding to Liverpool where I expected to be relieved by another Master.

The twelve days between the Panama Canal and Avonmouth I thought of little else other than the three calamitous floods that had engulfed the city of Johnstown. Pennsylvania, USA. And in particular the flood of May 31st. 1889 of which this lengthy narrative is all about!

In Wales a person finds more relatives per square-yard than in any other country. Some are blood-relations, others by marriage while friendly and caring neighbours within a hundred yards are frequently addressed as Uncles and Aunts. From a very early age I have known of dozens in many parts of the world whose relationship would be very difficult to trace!

Aunty Jane and Uncle Griff Williams had lived in Johnstown for many years before the flood of May 1889 having left the coal-mines surrounding Ystradgynlais in the Swansea Valley for richer pickings of the coal-mines of Pennsylvania. And Aunty Jane's cousin, 'Uncle' John Harris who had also emigrated from Ystradgynlais, was Chief of Police there.

On Wednesday, 31st. May 1889, after weeks of persistent rain the Conneghma Lake Dam burst and twenty million tons of water in a wall seventy-feet high tore down the valley and through the streets of Johnstown carrying everything and everyone before it, including Aunty Jane's only daughter Margaret Ada and her fiancé Robert Tilsley.

Almost nine months pregnant Aunty Jane and her family were forced by rising waters to seek refuge on the roof of their home and where the baby boy was born, later to be christened Moses Flood Williams!

It was days later when one of the recovery-teams found several bodies of victims and among them that of young Margaret Williams whose body was later identified by the shawl and the brooch she had been wearing that fatal night.

As our eastbound passage progressed and we approached the British Isles a host of urgent 'end of voyage' duties asserted themselves and thoughts of Johnstown slipped temporarily into my subconscious. The fine weather of the Caribbean seemed to follow us so I was able to bring the 'Official Log-Book' up to date as well as my 'Voyage Report' and 'Ship's Disbursement Accounts'. And by 'force majeure' all three tragic floods of Johnstown shelved for the time being.

On entering the Bristol Channel and a few miles north of Lundy Island we sighted the Royal Yacht 'Britannia' making an approach

Wreckage of the Johnstown flood, May 31st.1889 - Head of Main Street.

to the island. We heard over the VHF radio-telephone arrangements being made for a picnic to be held there. With adverse tidal conditions in Avonmouth I decided to occupy our time 'swinging ship' in the vicinity of 'Breaksea Lighthouse', to construct a 'curve of errors' for our radio-direction-finder.

Later the same evening we were eventually moored alongside the refrigerating berth in Avonmouth and the next day stevedores began discharging our frozen carcasses of lamb. Marine, Technical Superintendents and other representatives arrived on board and I was busily engaged with the ship's business throughout much of our stay in Avonmouth. Five days later, with all the Avonmouth part of our cargo discharged we sailed for Liverpool arriving there on Saturday August 20th. 1977 and where, a few days later I handed-over command of the 'Matangi' to Captain Symonds and proceeded home on leave pending further appointment.

It was only after I had settled into a First-Class seat on the train from Lime Street, Liverpool to Euston, London I was able to relax and review the whole voyage from beginning to end, including the contents of the newspaper brought by the Panama Canal Pilot which had reported the recent flood of Johnstown and comparisons of those in 1889 and in 1936.

In my comfortable corner-seat of the First-Class compartment the rhythmic click-click of the carriage wheels soon had its hypnotic effect on me and I dozed-off. There followed a kaleidoscopic series of dreams so vivid I was greatly relieved, even glad, to feel the train slowing on its approach to Euston Station where it finally ground to a juddering halt. I was still half-dazed when the voice of a burly porter, "D'yer 'ave much luggage Sir?" brought me to my senses.

The taxi ride from Euston to Liverpool Street was a virtual crawl at about the busiest time of the day in London, but I arrived in time to catch my train to Colchester. The bungalow on Mersea Island looked all the better for the extension that had been built during my absence at sea. And the list of 'do-it-yourself' now claimed every bit of my attention, so all thoughts of Johnstown retreated further into my subconscious. Shelved for an undetermined period of time.

As all seamen will tell you, however long the leave, whether it be for one week or more the end comes all too soon. And mine was no exception with the arrival in the post of the all-too-familiar green envelope from Liverpool. I was required to fly out to San Juan to take command of the Company's cruise-liner 'Cunard Countess'.

But this particular cloud had a silver-lining in that my wife was permitted to accompany me. There followed a few hectic days shopping and buying the sort of clothes suitable for cruising in the West Indies. Then, at last, it was time to catch the flight from Heathrow to San Juan Puerto Rico via Lisbon.

At San Juan airport we were met by my old friend Ian Boreland who drove us to the hotel where we were to stay the night until the 'Cunard Countess' arrived the following morning. When we finally arrived at the pier the next day passengers were still disembarking with the usual melee of taxis, coaches and mountains of baggage and distraught husbands being henpecked.

Staff-Captain Robin Wadsworth and I had been shipmates years ago, from the time we had shared 'digs' in Glasgow while awaiting the officers' accommodation in the 'Sylvania' to be readied for occupation. While the ship was being fitted-out in John Brown's shipyard, Robin had joined as Second Officer and I as Junior First Officer. And thereafter we had been shipmates from the 'maiden voyage' and for a further two years.

It had been a few minutes after midnight when we finally sailed from San Juan, so by the time we disembarked the harbour Pilot I was more than ready for bed. As my reader will appreciate it had been a long and tiring day. So, it was pure pleasure to leave the bridge to the officer-of-the-watch and rejoin Joan in the comfort of my air-conditioned quarters.

At sea the next morning I joined the other officers for breakfast in their Mess, where it was a pleasure to meet-up with several old friends and shipmates again. Joan enjoyed a leisurely breakfast of orange-juice followed by tea, toast and marmalade. When I returned to my cabin I studied the details for the eleven o'clock Church Service which I would be conducting in the ship's theatre.

And to remember when announcing the last hymn the age-old practise "during the singing of this hymn there will be a collection for maritime charities on both sides of the Atlantic"!

The remainder of the day would be a leisurely one except for the need to prepare notes for the evening 'Captain's Cocktail Party' in which I would be required to meet and greet the passengers for 'Main Sitting' at 5.45pm and those for 'Late Sitting' at 7.45 pm. At both 'parties' I would be required to make a speech in which I would welcome them on board, express the wish that they would enjoy the cruise, and remind them of Cunard's dual slogans, 'Getting there is half the fun' and 'Gracious living at its best', etc., etc., etc.

CUNARD COUNTESS
Caribbean Cruises

"CAPTAIN'S COCKTAIL PARTY"

LADIES and GENTLEMEN -

HAVING ALREADY GREETED YOU AT THE DOOR, IT ONLY REMAINS FOR ME TO ADDRESS YOU COLLECTIVELY. SO, ON BEHALF OF THE CUNARD LINE AND THE ENTIRE SHIP'S COMPLEMENT, MAY I WELCOME YOU ON BOARD THE 'CUNARD COUNTESS'.

THIS TRULY MAGNIFICENT CRUISE-LINER WAS CHRISTENED BY MRS NEIL ARMSTRONG, WIFE OF THE CELEBRATED AMERICAN ASTRONAUT WHO WAS THE FIRST MAN TO SET FOOT ON THE LUNAR SURFACE AND WHO UTTERED THOSE HISTORIC WORDS, "A SMALL STEP FOR MAN, BUT A GIANT LEAP FOR MANKIND".

IT IS IN HONOUR OF HIS REMARKABLE ACHIEVMENT THE PUBLIC ROOMS IN THE SHIP HAVE BEEN GIVEN ASTRONOMIC NAMES SUCH AS 'GALAXY LOUNGE', GEMINI RESTAURANT', 'THE NOVA SUITE', 'CLUB AQUARIUS', 'THE STARLIGHT ROOM', AND 'THE SPLASH-DOWN BAR'.

IN THE LONG AND DISTINGUISHED HISTORY OF CUNARD LINE THERE HAS BEEN A SUCCESSION OF WORLD-FAMOUS PASSENGER LINERS - SHIPS THAT ESTABLISHED PROUD TRADITIONS FOR QUIET, UNOBTRUSIVE, BUT EFFICIENT SERVICE TO THEIR PASSENGERS, BOTH IN PORT AND UPON THE HIGH SEAS.

IT IS AN IMPORTANT PART OF MY DUTY TO ENSURE THESE TRADITIONS ARE CONSTANTLY MAINTAINED AT ALL TIMES, SO THAT YOUR STAY ON BOARD WILL BE A COMFORTABLE ONE, A HAPPY ONE, AND ABOVE ALL, A MEMORABLE ONE.

LADIES and GENTLEMEN - THANK YOU.

Facsimile of Captain's Speech

THE CUNARD STEAMSHIP COMPANY

'CUNARD COUNTESS'

Tonnage: 17,586 Gross. Length Overall: 536ft. 7ins.
Breadth: 74ft. 10 ins.
Draught: 18 ft. 8 ins. Speed: 20.5 Knots.
Stabilisers: Two Fins-Brown's.
Crew: 350. Lifts: 2. Passenger Capacity: 750.
Passenger Cabins: 380.
Air-Conditioning: 100%. Passenger Decks: 8.
Medical Facilities: Fully Equipped Hospital Operating Theatre.
Male, Female and Isolation Wards, etc.
Main Engines: Four Turbo-Charged 7 Cylinder B. & W.
Diesels - BHP 21,000.
Variable-Pitched Propellors. Bow-Thruster 1000 HP.
Lifeboats/Cruise Launches.

Christened 'Cunard Countess' by Mrs. Janet Armstrong.
Wife of Neil Armstrong, American Astronaut.
First Man to step onto the Lunar Surface.
Ceremony in San Juan, Puerto Rico, 8th August 1976.

INTERLUDE - CUNARD COUNTESS

It was barely daybreak when we embarked the Dutch Pilot to take us into Wilhemstradt Harbour. The boat bridge swung wide-open to let us through the short canal. Most of the townsfolk on either side still abed. Often referred-to as the Dutch ABC islands of Aruba, Bonaire and Curaçao they are almost entirely dependent on the oil industry with the crude being brought from nearby oil-wells in the Gulf of Maracaibo in Venezuela. In Wilhemstradt there is also a healthy trade in precious stones and the jewellery that goes with them. There is a thriving ship-repair yard and dry-dock also.

As I have mentioned earlier La Guaira is a thriving commercial port and a naval base for the Venezuelan Navy. The main attraction for tourists is the capitol of Caracas high up in the mountains and reached by a winding road or by cable-car. One of the many attractions in Caracas is the 'Officers' Club' where the visitor can admire large murals depicting the peasant revolt led by Simon Bolivar and ably assisted by units of the South Wales Borderers who, to this day, have the 'Freedom of the City'. Viz. to march through the city with 'Fixed bayonets'.

As with all our ports of call it was early morning arrival and late evening sailings. It was nice to meet again our good friend and harbour Pilot for Grenada, John Rapier. Also our Agent Walter St. John, one-time captain of the West Indies cricket-team, his charming wife Yvonne and their two delightful children.

The French island of Martinique is best known for the terrible disaster when the volcano of Mont Pelee erupted and spewed thousands of tons of red hot ash over the island killing thousands of its inhabitants. The mulatto dancers are just as wild and abandoned as ever giving a typical vertical expression of a horizontal desire! I have always felt a brooding fear in Martinique that Mont Pelee will once again 'blow its top'. I can only hope I'm not there when it happens.

The island of St. Lucia has a thriving harbour at Castries where several cruise liners can be seen almost any day of the week. The magnificent hotel 'Le Toq' is owned and managed by Cunard. The central building is surrounded by a variety of attractive chalets and has its own private beach and swimming-pool. In the southern part of the island the two massive 'Pitons' are volcanic 'plugs' and Souffrier Bay is what was once the crater surrounded by a black volcanic sandy beach. And the island's hot sulphur-springs are a great tourist attraction.

A young Englishwoman in Castries had the contract to change the ship's many potted plants and flowers during our weekly visits to the island. On one such visit I found her busily engaged potting and repotting, when I noticed a particularly exotic bloom. When I told her I had seen an exact replica in a florist's window in Colchester. One can imagine my surprise when she told me she had once lived in Colchester. Then, correcting herself, saying, "Not Colchester exactly but West Mersea"

When I told her I also lived in West Mersea we both burst out laughing with the extraordinary coincidence. Furthermore she added, "Then you must know my uncle George Harrison, secretary of the Mersea Island Yacht Club". I didn't know him then but I certainly do now!!!

Our last port-of-call was at St. Thomas, Virgin Islands. On the American part of the group, handed-over by the British during the Second World War in exchange for fifty obsolete destroyers. The town and harbour of Charlotte Amalie is almost completely surrounded by high mountains making it an ideal shelter for ships, boats and yachts of all descriptions. Among other things it is also a duty-free zone where passengers and crew alike supplement their stocks of liquor.

By leaving Charlotte Amalie on or about midnight we were then able to arrive back in San Juan at six o'clock Saturday morning to repeat the process of disembarking and embarking passengers over and over again, week after week, month after month!

Perhaps I should apologise to my reader if I have inadvertently given the impression this is a travel brochure for West Indies

DAILY PROGRAMME

S U N D A Y   16 OCTOBER 1977
CAPTAIN: G. D. WILLIAMS   CRUISE DIRECTOR: GEOFF DENTON

BON APPETIT!

	Main Sitting	Late Sitting
BREAKFAST	7.30 am	8.45 am
LUNCHEON	Noon	1.30 pm
DINNER	6.30 pm	8.30 pm

Passengers are requested to note meal times and for their own comfort to take their seats promptly.

- **7.00 am** — For early birds, eye-opener coffee served on 5 Deck Aft.
- **8.00 am**
- **8.30 am** — HOLY MASS will be celebrated in the Nova Suite.
- **9.30 am** — Join Clay on 6 Deck Aft for a jog around the decks followed by some simple exercises.
- **10.00 am** — "Weight Watchers Weigh In" - check today and again on Friday morning. A prize will be given to the person gaining the most weight - Pool Side.
- **10.15 am** — PASSENGER BOAT DRILL The Captain requests that all passengers who embarked in San Juan attend wearing life-jackets.
- **10.30 am - 12.30 pm** — Change will be available in the Casino.
- **10.30 am** — Mid-morning bouillon served at the Pool Side.
- **10.45 am** — TRAVEL TALK ON THE ISLANDS - where to go, what to see and do - given by your Cruise Director, Geoff Denton in the Galaxy Lounge.
- **11.30 am** — SINGLES PARTY - Travelling alone or unattached and feeling friendly? Join the Cruise Staff for drinks and meet some new friends in the Aquarius Club with COAST TO COAST.
- **11.30 am** — TOTE ON THE SHIP'S RUN - Can you guess how far the ship has travelled since leaving San Juan until Noon today? To be held at the Pool Side.
- **11.30 am** — A member of the Cruise Staff will be in the Galaxy Lounge with tickets for any passenger wishing to visit the Bridge.

M*O*V*I*E P*R*O*G*R*A*M*M*E - in the Nova Suite, showing at 3.00 pm, 8.00 pm and 10.30 pm in English - "THE PEOPLE THAT TIME FORGOT"

- **Noon** — Hot dogs, hamburgers and iced drinks available at the Pool Side.
- **3.00 pm**
- **1.00 pm** — Informal meeting of the Rotarians and all Service Clubs in the CLUB AQUARIUS.
- **2.15 pm** — An introduction to gaming - CASINO
- **2.30 pm** — The CASINO opens for your gaming pleasure.
- **2.30 pm** — TABLE TENNIS TOURNAMENT on 5 Deck Aft.
- **2.45 pm** — Anyone for Bridge or Backgammon? Meet Fred Fels in attendance in the Card Area on 5 Deck Aft.
- **2.45 pm** — GOLF CLINIC - Improve your swing Join Mark Porter in the Gallery - 6 Deck.
- **3.00 pm** — Complimentary Dance Class - Join Bev and Juan and learn some new simple steps - Galaxy Lounge.
- **3.45 pm** — TRAP SHOOTING - Bridge Deck Aft. $1.50 for 4 shots.
- **4.00 pm** — Afternoon Tea served in the
- **4.30 pm** — Galaxy Lounge.

****

CAPTAIN'S COCKTAIL PARTY

Captain Williams and his Officers request the pleasure of your company in the Galaxy Lounge.

- **5.45 pm** — Party for guests on Main Sitting
- **7.45 pm** — Party for guests on Late Sitting

Please enter by the forward door on boat deck.

****

IN THE GALAXY LOUNGE - SUNDAY

S*P*E*C*T*A*C*U*L*A*R - Our glittering floor show at 9.00 pm and 10.30 pm featuring:
  ANNI ANDERSON   SWEET ELEGANCE
  MUNDANE THE GREAT

****

S T A R L I G H T   B A R   opens 8.30 pm

- **10.00 pm** — The CASINO opens and FLO GLENN entertains with songs at the piano.
- **10.00 pm** — CLUB AQUARIUS opens with the sounds of COAST TO COAST.

A MIDNIGHT BUFFET will be served in the Gemini Restaurant from midnight until 1.00 am.

Facsimile reproduction of Daily Programme.

Cruises. Rather clumsily, I've tried to illustrate what a 'rat-race' these cruises were for the ship's crew and how for my part the horror of disastrous floods and their disastrous consequences can be thrust into the background of one's consciousness.

Needless to say, each weekly cruise I invariably asked my table companions where they were from, to give conversation a 'kick-start'. But also in the hope of meeting someone from Pennsylvania, even Johnstown itself. But such was my kind of luck to be told they were from almost every State in the USA except Pennsylvania.

Sailors all know the Captain's steward is his 'Tiger'. And mine had a remarkable sense of humour and my table companions loved his keen wit and repartee. In all my seagoing experience I have found Americans to be charming, kind and generous. But there was one cruise when I found Elmer C. Winterbottom to be an aggressive, argumentative florid boor of a man whose little wife had no choice but to agree with everything he said.

One evening after dinner my 'Tiger' was serving coffee and when he approached Elmer C. Winterbottom with the customary question, "Coffee Sir?" the American replied loudly, "Yeah, hot, sweet and strong like my women." My 'Tiger' retorted with, "Certainly Sir, Black or White?"

But week after week, cruise after cruise, neither the passengers at my table nor those I met around the ship were from Pennsylvania much less from Johnstown. Until my fifth week sailing from San Juan I met the Gallaghers. Andrew Gallagher's father was a Scot who had emigrated to America and found work in the ironworks around Pittsburgh, Pennsylvania. Marrying a local girl they were blessed eventually with a family of two boys and a girl, Andrew being the eldest.

It was quite evident Andrew knew a lot more about the 1936 Johnstown Flood and the more recent one on 31st. May 1977. It was not the sort of topic to be discussed at the table but I invited him to my quarters for a drink the next day when Joan could engage his wife Pauline on subjects all women like best - clothes!

At eleven o'clock the next day, after my steward had deposited the tray of coffee and biscuits on the rectangular table, I asked Andrew if he remembered the 1936 flood of Johnstown. For a couple of minutes I had to wait his reply because Joan had just given him his coffee. "Black as night" he called it, "With no sugar." Taking an appreciative sip he turned to me and said, "I was eleven years old at the time, but it was the sole topic of conversation at home and in school. I gave a slight, deprecating cough before saying, "I don't suppose you had much in the way of television in those days."

"No I guess not," he replied, "But there was radio." He paused while he took another sip of coffee then added, "But I remember people being interviewed on the radio and there was a lot of criticism about the way they said it would never happen again." He gave his wife a quick glance and said. "You lost some kinfolk in this last flood didn't you honey?"

His wife Pauline nodded and whispered so low I barely heard what she was saying, "They were my cousins Rupert and Freda, they died in the flood". She took out a postage-stamp sized handkerchief and wiped her eyes, then went on to say, "they were supposed to have been coming to my birthday party Wednesday 30th. July." She turned to Joan and again whispered, "And they all said it would never happen again." With one of her meaningful stares at me Joan said. "Another coffee Andrew?" That was her way of telling me to change the subject!

That last night in Charlotte Amalie, St. Thomas, Virgin Islands will remain indelibly imprinted in my memory. The following day we would be flying home, not on leave, but for good and, hopefully, a long and happy retirement. The dancing in the 'Galaxy' ballroom was followed by the usual floor-show when Juan and Beverley, our entertainers, 'The Dancing Duo' excelled themselves. Then came our surprise when Geoff Denton the Cruise Director signalled the band for a particularly rousing clash of cymbals.

When everyone in the room had fallen silent with anticipation he beckoned Joan and myself onto the dance-floor and when we had joined him he gave a very touching little speech which ended with Beverley approached carrying a large box. There must have been several hundred people in the room including the band and entertainers and they all began chanting, Open it, open it, open it!" -

which I did forthwith and produced the most beautiful and exquisite Lladro statuette of two seagulls perched on a rock.

My embarrassment was happily relieved by the band who played, and the folks began singing, "For he's a jolly good......" Geoff then presented Joan with a beautiful gold 'Omega' wristwatch to thunderous applause. Two waiters then appeared carrying the largest cake I've ever seen. Approximately three feet by two feet and in large letters the words, 'Happy Retirement Captain'. And for the second time the lump in my throat was almost unbearable.

But it didn't end there. One of my junior officers came up to invite us to the Wardroom for a 'little ceremony'. (I was beginning to like this). On our arrival there it was to find every officer available, nursing sisters, beauty salon ladies and shop assistants all applauding our arrival. Champagne was thrust into our hands and we were then presented with a very attractive crystal-bowl and vase. And for the third time I was speechless with emotion. And that dear reader, is a strange and novel experience for an elderly retiring, Sea-Captain!

After less than six hours sleep we arrived back in San Juan early Saturday morning still feeling emotionally drained. But, as the Americans are so fond of saying, "The show must go on." Captain Doug Ridley returned from leave in time to join the usual 'conference' where there were a few laughs at my expense reading some flattering remarks in the 'Comment Cards'!

While all this was going on Joan had packed all our 'bits and bobs' and in no time we were being whisked to the airport for our flight to New York via Eastern Airlines, (First Class - compliments of their Chief Executive), followed by the long haul across the Atlantic to Heathrow and Home.

After nearly fifty years of a seagoing career it was, and still is, a strange feeling to arrive back home not quite knowing what to expect. For the first time in my life there was no expectation of being recalled or being 'On leave pending further appointment". Within a few days there came that familiar 'emptiness' in the stomach that comes with being hungry. And, bless her heart, Joan must have recognised the symptoms, she kept quiet saying nothing.

It was many weeks later when I was tidying-up my desk and browsing through old 'Captain's Reports', 'Cash Accounts' and stacks of letters that I came across that page of the 'Miami Herald' dated Sunday 24th. July 1977 reporting the third disastrous flood of Johnstown the previous Tuesday night.

Having read the article in the 'Miami Herald' for the second time, I began telling my wife about that first terrible flood in 1889. How one of the victims, Margaret Williams's body had been identified by the brooch she'd been wearing. And, how her mother, my Aunt Jane, on the rooftop of their home, had given birth to a baby boy, later to be Christened; Moses Flood Williams!

I have no knowledge of when Uncle Griff, Aunt Jane and their family removed from Johnstown and their return to Wales. No doubt it was the trauma of the disastrous flood and the loss of their only daughter that triggered that decision. On their return to the Swansea Valley they settled down in a hillside farm overlooking the village of Ystradgynlais and the River Tawe.

The four stalwart boys, David, Howell, Will and Moses were among the early founders of 'The First Swansea Valley Scout Troop' under the patronage of Lord Glanusk, and the leadership of 'Skip' Morgan, whose brother Llew. taught me in primary school. Theirs, I my add, is a fascinating story equally as interesting as 'The Forsyte Saga' if not more so.

In later years David became headmaster of a primary school in a village nearby. He and his wife Beatrice had a son Oswald who, during the First World War rose to the rank of Lt. Colonel. Will and Howell took advantage of the 'Baden-Powell Grant' to farm in Kenya. In 1937 during a prolonged period of drought and searching for water in a parched river-bed discovered a rich reef of gold which made them equally as rich.

In 1952 when Ystradgynlais was the venue of the National Eisteddfod, 'Uncle' Will had a Teak tree felled and from which was fashioned a Bardic Chair. It was intended Will would personally present it at the 'Chairing Ceremony'. But early one morning his 'butler' discovered his bloodied corpse mutilated by the drug-crazed Mau-Mau terrorising Kenya at that time.

The youngest son, Moses Flood Williams, became a successful journalist with a popular weekly magazine. For several years he and his wife lived in the semi-detached house 'Camnant' next door to my family home 'Glanffrwd'. But some years later when they when they moved to Wisbech, Cambridgeshire, Uncle Griff and Aunt Jane moved-in to replace them.

I can only hope and pray the foregoing 'thumb-nail' sketch of the Johnstown connection has not confused you unduly. For this I must apologise on grounds of being a clumsy amateur story-teller but the lapse of time has produced such a faded tapestry where some threads are worn while others are missing entirely. But such is life.

As I had begun my seagoing career before Uncle Griff. and Aunt Jane moved in next door I saw very little of them other than during short leave periods. Meanwhile, my two sisters were now married and living near Colchester while my brother Cedric, also married, was serving in the Royal Air Force and attached to the Air Ministry.

On the 31st. March 1936, while my ship 'Bangalore' was on the Japanese coast, my indentures expired and I was promoted Fourth Officer. A promotion which proved to be short lived when a huge item of cargo fell from a dizzy height and I was rushed into hospital in Kobe with multiple injuries!

In the weeks that followed my Mother was persuaded by my siblings to leave Ystradgynlais in exchange for a pretty little villa not far from my married sisters in Rowhedge. So, when eventually discharged from hospital I arrived back in the UK where I was met by my brother who drove me to our new home.

Later, I was told, as Mum was preparing to leave 'Glanffrwd' a tearful Aunt Jane gave her the brooch her daughter Margaret had been wearing when she had died in that disastrous flood of Johnstown in May 1889.

Not very long after the Second World War, in which my Brother, Squadron. Leader Cedric Watcyn Williams was killed when his 'Hurricane' was in a head-on collision with a 'Messerschmit 110', my dear Mother was advised to have this brooch cleaned by a reputable jeweller in Colchester but on hearing its history he very properly refused.

Putting his 'optic' to one side he said, "Mrs Williams, this attractive piece of costume jewellery has very little intrinsic value by itself, but from what you have told me about its connection with the Johnstown Flood in 1889 I truly believe it is a piece of American History." He paused while cleaning his spectacles then he added, "I beg you madam, never, never have that brooch cleaned"!

As my elder sister Win had no children of her own, my dear Mother left the brooch to my younger sister Mattie, who, in turn left it to her elder daughter Wendy, who kindly loaned it to be photographed as an illustration for this story. And it only remains for me to remind my reader when the Panama Canal Pilot handed me a copy of the 'Miami Sunday Herald' dated 24th July 1977 reporting the THIRD flood of Johnstown, it occurred to me, each time Johnstown suffered a calamitous flood the authorities claimed it could never happen again!

They can tell that to the occupants of 'Grandview Cemetery' on the hill overlooking Johnstown, Pennsylvania, USA and for my money they can also tell it to the Marines!

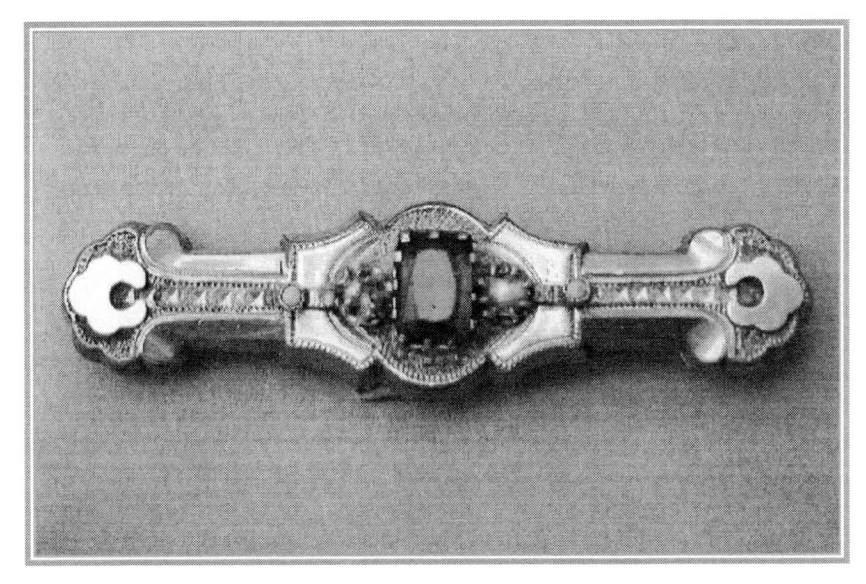

TO THE MEMORY OF MARGARET WILLIAMS WHO DIED IN THE FLOOD AND WHOSE BODY WAS LATER IDENTIFIED BY THE BROOCH SHE WAS WEARING.

EPILOGUE

Perhaps I should apologise to my dear reader for the appalling lack of detail in my story about 'The Brooch' and the disastrous floods that overwhelmed Johnstown, Pennsylvania. As may be seen by the correspondence included here with the civic authorities failed dismally to meet my expectations.

The few relatives of mine in possession of detailed information have sadly 'passed on' to what I can only hope and pray is a far better place than this tired old world. In their day they probably lacked the will or desire to put pen to paper and certainly lacked the advantage of a typewriter, much less the magical qualities of a word-processor.

However and hopefully the story I have told has facets of interest in its scope rather than what it lacks in detail. In this day and age where school-children are taught the skills of using computers there is little or no excuse for their not recording their family histories from one generation to the next.

Radio and television have made gigantic strides in my lifetime opening-up vast new fields of interest and entertainment. One can only speculate what future science may bring my children and my children's children, ad infinitum. Sadly, it is as though one has been deeply engrossed reading a very interesting book only to have it snatched away before learning how it all ended!

And Again That's Life.

Tel.(01206) 38 3980

'MEADOW END',
14 Broomhills Road;
West Mersea;
ESSEX,CO5 8AS

4th.May 2000

His Worship the Mayor;
CITY HALL,
Johnstown;
PENNSYLVANIA, U.S.A.

Dear Mr.Mayor;

In researching for my book "The Brooch" which has its Genesis in the flood of Johnstown May 31st.1889 I would be most grateful for certain information to which you have access.

Personal relationships are often difficult to define or crystalize but my mother's Aunt, Jane Williams, lost her only daughter, Margaret in the flood. When her body was eventually found in the rubble and mud itwas identified by the shawl she was wearing and the brooch by which it was clasped.

At the time of the flood Aunt Jane was pregnant with child and we were led to believe the baby boy was born on the roof-top of their home at Eben James' house at 236 Market Street and was later christened Moses Flood Williams.

The family later returned to the Swansea valley in South Wales and when Aunt Jane died she bequeathed the brooch to my mother because her name was also Margaret. And many years later my mother took the brooch to a jeweller's to have it cleaned. On hearing the story the jeweller refused to clean it because it held the residue of the mud hidden between the stones and THAT made the brooch absolutely priceless.

Aunt Jane's cousin John Thomas Harris was chief of police of the City of Johnstown under Mayor John Pendry. He died on the 9th.April 1911 and was buried in Grandview Cemetary. But as this is the sum total of my information any further detail you could offer will be acknowledged gratefully

Yours faithfully;

(Captain) Gwilym D.Williams.

PS My niece Wendy now has the brooch in safekeeping.

JOHNSTOWN CITY COUNCIL
"A Home Rule Municipality"
CITY HALL
401 MAIN STREET
JOHNSTOWN, PENNSYLVANIA 15901

814-533-2001

DR. DONATO B. ZUCCO *Mayor*
MARTHA BANDA
JOE GALLO
ADAM HENGER
NUNZIO JOHNCOLA
NANCY J. MALLOY
ANTHONY R. PINIZZOTTO
RON R. STEVENS
BRIAN SUBICH

May 15, 2000

Captain Gwilym D. Williams
'MEADOW END'
14 Broomhills Road
West Mersea;
ESSEX
ENGLAND
CO5 8AS

Dear Captain Williams:

Thank you for your May 4th letter and sharing the information regarding the work you are doing in conducting research for your book.

I am sending your letter to Richard Burkert, Executive Director of The Johnstown Area Heritage Association. Richard, is I believe, an individual who can provide you with information that may be helpful.

I wish you success in your venture and if I can be of any additional help, please feel free to contact me.

Sincerely,

CITY OF JOHNSTOWN

Dr. Donato B. Zucco
Mayor

DZ/dmk

P.T.O

Richard Burkert's Address

WORKING TO MAKE JOHNSTOWN FRIENDLY, SAFE AND CLEAN

Tel.(01206) 38 3980

'MEADOW END',
14 Broomhills Road;
West Mersea;
ESSEX,CO5 8AS

27th.May,2000

Richard Burkert, Esq.;
Executive Director;
THE JOHNSTOWN AREA HERITAGE ASSOCIATION:
P.O. BOX 1889.
JOHNSTOWN, Pa. 15907
U.S.A.

Dear Mr.Burkert;

In his reply to my letter, His Worship, Dr.Donato B.Zucco, Mayor of Johnstown, mentioned he had sent my letter to you. There is, therefore no point in my repeating all those details other than to say I am researching for the book I hope to have published.

"The Brooch" is about a voyage from Avonmouth U.K. to Bluff, New Zealand via the Panama Canal when I was Master of the Cunard cargo-ship "Matangi". And on our arrival back at the Canal on the homeward passage the pilot brought with him a copy of 'The Miami Herald' dated Sunday July 24th.1977 in which was reported the recent (and third) flood of Johnstown.

You can imagine the impact this news had on me when I vividly remember when, as a child, I had heard tales of the flood of 1889. On that horrific occasion my mother's Aunt Jane had given birth to a baby boy who was later christened Moses Flood Williams. Their daughter Margaret and her fiance had perished in the flood, her body being later identified by the shawl she was wearing and the brooch which secured it. !

Many years later when Aunt Jane died she beqeathed the brooch to my mother because her name also was Margaret. And several years even later mother took the brooch to a reputable jeweller to have it cleaned. But on hearing the story of how the residue of mud was embedded among the 'stones' he refused to clean it, saying the trinket had incalcuable value as it was now of historical value. When mother died she left the brooch to her daughter Matilda, (my sister) who has since given it to Her daughter Wendy who treasures it above all else.

Enclosed a phot-copy of another relative, (Uncle John Harris) who was Chief of Police at the time of this terrible tragedy in the history of Johnstown. I'm sure it will be of inestimable value to the historical pages of your City and to your Mayor.

Yours Faithfully;

(Captain) Gwilym D.Williams

Tel.(01206) 38 3980

'MEADOW END',
14 Broomhills Road;
West Mersea;
ESSEX,CO5 8AS

4th.July,2000

Dr.Donato B.Zucco,
His Worship The Mayor,
JOHNSTOWN CITY COUNCIL,
City Hall,
401 Main Street;
JOHNSTOWN, PENNSYLVANIA 15901
UNITED STATES of AMERICA.

THE FLOOD BOOK JOHNSTOWN
May 31st. 1889

Dear Doctor Donato;

With reference to my letter dated 4th.May and your kindly reply dated 15th. in which you gave me the address of Richard Burkert, Executive Director of the Johnstown Area.

I duly wrote to Mr.Burkert on the 27th.May enclosing a small booklet entitled "The Memoirs of John Thomas Harris" written by Henry Wilson Storey dated "Thanksgiving Day 1911"

As a historical little document I considered it prudent to post it in a protective 'jiffy-bag' for safety's sake but to date I hve not received a reply from Mr.Burkert acknowledging receipt of it which gives rise to some anxiety on my part.

I hesittae to take up so much of your valuable time but I would be eternally grateful if you could check if Mr Burkert has received the booklet and my letter enclosed with it. I would be devastated if it has been lost in the post.

As an additional piece of useless information the date above also marks the inauguration of the Cunard Steamship Company. If by chance you have ever enjoyed a cruising holiday in either "Cunard Adventurer" or "Cunard Countess" I might have been the Master. (stranger things are known to have happened).

Yours sincerely;

Captain Gwilym D.Williams

JOHNSTOWN CITY COUNCIL
"A Home Rule Municipality"

DR. DONATO B. ZUCCO *Mayor*
MARTHA BANDA
JOE GALLO
ADAM HENGER
NUNZIO JOHNCOLA
NANCY J. MALLOY
ANTHONY R. PINIZZOTTO
RON R. STEVENS
BRIAN SUBICH

CITY HALL
401 MAIN STREET
JOHNSTOWN, PENNSYLVANIA 15901

814-533-2001

July 11, 2000

Captain Gwilym D. Williams
'MEADOW END'
14 Broomhills Road
West Mersea;
ESSEX
ENGLAND
CO5 8AS

Dear Captain Williams:

This is in response to your July 4th communication regarding your concern as to the receipt of your letter and attached documents by Mr. Richard Burkert of The Johnstown Area Heritage Association.

After receiving your message my office spoke with Mr. Burkert and he did indeed receive your letter and booklet and informed us that he and his historians were in the process of researching some information for you in preparation of his response to your inquiries. He exclaimed that he receives many requests for historic information but that your letter and document was one of the most interesting he has ever received. He noted that he is eager to respond to you but needs to verify and research the information in order to be as accurate as possible. He apologized for the delay but indicated that The Heritage Association was indeed working to answer all your questions and send you pertinent information.

Thank you for the insight regarding the date of your letter of July 4th as being the inauguration date of the Cunard Steamship Company. I have not had the pleasure of a cruising holiday on either cruise line but congratulate you on your association with this historic date and Company. July 4th is also a day which is commemorated with much festivity in my country as the date of the birth of the United States, so I join you in celebrating this memorable occasion.

I am sure you will hear from Mr. Burkert as soon as he has researched and processed the historic information for you. Best wishes as you continue with your manuscript and if I can be of any additional help, please feel free to contact me at any time.

Sincerely,

CITY OF JOHNSTOWN

Donato B. Zucco, Ph.D.
Mayor

DZ/dmk

WORKING TO MAKE JOHNSTOWN FRIENDLY, SAFE AND CLEAN

EASTER SUNDAYS

It was Easter Sunday morning in 1919 - a few weeks before my fourth birthday 7th May 1915 and, incidentally, the sinking of the 'Lusitania'. The previous day my Mother, brother and two sisters had joined a huge throng of people converging on our local railway station. Even from some distance away we could hear the brass-band playing popular airs and marches. There was a subdued air of excitement and anticipation while we waited for the arrival of the 'special' train from Brecon. Since the Armistice had been signed - 11th. Hour, 11th. Day, 11th. Month 1918 - hundreds of service-men and women were now at last returning home. Flags and coloured bunting adorned the station roof-tops. As the train arrived at the station carriage-doors flung open, servicemen leaped onto the platform to be hugged and kissed, while my childish eyes were focussed on the gleaming hissing locomotive.

And now, in St. Cynog's Church, seated in the family pew immediately behind Colonel and Mrs Gough, I was wedged between Grandad and Uncle Mike (to ensure my good behaviour). With minutes to go before the eleven o'clock service began, the church was already full. Not far from where we sat I could see Mum at the organ playing soft incidental music. And although I couldn't see him behind the heavy curtains I knew my brother Cedric was zealously pumping air into the organ. While my Sister Mattie was somewhere among the ladies section of the church choir.

Many of the service personnel in the congregation had been among those who had returned home the day before. Also Scouts and Cubs from the 'First Swansea Valley Troop' - Guides and members of St. John's Ambulance Brigade all in uniform. My eldest sister Win stayed at home to cook the Sunday dinner to which Mum's brother Uncle Mike had been invited.

The church service had advanced as far as the reading of the First Lesson and the curate, Mr Jenkins returned to his seat while Mum played the introductory bars for the 'Te Deum'. We all sat down as the rector prepared to read the Second Lesson at the end of which Uncle Mike bent his head to whisper something in my ear. Obediently and without question I stood up and at the top of my voice yelled, "Play up Ada!"

Grandad hissed, "Keep quiet you little scamp", while Colonel and Mrs Gough, and at least half the congregation turned their heads open-mouthed with amazement, my poor Mum, her face scarlet with embarrassment, played the introductory bars for the 'Magnifcat - My Soul shall magnify the Lord and my Spirit hath rejoiced in God my Saviour..............' Meanwhile Uncle Mike looked straight ahead - the picture of innocence!

Far too young to know or appreciate it at the time, although Grandad knew only too well, his son, my Uncle Mike was and always had been a practical joker. It was also the fact that Uncle Mike was a brilliant engineer, this side of his character was tolerated, even forgiven. In the early stages of the industrial revolution he was very much in demand by various works and factories to attend to some stubborn machinery.

He had stumbled on the gyroscopic effect on the flywheels of machinery, especially high-speed engines without consciously being able to explain it. Main-bearings were found to be wearing unevenly with calamitous results. To the horror of owners and managers alike he would insist on the engine being re-sited which invariably resulted in a satisfactory operation. He was also some-

Lusitania, sunk on the day of my birth.

thing of a 'ladies' man' and an especial favourite of Madame Adelina Patty the world-famous diva and was always welcome at 'Graig-y-Nos' castle when she was in residence. Of course I only learned of this at a later stage in my own rather 'chequered career!'. For the rest of my life, even during my fifty years of a seagoing career, various Aunts, Uncles and cousins have taken a great deal of satisfaction and delight in telling this story, as much to embarrass me as to amuse anyone who cared to listen. It is not that I mind or care very much but in the years to come, and very curiously there came a strange almost incredible sequel to that event so many years ago.

It was now Easter Sunday morning in 1959 and within weeks of my forty-fourth birthday, the Cunard luxury cruise-liner 'Caronia' (the millionaire's yacht) had just arrived alongside the Pier in Kowloon, Hong Kong, on her annual "Around the World Cruise'. Her eight navigating officers, of which I was one, having been 'on stations' since dawn, were now relaxing in the wardroom enjoying freshly-brewed 'Cona' coffee and reading English-language newspapers that had just arrived on board.

A column on one of the inside pages caught my eye, it listed the times of various church-services to be held that day in the Colony. Perhaps it was with 'tongue-in-cheek' that I read aloud the following entry. "11 o'clock Easter Sunday Service at St. Steven's Church, Kowloon - anyone interested?" Much to my surprise four of my fellow officers replied, "OK Willie, I'll come with you," and, "OK I'll come too."

But where on earth was St. Steven's Church? That was the rub. I 'phoned the 'American Express Travel Bureau' on board and they promised to ring me back. Sooner than expected they rang to tell me St. Steven's Church was on the corner of Simla Road and Cartwright Avenue - a mere ten minute walk from the Pier and 'Caronia'. And so it was agreed that after breakfast we would meet again in the wardroom by no later than ten-thirty all spick-and-span and ready to sally forth!

It was a fine sunny morning and not too warm and we found it to be a very pleasant walk to St. Steven's and as we approached the church we remarked on the number of people converging from all directions. As expected there were a large number of Europeans and a fair number of Chinese also. In fact, there were so many people attending we were very lucky to find places to sit.

The Easter Sunday Service followed the same familiar pattern I had known all my life and not unlike the church-services held on board every Cunard ship when at sea. Eventually, the First Lesson was read by the priest, Rector or Vicar, and followed by the singing of the 'Te Deum'. It was immediately after the reading of the Second Lesson, when it would be followed by the introductory bars of the 'Magnifcat' - instead there was a long pause, an extended silence. The Rector, even the whole choir were looking around anxiously, and at that precise moment in a sort of choked whisper I blurted out, "Play up Ada" and with that the organ blared out the opening bars of the 'Magnifcat' - "My soul shall magnify the Lord and my Spirit hath rejoiced in God my Saviour................"
On the walk back to the ship my fellow officers, almost in unison asked, "Why in hell's name did you say that Willie?" I could only reply, "I don't know chaps, it just came out." Would they have believed me? Or would they have understood? I only hoped and prayed they wouldn't repeat the question.

I needn't have worried they never did!!!

OBSESSION

The event I am about to relate happened over forty years ago during the Second World War at sea. I still suffer the occasional nightmare in which the horrifying scene is repeated over and over again and when it occurs I wake up bathed in perspiration and mumbling some sort of protest. On such occasions my wife sympathetically makes a brew of tea after which I enjoy a dreamless and restful sleep until her little radio calls us at the set time to face a new day. Even so, the memory of the nightmare haunts me for several daylight hours until the hum-drum normality of daily life reasserts itself.

It so happened while enjoying a few pints at our 'local' a very close friend and I were exchanging a few confidences and somehow the subject of dreams and nightmares came into the conversation. Apart from my wife I have never told anyone about my recurring nightmare, but on this occasion, and knowing Charles wouldn't laugh, I told him the whole story leaving out nothing. In fairness to my friend he listened attentively without interruption other than to clarify a small matter of detail.

When I had finished there was a longish period of silence during which I headed for the bar to replenish two empty pint-pots. While thus employed on a small but equally as important an errand must have given Charles the opportunity to mull-over what I had been telling him because, immediately after exchanging the age-old expression 'cheers' followed by an appreciative sip of the 'amber nectar' he began.

"You may or may not have heard about it G.D. (my friends have always called me by the first two initials of my name), but there have been cases parallel if not identical to yours, where the sufferer is advised to put it all down on paper." He paused to take another sip then went on. "What I mean is - if you write about your experience, just as you've told it to me, it exorcises it from your memory - it removes all traces of an unhappy episode from your subconscious - see what I mean?" I gave a little shrug then replied, "It sounds feasible Charles, I'll give it some thought - never venture, never gained, eh?" And with that we dropped the subject in favour of another pint.

After watching the ten o'clock news on the 'telly' and enjoying our last cup of tea before bedtime I told Joan what Charles had suggested. When she had washed, dried and put away the tea-things she said, "I think Charles knows what he's talking about, he always has his feet firmly on the ground, so why not do as he suggests - write it all down omitting nothing."

So, dear reader, this is my story - such as it is:-

In the early hours of March 17th. 1943 (St. Patrick's Day), while homeward-bound across the North Atlantic in Convoy HX 229 my ship 'Nariva' was torpedoed. From about seven o'clock in the evening I had been 'standing-by' the four-inch gun on the poop with the rest of the gun's crew, as other ships in the convoy had been attacked. For hour after hour we had stamped our feet and flailed our arms to keep out the bitter cold, until, at a few minutes before eight bells (midnight) I was called to keep my watch on the bridge. For the first two hours there came a lull in submarine attacks, giving the 'old man' (Captain Dodds) and myself enough time to enjoy mugs of steaming hot cocoa made by senior cadet Ron Bryden.

Shortly after 2.30 a.m. there came the distant rumble of another ship having been hit and this was followed by others even closer. Then came a massive explosion in the next column to ours on the port side. I went over to the port wing of the bridge to watch this ship drifting by as we steamed inexorably onwards At that precise moment I saw what looked like a porpoise approaching 'Nariva'. A second later, before I could utter a word, I saw a huge green flash underwater as a torpedo exploded against the ship's side between numbers one and two cargo holds and the 'Nariva' bucked like a startled horse.

Luckily for us and due to a full cargo of frozen meat the 'Nariva' took a long time to sink, giving us ample time to prepare and launch all four lifeboats. A few hours later in the grey light of dawn we were sighted by and picked up by HMS 'Anemone', one of the corvettes escorting the convoy.

During the following afternoon, at the height of a typical North Atlantic gale another lifeboat was sighted a few cables away. Lt. Commander Pat King, RNR and ex-Chief Officer in Orient Line showed superb seamanship as he manoeuvred 'Anemone' alongside the boatload of survivors from the stricken ship 'Canadian Star'. Then, with a rope 'scrambling net' over the side of the corvette the naval crew hurriedly but skilfully helped these survivors on board in spite of the way the lifeboat rose and fell, frequently crashing against the side of the corvette in the heavy seas and swell.

I and a dozen other survivors from the 'Nariva' watched in amazement as a teenaged girl was literally snatched aboard the corvette by her long blond hair. And then, a little baby was tossed upwards by its father, a Royal Air Force Officer, to be caught skilfully, safely, by one of the sailors. But a young woman, whom we discovered later was the wife of the air-force officer, was halfway up the scrambling-net when the rising lifeboat smashed her against the ship's side and her body fell lifeless into the raging seas.

Eventually, all but one survivor had been safely brought aboard the 'Anemone. The exception being an elderly man whom, we learned later, had been the carpenter on the 'Canadian Star' and he was now seated at the bottom of the lifeboat, unable to move because one of the buoyancy-tanks had broken loose and become wedged across his legs and, try as he might, he couldn't free himself.

Each time the boat was lifted high on the crest of a wave we watched breathlessly as the sailors strove to save him. At times they managed to grab his arms to pull him free but after several attempts I couldn't help screaming, "For Christ's sake be careful, or you'll wrench his arms off." And in the peak and stress of emotion I thought I heard a hidden voice telling me to jump into the boat to save the old man. But suddenly the boat crashed heavily against the ship's side so violently the poor old man fell backwards with his head and shoulders half-hidden in the empty space under the side-thwart from which the buoyancy-tank had broken loose. With every movement in the heavy sea running the water in the boat kept sloshing over his head and face until, at last, shocked and overcome with grief, we watched him die before our very eyes.

It was a scene I shall never forget and, for over forty years I have nursed a horrible feeling of guilt that, regardless of myself being a survivor, a passenger even, but I know I should have jumped into the boat in order to save that poor old man's life. In broad daylight I remind myself it was not up to me, the crew of the 'Anemone' had done all that was humanly possible to save him. Yet, I keep having these recurring nightmares in which I relive the scene and I keep hearing this mysterious voice saying, "Jump into the boat you coward - jump!" And That is my feeling of guilt - my obsession! It remains to be seen if it exorcises the scene from my subconscious. If it does - perhaps I will let you know!!

RMS Nariva

HMS Anemone

THE ARAB BEGGAR

Yet another cruise of the 'Caronia' ended where it had begun, alongside Pier 90 in New York. Hundreds of wealthy American passengers disembarked to proceed homeward while the ship's crew were feverishly preparing the ship to receive hundreds more. Tons of fresh stores, thousands of pieces of freshly-laundered bedroom and kitchen linen were exchanged while the ship's fresh-water and fuel-tanks were being replenished. And all this activity in preparation for the forthcoming 'Autumn Mediterranean Cruise' with Captain Fred Watts in command.

While many of the ship's officers were able to enjoy the flesh-pots of Manhattan, I busied myself in the chartroom putting away used charts in their respective folios and selecting those that would be required for the next cruise. There now followed hours of calculating Courses and Distances between ports and plotting them on the pertinent charts. Then, referring to the Company's itinerary, giving the times of arrival and departure at each port, calculate the speed required and the number of revolutions per minute as an approximate guide for our Chief Engineer.

Three days later our departure from New York was something of a repeat of all the others with lavish champagne parties on board and on Pier 90. The passengers on board waving farewell to their friends and relatives they were leaving behind. Flags and bunting, balloons and colourful streamers almost filled the gap between ship and shore, with music, music, music.

With her gangways landed, moorings slipped fore and aft and the deafening three long blasts from her whistle 'Caronia' began moving astern and away from her berth alongside Pier 90. By the time her bridge cleared the end of the Pier she would be making the better part of fifteen knots. And the brown muddy water of North River is churned into a froth as her engines go ahead and she turns in mid-stream to head down-river. Another long farewell blast from her whistle echoes through the concrete canyons of Manhattan. 'Caronia' - 'Green Goddess' - 'The Millionaires' Yacht', is on her way to exotic countries and ports of call.

A few weeks later on a Sunday morning the 'Caronia' is safely moored alongside the quay in Alexandria Harbour in Egypt. Her navigating-officers were relaxed and enjoying freshly-brewed 'Cona' coffee while reading English-language editions of newspapers brought aboard by the local Cunard representative. A column in my copy gave details of Church Services being held in the city including one at eleven o'clock in St. Peter's Church, Mohammed Ali Square.

Unlike the previous occasion when I had invited my fellow-officers to join me, the response this time was almost instantaneous, when three others expressed their willingness to accompany me. It was agreed the best way to find St. Peter's Church would be to hire a taxi at the main gate, but when the Captain heard of our intention he sent word he wouldn't be requiring the Agent's car so it was at our disposal.

At a few minutes before eleven o'clock the chauffeur brought the car to a halt immediately opposite the entrance to St. Peter's Church and we four churchgoers climbed out. When inside and our eyes had become accustomed to the gloom, Chief Officer Mort Hehir led the way to a pew halfway down the central aisle. I couldn't help but notice the number of unoccupied pews there were in this beautiful old church.

As we sat admiring the internal architecture I espied the Rector emerge from a doorway to approach the lectern where he began adjusting the purple ribbon to mark the two Lessons. Having done so, he then came to where we were seated and with a shy smile asked, "Would one of you gentlemen care to read the Lessons this morning?" Mort Hehir instantly replied, "Yes Padré, and pointing his thumb in my direction said, "He will." Simultaneously Andrew Thompson also said, "Ye Padré", and pointed in my direction. They were both my senior officers!

Smiling his thanks the Rector then asked if we were from a ship in the harbour. Mort Hehir explained we were from the cruise-ship 'Caronia'. "Ah yes," said the Cleric, "She really is a beautiful ship." He paused for a second then said, "Perhaps you would care to join me for coffee in the vestry after the Service." And we nodded our acceptance with thanks.

Over coffee I commented how few parishioners had attended the Service and the Rector explained. "As you probably know relations between Egypt and the UK have been at a very low ebb since the Suez affair." We nodded appreciatively. The climate between the two countries remained the main topic of conversation thereafter until Mort Hehir remarked it was nearly time for lunch and invited the Rector to join us. He thanked the Chief Officer but declined the invitation pointing out that his every move was being carefully watched by the authorities. With that we all shook-hands and with customary expressions of goodwill found our way out of the church to the Agent's car and our return to the happier atmosphere of the 'Caronia.

My three companions were already in the car but just as I was about to enter, I was accosted by a scruffy old Arab beggar mumbling something unintelligible while holding out a battered tin mug. One eye was weeping copiously with advanced glaucoma, but the other eye was bright with intelligence and seemed to penetrate my brain. I searched into my trouser pocket for small change but it only produced a two-piastre note which I stuffed into his tin.

The old beggar bowed several times and pointing a gnarled finger at his weeping eye mumbled something which sounded more English than Arabic. "One eye on fire Effendi". Then he pointed the same finger at me and croaked, "One eye on wire." With that he shuffled away still mumbling to himself, while I climbed into the car. In between hoots of laughter the Chief Officer said. "What did the old beggar say Willie?" I told him what it sounded like to me. Andrew Thompson then said, "Old men like that around my home in South Africa are often credited with second sight!" I shivered with apprehension.

During the drive back to the 'Caronia' much of our conversation concerned the Anglo-Egyptian diplomatic relations and how it had affected church attendance. Personally I was relieved to arrive back on board in time for a few 'gins' before lunch. But when the Chief Officer told our fellow officers I had given the old Arab beggar a two-piastre note one of them gave a loud chuckle and said, "Christ Willie, you have given that old beggar enough to keep him in hashish for a month or more." The others then wanted to know what the old man had said and I told them. "He pointed a finger at his one eye and said, 'One eye on fire Effendi'." Then pointing it at me he said, "One eye on wire." At that precise moment in the friendly atmosphere of the officers' wardroom I felt a strange weird premonition.

On our arrival at the Lebanese port of Beirut I accepted the offer to join our two nursing-sisters for an afternoon tour of the City. This was by courtesy of our friends in the Thomas Cook's Travel Bureau who often managed to arrange a car, for our use. There were still signs of conflict evident on many of the buildings, but we spent quite some time admiring the interior of the Sultan's Palace. The longest and certainly the most interesting part of the tour was on foot exploring the 'Gold 'Siq' Market'.

In Istanbul there was far too much chart work to catch-up with. So there was no chance of going ashore there. Some of my fellow-officers went on a tour of the City but they all managed to enjoy the night-spots of which there were many. They didn't return on board until the early hours of the next day feeling no pain at the time but still somewhat 'woozy' when we sailed shortly after lunch. The wages of sin is breath!

As was my duty on arriving and leaving port I stood alongside the Turkish Pilot who began advising our passage through the Bosphorus and into the Black Sea. But when I was relieved on the bridge by Zulu Thompson the scenery was so magnificent I asked Captain Watts if he would like me to take his cine-camera up the mast for some breathtaking 'shots'.

I had climbed the mast on several occasions and remembered there were 86 rungs up the iron-ladder to the crowsnest. Before I was halfway up I felt glad I'd stopped smoking for over eighteen months. While I was busy filming both banks of the Bosphorus I became aware of the able-seaman on lookout tapping me on the shoulder and shouting anxiously, "One of those overhead cables looks very low to me Sir." And without even bothering to look I replied, "Yes Mason, they always do, it's what is known as an optical illusion." My words had barely left my lips when there came a massive jolt and the mast shook violently as our topmast struck one of the wires.

My immediate thought was of a thousand volts or more pouring through the mast until I realised we were standing on the wooden grating covering the floor of the crowsnest. I warned the able-seaman not to touch any of the metalwork surrounding us. Peering down I could see the 'Caronia' closely resembling an arrow on the string of a 'long-bow'. Our engines were going astern to relieve the stress on the overhead cable. Glancing upwards I then saw the wire beginning to unravel where it had been caught on a shackle. Suddenly, with a loud 'ping' it parted completely with one frayed end whipping across the waters of the Bosphorus while the other end sliced across to the opposite bank.

Minutes later, freed from entanglement, I felt the engines going 'ahead' and the 'Caronia' resumed her passage through the Bosphorus none the worse for the encounter. On reaching the Black Sea at the eastern end of the straits the Turkish Pilot disembarked still looking a bit shaken from the experience. On my return to the bridge below Captain Watts greeted me with, "Is my camera alright Williams?" (some people have no soul).

Our passage now took us across the Black Sea to Yalta on the Crimea where leading Russian politicians have their 'Dacha' summer houses. It is also where President Roosevelt and Prime Minister Winston Churchill met President Stalin to discuss plans for 'World Peace'.

For several days thereafter I spent hours searching through back-numbers of Admiralty 'Notices to Mariners' in expectation of finding a mention of an additional cable being triced-up across the Bosphorus, but without success. To this very day, whenever I see or hear a 'barman' use a cocktail-shaker I am reminded of the time when I was shaken around the crowsnest of 'Caronia'. And I vividly remember the old Arab beggar who croaked, "One Eye On Fire, Effendi and One Eye on Wire."

MY LUCKY STAR

It never ceases to amaze me how a mere word, a song, a smell even a sound can trigger one's memory of an event of long ago.

In the latter half of 1936 I was attending the Sir John Cass Nautical College in London studying for my Second Mate's ticket. or to describe it more accurately, examination for their Board of Trade Certificate of Competancy. At this time Captain Cameron was the college Principal. and Captains, Aubrey-Smith, Thorton and Murray were the instructors.

Captain Aubrey-Smith's subjects were 'Seamanship' - Chartwork and 'Shipmaster's Business' of which he was the author. Captain Thornton taught us 'shipbuilding' and nautical instruments, including the mysteries of the 'sextant'. Captain Murray's subjects were 'knowledge of principles' (KOP) and meteorology, he was wont to remind us 'meteorology' was NOT an exact science but that it was a fascinating one. Among other things, we learned that when the ice-cold waters of the Labrador Current met the relatively warm waters of the Gulf Stream, (around the Grand Banks of Newfoundland) one could expect sea-water temperature below 'dew-point' and fog imminent. A truism that has remained indelibly printed in my memory.

Recently, having observed a 'near-total-eclipse' of the sun I began browsing through old copies of 'Master's Voyage Reports' and came across one that captured my attention. This was my 'Voyage Report' to management from the Cunard cargo-vessel "Saxonia" dated 18th.August 1968. What intrigued me was the brevity with which I had described the overnight passage from Norfolk, Virginia to New York when, in actual fact, it had been a very hectic one indeed.

Not wishing to bore my reader with the full content of the report I will simply quote verbatim the particular paragraph that illustrates how brevity fails to convey how a very kind and generous action of a fellow seaman saved me the stress and anxiety I would otherwise have suffered that night.

INTRODUCTION

REGULATIONS FOR PREVENTING COLLISIONS AT SEA

Rule 16.

(a) Every vessel, or seaplane when taxi-ing on the water, shall, in fog, mist, falling snow, heavy rainstorms or any other condition similarly restricting visibility, go at a moderate speed, having careful regard to the existing circumstances and conditions.

(b) A power-driven vessel hearing apparently forward of her beam, the fog-signal of a vessel the position of which is not ascertained, shall, so far as the circumstances of the case admit, stop her engines, and then navigate with caution until danger of collision is over.

(c) A power-driven vessel which detects the presence of another vessel forward of her beam before hearing her fogsignal or sighting her visually, may take early and substantial action to avoid a close quarters situation but, if this cannot be avoided, she shall, so far as the circumstances of the case admit, stop her engines in proper time to avoid a collision and then navigate with caution until danger of collision is over.

Before the Second World War, candidates for 'Mates & Masters' examinations were required to learn ALL thirty-one Articles parrot-fashion. (In my opinion the ONLY way to know their contents perfectly). Today the candidate is only required to know the gist of their content. (not quite the same thing).

Where the arrival of a cargo-vessel is important when stevedore gangs have been ordered beforehand, a late arrival can incur certain penalties. With passenger liners it is even more important when boat-trains, coaches, cars, air-flights even hotels have been pre-arranged. The ship's master has no-one on whom to rely other than his own judgement. As the American President once said, "The Buck Stops Here".

The brief paragraph in my voyage report to which I refer is quoted as follows: -

By 4.15 pm all cargo work was completed and at 4.56 pm 'Saxonia' left her berth, (in Norfolk, Virginia, USA), to proceed on passage to New York. The overnight run up the East Coast was made under a blanket of coastal fog for much of the time during which our radar had broken-down and not operational. However, our ETA (Estimated Time of Arrival) was met by arriving at the 'Ambrose Tower' (Pilot Station) on time and 'Saxonia' finally berthed alongside Pier (in New York at 1.15 pm on Tuesday as expected.' Unquote.

The reader will no doubt, agree the foregoing paragraph is a reasonable example of brevity, without frills, embellishment or exaggeration. But what now follows is a much more accurate and detailed account off what and how it all happened on that, never to be forgotten passage between Norfolk, Virginia, and New York on the night of Monday 5th. August 1968.

Following our departure from the berth in Norfolk, Virginia and while steaming down the buoyed channel we came within sight of a Blue Star Line cargo/passenger ship alongside one of the lower piers. The Pilot and I agreed she was indeed a truly beautifully designed ship. Her funnel was painted in the usual colours with the familiar motif typical of Blue Star Line. But, instead of the black hull of other Blue Star ships this hull was painted white, known to most seafarers as being on the America, Australia and New Zealand service. Our Pilot confirmed the 'Washington Star' was due to sail within the hour.

At Cape Henlopen the Pilot was disembarked, the engines were rung Full Ahead and Course set northwards. I made out the radio signal to New York giving our ETA for 11.00 am the next day. Before handing-over the bridge to our Third Officer I glanced ahead towards the horizon and didn't like what I saw. A thin brown haze that could only spell one thing. Mid-Summer coastal fog, then, in answer to my query our Radio Officer informed me our ETA message had already been transmitted. There was little I could do immediately but to await events.

Within twenty minutes visibility was slowly deteriorating to less than a mile so I ordered the engines 'On Standby' and a lookout posted forward on the foc'sle-head. At that critical moment our Third Officer reported the Radar has ceased to function. Taking a walk out to the port wing of the bridge I caught sight of the white hulled 'Washington Star' half-a-mile astern and overtaking us rapidly.

On sudden impulse I shouted to the Third Officer to bring out the Aldis signalling-lamp and told him to call the Blue Star cargo-liner. I saw the flashed acknowledgement letter 'T' and told the officer to send the following message. "From Saxonia please call on VHF channel sixteen." The response from the Washington Star' was immediate because we could hear him calling on the radio-telephone.

"Hello Saxonia this is Washington Star, OVER." Within seconds I made my reply, "Hello Washington Star, I am bound for New York and my radar has failed can I tuck myself behind you? OVER." His reply came immediately, "Hello Saxonia, yes by all means keep astern of me, we are bound for Baltimore but I'll keep you informed of our distance apart every ten minutes until we turn off for the Delaware," then he gave a chuckle before adding, "It'll be like station-keeping in convoy during the war."

True to his word every ten minutes the Master of the 'Washington Star' called me on the VHF radio-telephone to inform me of our respective distance apart. Sometimes we would be four or five cables, (a cable being 200 yards), at other times a little more in which case `I would 'phone the engineer on watch to either increase or decrease the propeller revolutions.

At other times he would call to say he had the echo of a ship either to port or starboard and whether or not we were on a collision-course or passing clear. His regular reports were so informative they helped considerably to ease my anxiety. Of all the weather conditions one can encounter at sea, fog is most certainly the worst, especially without the navigational aid of Radar.

For mile after mile, hour after hour, we followed the 'Washington Star' at a moderate speed as required by the International Rules for the Prevention of Collision. Until at about fifteen minutes past midnight came another call from the ship ahead. This was from the Master of the 'Washington Star' to say he was now altering Course to steer for the Pilot Station near Cape Henry and the Delaware River.

He went on to say there was nothing on his Radar ahead of me and that he would still keep me informed until he was obliged to manoeuvre his ship while embarking his Pilot. I thanked him for this information and for all the help he had given me. Half-an-hour later he made his final call to say the course ahead of me was still free of echoes and to wish me luck and a safe arrival in New York. I reciprocated his sentiments and thanked him for his consideration and help. I then resumed my vigil outside on the port wing of the bridge peering into the grey swirling fog and listening, always listening. Listening for any tell-tale sound, or the fog-signal of a vessel in response to our own whistle giving one long blast every two minutes. I shivered as the fog penetrated my bones.

Becoming increasingly heavy and saturated with the moist, clammy atmosphere, my duffle coat weighed heavily on my hunched shoulders. I was suddenly startled with the voice of my Second Officer saying, "This will warm you up Sir," as he handed me a mug of scalding hot cocoa. I thanked him and took a sip of the thick, sweetened brew. "The clouds are breaking overhead Sir," he added, "I can see a couple of stars." Glancing upwards I too saw a couple of stars but I was in no mood for idle chatter so I just grunted, "We're not going that way Second Mate" He took the hint and went back into the wheelhouse.

A few minutes later lo and behold, what had been a dense blanket of fog became a few wisps and quite suddenly it cleared altogether and we had maximum visibility with a myriad of stars twinkling in a cloudless sky. After an interval of five or ten minutes during which time I finished-off my cocoa I grew confident we had left fog far behind and told the Second Officer to phone the engine-room for maximum revolutions. I then handed-over the bridge to him with instructions to call me the instant visibility reduced.

Below in my quarters I was glad to get rid of my sodden dufflecoat then decided on a hot bath to soak the weariness out of my bones before climbing into bed where, within seconds I was fast asleep. I had been awake and on my feet for nearly twenty-four hours and for a large part of that time outside on the bridge in the midst of fog.

I was awakened by the voice of my steward wishing me a breezy, "Good morning Sir, it's just gone seven o'clock, Sir, and here's your tea, toast and marmalade as usual Sir." He placed the tray on the table and rambled on, "It's a beautiful sunny morning Sir, shall I draw your bath now or wait 'til you ring?" His chirpy voice irritated me somewhat until I realised, how was he to know I'd been on the bridge all those hours?

After I had shaved and showered I ambled on to the bridge a few minutes before eight o'clock to find the Chief Officer writing-up the log. "Morning Peter" I greeted him, "How are we doing?" He looked up and returned my greeting with a wide grin, "Good morning Sir, we've been doing very well since last night's fog", he pointed to a position on the chart and continued, "You'll be pleased to know we'll make the 'Ambrose Tower' right on the ETA you sent last night." He made a few minor calculations then added, "We should be embarking the 'Sandy Hook' Pilot at eleven o'clock Sir."

He followed me out into the wheelhouse saying, "That was a neat little stunt you pulled, following behind the Blue Star boat." "It was pure inspiration my dear Watson", I replied, "And it took a load off my mind after the damn Radar broke down, I can tell you." I'll keep that in mind if it ever happens to me,' replied the Chief Officer. At that moment our tall young Third Officer arrived on the bridge just as the quartermaster rang 'eight bells', so I strolled out on to the wing of the bridge while the two officers carried out the change of watch procedures.

And indeed, my steward had not exaggerated, it truly was a beautiful morning and I began my regular morning perambulations breathing deeply the crisp, invigorating morning air. A few minutes later I was joined by the Chief Engineer who wished to consult me about some engine-repairs he was anxious to tackle while we were loading additional cargo in New York. Then I accompanied him down to his office where I read, approved and signed a few stores requisitions he needed urgently. After which he invited me to join him with coffee, which I gladly accepted, but not before ringing the bridge and telling the Third Officer I was with the Chief Engineer and to inform me when 'Ambrose Tower' was sighted.

Well, dear reader, I have tried to illustrate how a simple and brief paragraph in a 'Captain's Voyage Report' can hide a multitude of emotions and anxieties. It also goes some way to indicate the truth of the legend that rests on the desk of the President of the United States, "The Buck Stops Here'.

There is little more to add, other than to say, we eventually arrived at the 'Ambrose Light' precisely at eleven o'clock in the morning as predicted in my original message to our New York office, and as promised by my Chief Officer. A few minutes later we had embarked the 'Sandy Hook' Pilot and proceeded up the River Hudson towards New York. Passing under the recently-built Verazzano Bridge we came within sight of the Statue of Liberty which quickened my pulse-rate as it never failed to do.

By 1.15 pm we were safely moored alongside the Cunard Pier at the foot of 52nd. Street, Manhattan and happy to welcome aboard two old shipmates, now Assistant Superintendents, Johnny Hughes and Geoffrey Hunt who joined me for lunch. Over coffee I gave them a detailed account of how, when our Radar had broken down, the Master of the 'Washington Star' had so kindly guided me through dense impenetrable fog. It was when John asked me the name of the helpful Master I realised, with dismay that I had never thought to ask him. It seemed only natural that, as we had kept in touch over the VHF radio-telephone we had habitually addressed each other as 'Cap'n'

Who knows, perhaps, one day, he will read these few lines or, one of his officers who served with him on that occasion. In that case please accept my most grateful thanks for the assistance rendered me at such a critical time. An assistance that took such a load off my mind. To them, each and everyone, I can only repeat what our Lord Jesus Christ once said to his disciples, "Go Thou and do Likewise." (AMEN).

Saxonia

WHAT PRICE LOYALTY

By 1950 it was generally accepted the fate of the once-famous Cunard Steamship Company was sealed. Increasing competition from several airlines to Canada and the United States of America made it inevitable. At about this time there were a few prototype flying-boats built by Saunders-Roe anchored off Calshot close to Southampton. These were the 'Princess' type nearly twice the size of their predecessors the famous 'Sunderlands' which had served the country so well during the Second World War. These 'Princesses' were idly awaiting more powerful engines to make them economically viable.

At a regular meeting of ships' officers with management in Cunard Buildings Liverpool, I made a futile attempt to persuade the Chairman and General Manager to consider an idea I had nurtured for several months. This was intended to give the Company a 'boost' by offering prospective passengers the exciting option of travelling 'Out by Princess and home by Queen' or vice-versa.

Puffing at his enormous briar-pipe the Chairman snapped, "Rubbish Williams, we've been a successful shipping company for over a hundred years and I have no doubt we will remain so for many more years to come." Stung by his remark I replied somewhat tartly, "Then you are putting all your eggs in one basket Sir." Without even appearing to have heard my reply he turned to the General Manager changing the subject altogether. Leaving me to study the bubbles arising from my 'gin and tonic' and the poem 'Invictus', 'My head is bloodied but unbowed.'

In the ensuing years the popularity of crossing the Atlantic by ship gradually waned and Cunard were obliged to take out of service their least economic vessels. The few that remained went cruising during the 'off-peak' seasons. 'Queen Mary' was sold to an American consortium and 'laid-up' permanently as an 'hotel-cum-conference centre' in Long Beach, California.

The 'Queen Elizabeth' found a similar home temporarily in Miami, Florida but the consortium broke up and she was eventually sold to the Hong Kong Chinese shipping magnate C.Y. Tung. On passage from Miami to Hong Kong her last Master, Commodore Geoffrey Thrippleton Marr was induced to act in an advisory capacity. His book 'The Queens and I' give a lurid account of that voyage, which amounts to a catalogue of mishaps. And her last Chief Engineer, Ted Philips also went with her as advisor to the Chinese engineers.

After a most eventful and hair-raising passage she eventually arrived in Hong Kong to be renamed 'Seawise University' but while alongside the fitting-out berth she caught fire in the most dubious circumstances, to become a total constructive loss. To this very day, many Cunard employees and ex-employees remember the 'Queen Elizabeth as 'the ship that died of shame.' More of this to follow.

I have no desire to bore my reader with details and numbers of Cunard ships taken out of service, sold to foreign owners or taken to the breaker's yard. I will draw a veil over the eventual demise of the Cunard Line as a shipping company until bought by Trafalgar House Investments to prolong the agony. A few years later the T.H.I. Group was bought by the Norwegian conglomerate Kvaerner who soon managed to hive-off the shipping division to Miami-based Carnival Cruise Lines where Cunard is so diluted it barely exists.

While the Cunard fleet was being dismantled, hundreds of employees were being made redundant. In fairness to those saddled with the task it must be said they rejected the age-old pattern of 'last in, first out', in favour of judicious selection. Suffice to say it was as unpalatable to them as it was to the victims of the axe. The way in which this process affected my career is only the beginning of how redundancy affected dozens of ex-shipmates and there experiences, whether for better or for worse. I will leave to my reader to judge!

In 1965, after a brief spell ashore in London as Assistant Superintendent in the Surrey Commercial Docks, I received instructions to join the Company's 'Carinthia' in Liverpool as Chief Officer for one voyage to Quebec and Montreal. I was told John Mortimer was to proceed on leave and would be rejoining the ship on our return to Southampton via Le Havre. Already packed, in anticipation and having brought me up to date with all I needed to know, we shook hands and with a grin John wished me 'good luck' before dashing off to catch his taxi.

There followed several days alongside the Company's berth in the Huskisson Dock where her eastbound cargo was being discharged into the transit shed, followed by westbound cargo being loaded into the ship's four cavernous holds. During this time Captain Goodier was enjoying a few days at home with his family. He would arrive on board in time to take his ship out of the Huskisson Dock and alongside 'Prince's Landing Stage' where we would embark our passengers.

I had sailed with Les Goodier for several years in the old passenger ship 'Scythia' where he was Senior First Officer and I Junior First Officer. And more recently had met him frequently when he had become Master of a cargo ship while I was ashore in London. In all those years I had disliked his abrasive and boorish character Now we were about to become shipmates again I felt glad it was for the duration of just one voyage.

Prior to sailing we received word that two Company officials from personnel department would be joining the ship immediately on arrival at Quebec. It appears their brief was to explain the terms of redundancy payments to all members of the ship's crew while on passage up-river and during the ship's stay in Montreal. I would be required to arrange for them to meet groups of the deck department when convenient.

The westbound passage across the North Atlantic was very much routine and in moderate weather. Most mornings when coming off-watch at 8.00 am I would shave and shower before going down to breakfast in company with my young watchmate 'Ding-Dong' Bell. On return to my quarters I would apply myself to bringing the Log-Book up-to-date, followed by those tedious calculations of ship's stores, fresh-water and fuel-oil consumption to arrive at the ship's draft and trim. On most mornings my work would be interrupted by the 'Old Man' inviting me to join him in his quarters for morning coffee and a 'chat'.

I soon discovered the 'chat' invariably took the form of his speculating on the worst possible scenario as an option to being made redundant. He was resigned to being reduced to being Master of one of the cargo ships. He was of the opinion that cargo ships were a preference to making small-talk to awkward passengers. Never, but never did Les Goodier ask how I felt about being made redundant and what I thought my prospects would be if the unthinkable happened. I was always glad to escape and join my fellow officers for a pre-lunch pint!

In the solitude of my cabin, I have to confess, there was little else to occupy my every thought. I had a wife and three children who looked to me as breadwinner. To feed and clothe them and keep a roof over their heads. We had recently bought our home in Westhorne Avenue midway between Eltham and Catford and the mortgage repayments took a hefty slice out of my salary. And even in bed when sleep finally overtook me I would suffer the most appalling nightmares.

Eventually, when alongside our berth in Wolfe's Cove, Quebec, our two Company officials, Messrs Bown and Whitehead came on board and began interviewing members of the ship's crew as previously arranged. Due to essential commitments it had been tacitly agreed my deck-department Petty-Officers and Ratings would be left until our arrival alongside in Montreal early the next day.

Without further boring my reader with the nuts and bolts details of our interviews, let it suffice that, so far as the officers were concerned, redundancy payments would be in the order of one month's salary for every year's service to the Company. Not a King's ransom by any stretch of the imagination, but, with considerable financial restraint, would support a family for as long as it would take to find alternative employment. (at middle-age this could be over simplification).

Be that as it may, we were soon homeward-bound again for which I was truly thankful. I had had enough coffee and 'cozy chats' with Goodier to last me a lifetime. 'Carinthia' was to resume her previous year's commitment to the Canadian Government making Rotter dam the terminal port for military and civilian personnel. But as I was due to be relieved by John Mortimer in Southampton this change in itinerary didn't affect me.

It was early morning when we finally tied-up alongside the Gare Maritime in Le Havre. So near to my watch at 4.00 am I decided to stay on the bridge in order to bring my Log-Book and 'Voyage Report' up-to-date as the turn-round in Southampton would take only a couple of hours.

As I wrote the various entries in the log-book I became aware of the wind howling through the rigging and the noises of rigging frapping against masts and samson-posts. Through the chartroom window I could see the faint light of dawn through a heavily overcast sky. A French tug started tooting its whistle and suddenly I heard the loud twang of a towing wire parting. I rushed into the wheelhouse to see the cross-channel ferry 'Dragon' bearing down on us. Log-book and 'Voyage-Report' would have to wait, I dashed downstairs to the Captain's cabin and, shaking him awake, warned him of the impending impact.

I must have made the main stairs down three at a time to 'A' Deck and for'ard to the seamens' quarters where I awoke all hands shouting "All hands on deck." If anyone entertained some doubt about my clamour they were soon dispelled by the shuddering impact of the 'Dragon' landing heavily alongside.

I was soon joined on the foc'sle-head by the Bosun and several others. The carpenter and joiner followed me up to the boat-deck where we found most of the damage caused by the impact. Fortunately the cross-channel ship had landed broadside onto the port side of the 'Carinthia' so that although the damage was considerable, it was mostly superficial. Within a few minutes the tugs were again made fast to the 'Dragon' and slowly towed her away from the ship's side.

For the rest of the forenoon we were kept busy listing all the damage above and below deck. I advised Les Goodier to write a letter to the Captain of the 'Dragon' holding him and his ship responsible for all damage 'seen and unseen'. His reply was, "You've more experience of this sort of thing, as a Superintendent, so you'd better write it, I'll sign it." This was later handed to our Agent in Le Havre to be given to the Master of the cross-channel ferry.

Meanwhile, for much of the passage across to Southampton I was kept busy collating and typing lists of damages. It was dark by the time we arrived alongside our berth, where we were boarded by the usual Superintendents who had been informed by our Le Havre manager of what had happened. Mike Hunt, Denis Atkinson and my old friend Ian Borland settled themselves on my settee to begin going through my 'Voyage Returns' and the lists of damage caused by the 'Dragon'. Meanwhile those officers who had made the voyage together with those returning from leave were told to remain in the wardroom to learn their fate from Captain Borland.

Pointing to my booze-locker I told them to 'help themselves' and turning to Ian I suggested he interviewed the officers in my cabin, while I repaired to the chartroom to finish the log-book and 'Voyage Report'. I was about to leave the room as Mike began pouring whisky into three glasses. Then he turned to Ian and said, "Go on Ian, put the poor bugger out of his misery and tell him."

Ian got to his feet and came towards me with hand outstretched. "You wouldn't mind wearing four gold rings on your sleeves would you?" I gave his hand a squeeze, the lump in my throat prevented me from saying anything, so I stumbled upstairs to the chartroom. It took several minutes to compose myself, then set about completing log-book entries and 'Voyage Report'. I was on cloud nine - or was it ten?

One of the lady assistant pursers typed my 'Voyage Record' in a fraction of the time it would take me. One copy I took to the Captain's quarters, but I met him in the alleyway dressed in civvies. "What have you got there?" he asked, and I told him it was his copy of my 'Voyage Report'. "Stick it up your arse" he replied, "I've just been made redundant." With that curt remark he carried on down the stairs.

Minutes later I returned to my cabin to meet Freddy Watts, the Junior First Officer, coming out. To my unspoken question he simply turned his thumb down. Poor old Fred, my emotions were both mixed and confused - sorry for him - yet relieved and happy for myself. What Price Loyalty?

Mike Hunt and Denis Atkinson had already left the ship and Ian urged me to pack hurriedly explaining that tugs for 'Carinthia' had been brought forward as the 'Queen Elizabeth' was due and would need them. Bless his heart, Ian drove me to Central Station to catch my train and, with time to spare, we enjoyed a quick pint in the station buffet. Needless to say it had been a very long day!

OF AFFLUENCE & EFFLUENCE

PREFACE

In all Cunard passenger ships the Captain; Staff-Captain; Chief Engineer; Principal Medical Officer Surgeon; Purser and Staff-Purser were hosts at their own tables in the first-class restaurant. The table for navigating and radio officers were determined by the Company's General Manager and never changed without his authority.

To the 'Caronia' - 'The Green Goddess' as an example. When on the North Atlantic run the forward restaurant, 'Balmoral' accommodated the first-class passengers while the aft restaurant 'Sandringham' catered for the cabin-class passengers. But when cruising the allocation of passengers was determined by the 'fare-rating'.

When cruising the Captain occupied the head-table in 'Balmoral' while the Staff-Captain would 'host' a table in the 'Sandringham'. Other senior officers would 'switch' around as convenient and 'diplomatic'. Engineer-Officers had their own Mess adjacent to the engine-room lift while other officers, male and female, were seated variously as dictated by passenger numbers or other reasons.

All officers were required to 'dress' for dinner except on sailing and arrival nights. On the North Atlantic run mess-kit comprised the short navy-blue jacket and trousers, starched white collar and shirt with either waistcoat or cummerbund and of course black shoes. Gold-lace rings on sleeve cuffs to indicate rank, the gold rings being separated by white for pursers, purple for engineers, green for electricians and radio officers. The Captain and all navigating-officers had no distinctive colours between the gold rings indicating their executive status. When cruising short white mess-jackets were substituted with badges of rank on shoulder-straps instead of on sleeve-cuffs. Campaign and other medals to be worn on special occasions as directed by the Master.

First Officer Gwilym D. Williams
North Atlantic run
(Mess Kit)

It had always been a policy of The Cunard Steamship Company to retire members of its sea-staff at 63 years of age. Perhaps directors, management and superintendents recognised the heavy toll and stress suffered by them owing to the hazards and vagaries of weather conditions in the North Atlantic Ocean. After all, seamen worldwide often describe the Atlantic as being nine months of bad weather and three months of Winter!

Be that as it may, my five weeks leave entitlement expired on the 7th. May 1978 and a new phase in my lifestyle began with retirement. Perhaps my reader will have deduced I was born the same day the Cunard liner 'Lusitania' had been torpedoed and sunk by a German submarine 63 years previously. In this barbaric attack on an unarmed merchant ship 1198 lives of passengers and crew, of men, women and children had been lost.

Within a few days I had received letters from various Company officials congratulating me on my retirement, thanking me for years of devotion to duty, loyalty to the Company and other expressions of meaningless clap-trap. Of much more substance I had been wined and dined. presented with a gold watch and an illuminated scroll recording years of service. There was also the prospect of a modest monthly pension. Two years before qualifying for the State Pension.

But now, having caught-up with most odd-jobs in and around our home, a list of which had been diligently kept by my dear wife Joan. The novelty of being unemployed for the foreseeable future was wearing thin.

Day after day, as I carried out various chores in and around our bungalow I began giving serious consideration to the problem which had come uppermost in my mind. Then, one sunny afternoon as I strolled back to the car park in Colchester, and on impulse, I called in at the 'Job Centre' in the High Street.

"Take a seat" said a buxom blonde in 'Reception', pointing to rows of cheap plastic chairs most of which were already occupied by a motley collection of young men and women. I began to regret not having brought something with me to read. Instead, to while away the time, I began a furtive study of my fellow job-seekers and found they had one thing in common. They were all so unkempt in appearance I wondered if any of them had a snowball's chance in hell of being offered employment. In their late teens or early twenties, I even speculated what sort of employer would dream of taking them on.

"Williams" came the voice of the overweight blonde. Momentarily I paused wondering if the call was intended for me. After all, for over fifteen years I had been accustomed to being addressed as 'Captain Williams'. Then, seeing a pudgy finger pointing in my direction and beckoning, I was left in no doubt it was me being called.

Dutifully I followed her waddling backside along a corridor until, stopping at a certain door she knocked and on hearing a voice in answer to the knock. "Come in", she gave a brief nod to me to enter then waddled her way back to 'Reception'.

The dark-haired young woman seated at a desk was studying the contents of a pink-folder and without a glance in my direction said, "Please be seated". I noticed her hair was tied back in a 'bun' at the nape of her neck. Pale-faced without any sign of make-up she was wearing spectacles supported by a thin gold chain. Suddenly, she dropped the pink-folder into a wire basket and drawing a writing-pad forward she looked at me and, in a rather husky voce said, "May I have your name, address, date and place of birth please?".

There followed a veritable host of searching questions to which I gave answers as truthfully and as accurately as I possibly could. Every once in a while she would interrupt apologetically to clarify or to elaborate certain details. She wanted to know about my past employment and other details of my seagoing career.

Eventually she appeared to have all the information required and pushing the writing pad away cupping her chin in soft white hands she first gave a little cough then began. "I have never interviewed a shipmaster before", she paused for a few seconds, "And come to think of it I've never interviewed anyone of your age either." Again a short pause, "You see I am at a loss to fully appreciate your employable potential." This time the pause was of longer duration. The, looking directly into my eyes she asked, "What actually does a Captain do?"

I was taken aback by her question I was temporarily quite speechless. Then I gave a little laugh and asked her what school she had attended to which she replied, "My schooling has nothing to do with it, I've already said you are the first shipmaster I've ever interviewed for a job so, as briefly as possible tell me what a Captain does."

Vaguely remembering a book I had once read by Charles Cotter, (Extra-Master) and his introduction to it, I began as follows:-

"The shipmaster's function ideally should be something of an artist in his profession. Embracing all aspects of his responsibilities towards his passengers and crew, to their welfare, health and lives. He should be well-versed in the Merchant Shipping Acts, to prepare himself for marine and Medical emergencies and to exercise discipline firmly and fairly. Finally he should be a well-informed ambassador of his country," I drew a fresh breath before saying, "In the words of the Merchant Shipping Acts, the ship's commander is Master Under God and invested with almost absolute power."

My dear wife has often accused me of not knowing when to stop once I start talking. This time I stopped abruptly and in a state of shock when I noticed the young girl who had been interviewing me was actually 'crying'. I stood up from my chair and leaning across the desk apologised profusely. "My dear young lady", I stammered, "I had no wish or intention to upset you." With that I proffered her my handkerchief, silently thanking God I had taken it clean from my wardrobe that same morning!

Looking at it she first gave a smile of thanks followed by a weak little chuckle. "Please don't apologise Captain Williams, it was entirely my fault for asking you such a stupid question." She dabbed her eyes a couple of times then blew her nose before regaining her composure, then said, "Why don't you go down the Hythe and have a word with the harbour-master Captain Goody? I am sure he could help you better than we could."

Bless the girl I thought, I hadn't even entertained the idea. Then, putting thoughts into words I said, "What a brilliant idea, thank you very much, I'll do just that tomorrow morning." To which she replied, "And I'll telephone him to expect you, he often rings to ask if we have a young seaman or engine-room rating, or even a cook on our books."

After more words of appreciation and thanks I bade her a good day and made my departure. Halfway down the stairs into the street I realised I had left my handkerchief with her but, giving a shrug I dismissed the thought, she was more than welcome to it. It was when threading my way out of the car-park I metaphorically kicked myself (you can't do it physically when you're driving a car!) - realising what a bloody idiot I was for not having the common courtesy to enquire the young lady's name.

During the nine mile drive home from Colchester to our home in West Mersea I couldn't help but wondering why I hadn't thought of paying a visit to the Harbourmaster. I had to content myself in the knowledge that it was only on the spur of the moment that I had entered the 'Job-Centre' in the first place. Anyway, I thought, no harm done and I resolved to keep my word and visit the Harbourmaster next day.

When approaching the sharp bend opposite the olde-world pub 'Peldon Rose' I joined a queue of vehicles delayed by high water over the Strood which joins Mersea Island to the mainland. I cursed my stupidity for not having consulted the 'tide-tables' earlier. It now meant my being late for lunch and the usual admonishment from my long suffering wife.

Throughout the ensuing delay I sat in the car listening to the radio and mulling-over what I should say to Captain Goody, the Harbourmaster, the next day. Speculating whether he would be older or younger than me, and what kind of reception he would extend to a retired Cunard Master.

Anticipation and speculation were put to one side as the traffic ahead of me began to move and my attention concentrated on the car immediately ahead. On the Strood itself were isolated pools of sea-water as we slowly crossed and my temper sorely tried as some mindless oaf driving on the opposite direction would send a heavy spray over my car. Each and every time this happened I remembered the advice from the manager in Underwood's Garage,

"Never, but never buy a second-hand car in West Mersea, chances being it has been driven through saltwater countless times."

Eventually arriving at our attractive bungalow in West Mersea. I was somewhat relieved to be greeted with a bright smile and the remark, "I guessed you were held-up by the tide so I delayed lunch 'til now." Greatly relieved by such a nice greeting I rewarded her with an affectionate kiss and a gentle pat on her comely bottom.

The Colchester town hall clock could be faintly heard as I knocked and entered the Harbourmaster's office on Hythe quay. Seated at his desk, he was much younger than I had expected but there was no mistaking the tanned features and clear eyes of a seaman. With a quick glance at my calling-card Captain Goody introduced me to his deputy, Peter Powell and pointing to a vacant chair said, " Miss Langhorne in Colchester Job Centre told me to expect you Captain Williams, " he paused a few seconds then continued, "In what way can we help you?"

I proceeded to explain I had recently retired on pension from Cunard Line at 63 years of age and it would be another two years before I became eligible fo my 'old age pension'. As I spoke I saw they were nodding their understanding which encouraged me to continue. "So you see gentlemen, should a suitable vacancy occur in any ship in the port I'd be most grateful for a call - Miss Langhorne told me you occasionally 'phone her to enquire if she had a Mate, a seaman or cook looking for work.

Having discussed and thoroughly exhausted the topic of my hopes for a bit of 'pin-money', the conversation then became more general. Ken Goody asked about my qualifications and where I had studied for my certificates of competency. The whole atmosphere in his office changed markedly when we discovered we had both studied at the Sir John Cass Nautical College in London and, by a strange coincidence, he was actually at the college studying for his Mate's 'ticket' when I was also there studying for 'Extra Master' - But of course completely unaware of each other at the time.

Furthermore, and much to our surprise and delight, I learned that while Ken had studied at the Sir John Cass College he had stayed at 'Seamark' the Merchant Navy Junior Officers' Club of which I had been a founder member. I explained how, in 1936 the Club had grown from a sixpenny snack in the apartment occupied by Harry Chappell, curate to Tubby Clayton, vicar of All Hallows Church on Tower Hill until the premises in '7 The Crescent' had been provided by Lord Wakefield.

Captain Goody the Harbourmaster then asked if I had always served in Cunard, to which I replied I had first served my apprenticeship and as third Mate in the Hain Steamship Company and from 1939 to 1945 with Royal Mail Line and thereafter with The Cunard Steamship Company until retirement in 1978 at 63 years of age. Ken Goody then said he had served his apprenticeship with Thompson's King Line and had then joined Esso Tankers with whom he served until applying to Colchester Council for the post of Harbour Master in 1974.

Asking me in which Cunard ships I had sailed I enumerated them chronologically, beginning with 'Mauretania', 'Scythia', 'Media', 'Britannic', 'Caronia', 'Queen Mary' and 'Queen Elizabeth'. I also mentioned I had been temporary assistant superintendent in London on several occasions, terminal manager in Southampton for the container ships and relief operations manager in San Juan, Puerto Rico for Cunard's cruise ships. I doubt very much if any of my curriculum vitae impressed them unduly. (seafarers are not easily impressed!).

On the wall behind Ken's desk I noticed the times of high and low water and not wishing to try Joan's patience for a second time. I thanked them both for their hospitality and with mutual expressions of good luck and a promise from Ken to let me know if a pin-money job came along. I made my departure, climbed into my car and and headed for home. During the journey home I felt something bugging me, and not knowing the cause it left me quite irritable. That is until approaching the Strood and seeing the water on either side helped crystallise the problem.

Ken Goody had mentioned the name of the girl who had interviewed me in the 'Job-Centre' and he had called her Miss Langhorne and it had all clicked into place. In the officers' wardroom of the 'Mauretania' there had been a framed photograph of the famous American author 'Mark Twain' whose real name, as everyone, (except me), should know was Samuel Langhorne Clemens.

A few months later as I toiled in the garden, an occupation for which I was ill-fitted, having spent most of my life at sea when my wife called out to say I was wanted on the telephone. I gave a sigh of relief and, with a grimace of distaste, wiped my hands free of compost. The caller was none other than Captain Goody, the Colchester port Harbourmaster who wanted to know if I was still interested in earning a spot of 'pin-money'.

Frankly I had all but forgotten our interview of some months previously. However I was immediately intrigued when told a ship at the Hythe required a Mate at short notice. Ken Goody went on to suggest that if I was interested I should repair on board that very afternoon to meet the skipper, Dennis Murray. When I pressed Ken Goody for further details about the ship and the trade it was on he gave pressure of work as an excuse so I thanked him for the tip-off and told him I would be on board the 'Errwood' at two o'clock that afternoon.

I told Joan all that I knew, (which wasn't much) while washing my hands then we had our customary aperitif, she a dry Martini and my usual pink-gin before lunch. Joan kept up a barrage of questions, (to which I had no answers). I was glad to make my escape to fetch the car out of the garage. My parting words were something to the effect that I would tell her everything when I returned from the Hythe then I let out the clutch and drove off.

For once I left the car-radio switched-off, I was in no mood to listen to any kind of music or idle chatter. A thousand questions went through my mind repeatedly. What kind of ship was this 'Errwood' and what ports and countries was she trading? What and how many crew did she carry? More importantly what sort of chap, would the skipper Dennis Murray turn out to be? What sort of pay would I be earning and what overtime might be involved? These and a thousand questions made my head ache so much I was relieved to reach the Hythe Quay where the 'Errwood' was moored alongside and I drew up near the gangway.

As I climbed out of the car I studied the little coaster with a critical eye. That she was a 'tanker' of sorts was evident and not the 'dry-cargo' vessel I had expected. Her hull was painted black but the bridge and accommodation aft was white as was the raised foc'sle-head beneath which I could read the name 'Errwood', a name familiar to many people in the Lake District.

Suddenly the 'Errwood' faded out of focus as my memory carried me back to the wet and dreary afternoon in November 1932 when an apprentice on the SS 'Tremorvah'. My very first voyage had taken me to Vancouver in British Columbia we had loaded a full cargo of wheat consigned to J. Arthur Rank flour-mills in Glasgow. After a long tedious passage up the River Clyde we were now approaching the many shipyards on either side of the river. And suddenly we came within sight of a half-completed skeleton of the most enormous passenger-ship on one of the slipways. Hung over the stern of this leviathan I saw a notice-board with the legend 'John Brown's Shipyard Number 534'. Never in our lives had we ever set eyes on such a leviathan. I vividly remember imagining a mysterious voice whisper, "One day my son, you will be the senior First Officer of that magnificent liner".

And, as I stared, but unseeing, I remembered the day when I had climbed out of the taxi at Ocean Terminal at Southampton, I had stared at that magnificent liner. Admiring her sleek lines, the gleaming black hull with white superstructure. Three enormous red funnels with black tops and two tapering masts. And what was most important, under her port bow, in letters three feet tall the magic name, 'Queen Mary'. And I remember, almost as in a dream searching my pocket for the letter appointing me 'Senior First Officer'.

A shiver ran down my spine which snapped me back to the present and to focus my eyes on the 'Errwood'. Behind the bridge I noted the short squat funnel painted a light green and upon it the letters 'E.S.L' which conveyed nothing to me at the time, but later I came to know as 'Effluent Services Limited'. I recognised the Harbourmaster Ken Goody and Miss Langhorne had played their part on my behalf, so it was now up to me. Squaring my shoulders I made for the gangway and the Captain's cabin.

My knock at the door of the 'Captain's' cabin was acknowledged by a soft voice saying "Come in". The burly figure facing me arose to his feet and with a friendly grin said, "So you're the 'big ship man' looking for some pin-money". He held out his hand to give me firm handshake. Indicating the settee, and much to my surprise, he added, "This calls for a drink," and turning to a locker behind him produced a bottle of Gordon's Gin, a bottle of Indian Tonic and two glasses. As he poured out two liberal measures into each glass he ruefully apologised for not having ice or lemon.

Looking over the tops of our glasses we first eyed each other then mumbled the age old cliché "Cheers". I had a distinct feeling I was going to like this chap and felt certain we were going to get along with each other. By the time Dennis Murray had topped up our glasses for the second time I was actually convinced of it.

In answer to his last question I gave him a brief resumé of my seagoing career beginning with my four-year apprenticeship, followed by two years as Third Mate with The Hain Steamship Company. There followed seven years with Royal Mail Line including the Second World War and being torpedoed while Second Mate in the 'Nariva' In 1946 I had joined Cunard Line and having served as a watchkeeping officer in 'Mauretania', 'Scythia', 'Media', 'Caronia', 'Queen Mary' and 'Queen Elizabeth'. Eventually being given command as Master until finally retiring in 1978 on my 63rd. birthday.

Having given the Skipper a thumbnail sketch of my career I took a long sip of my gin and tonic, I now asked him about his own career. He gave a shrug then laughed before saying, "You might not believe this but I served twenty-three years in the Royal Marines before being invalided out six years ago." He paused for a second before continuing,"I was lucky to land the job as Mate of this ship for four years until the Skipper retired two years ago, then I was offered the Skipper's job and that's about all there is to it." He gave another shrug before adding. "I think I've been bloody lucky, that's all."

There were dozens of questions I wanted to ask the Skipper but he forestalled me with, "Look Cap'n Williams, if you take this job there will be time aplenty to exchange reminiscences, but first things first." He drained his glass then abruptly said, "Do you want the job or not?" Without hesitation I replied, "Yes Skipper, I have a gut-feeling we're going to get along just fine." I also drained my glass before adding, "Where do I sign?" We both laughed and shook hands for the second time.

There are a few Articles of Agreement between a ship's Master and his Crew, two of which are best known. 'Foreign Going' (or sometimes called 'Deep Sea'), and 'Home Trade' Articles. 'Home Trade' is best described in the British Merchant Shipping Acts as that area contained between the Elbe and Brest. The difference between these two sets of ''Articles' being too diverse to discuss here. Of these 'Articles of Agreement' there are two copies, one to be lodged with the Superintendent at a local Mercantile Marine Office and one to be retained by the ship's Master. Having signed both copies I was now legally bound to serve the said Master loyally and diligently! To the best of my ability.

"Come on then", said skipper Dennis Murray, "I'd better show you around." And pausing only to put bottles and glasses away he led the way from his quarters through a narrow door into what I could see was the ship's chart-room. On various shelves I could see familiar volumes of Admiralty Tide Tables, Radio-Signals, Alt-Azimuth Tables etc. The chart table had the usual number of drawers in which I guessed rightly, were various folios of Admiralty Charts. And on the after bulkhead the usual matching pair of brass clock and aneroid barometer.

Dennis led the way through another door into the wheelhouse. The first thing I noticed was the huge mahogany steering-wheel certainly bigger than any I had ever seen even in ships two and even three times the size of the 'Errwood', I was even mildly surprised to see the typical electronic 'aids to navigation' such as Kelvin Hughes Sounding Machine, Decca Navigator and even a Radar with a nine-inch Monitor Screen and on the after bulkhead a locker for International Signal-Flags In fact, apart from actual dimensions, which were rather small, this wheel-house had pretty much the same items one would expect to find in any other vessel regardless of size, tonnage or trade.

Skipper Dennis Murray lost no time pointing out all these various features with justifiable pride. Evidently he was happy to be a big fish in a small pool. (and I had sailed in some of the biggest 'pools' in the world!). For the whole time I had been on board the

'Errwood' I had been vaguely aware of a strong but wholly unfamiliar odour pervading the atmosphere but being ignorant of tankers I hadn't remarked on it.

So it came as something of a shock when I asked Dennis about his cargoes his eyebrows arched upwards in surprise and he said, "I thought you knew - we carry treated sewage from the plant." He pointed through the wheelhouse window to a large industrial complex a few hundred yards away across the quay, "And out to the 'Dumping-Ground' a few miles out to sea off the port of Harwich and near the 'Sunk' light vessel. You will see the area marked on the Admiralty Chart."

Never since that day in 1932 when I climbed on board the Hain Steamship Company's tramp-steamer S.S. 'Tremorvah' in Cardiff had I suffered such fleeting emotions of qualms and dismay as I now suffered. But I had already signed on the dotted-line and fully committed.

There and then, I had the feeling that Dennis Murray sensed my reaction to what he had said. Looking at his wrist watch he said, "Look G.D., it is now coming up to four o'clock, you have to go home to collect your gear and be back on board by midnight tonight." He paused a few seconds then, shrugging his broad shoulders added, "And if you're not on board by then it's no sweat, I'll have to go without you and no hard feelings."

RMS QUEEN MARY

Ship's Company

Master	1
Staff Captain	1
Navigating Officers (All Master Mariners)	8
Radio Officers	12
Carpenter (Shipwright)	1
Assistant Carpenters	4
Bosun	1
Bosun's Mates	4
Masters-at-Arms	8
Fire Patrols (Clocks)	6
Storekeeper (Deck)	6
Lamp-Trimmer	1
Quartermasters	6
Able Seamen (All Lifeboat Tickets)	60
Ordinary Seaman	8
Purser	1
Staff Purser	1
Assistant Pursers	18
Lady Assistant Pursers	6
Baggage Masters	3
Interpreter	1
Printers	6
Musicians (Geraldo)	22
Photographers	3
Telephonists (Exchange)	6
Principal Medical Officers (P.M.O.)	1
Surgeon	1
Nursing Sisters (State Registered)	4
Physiotherapist (State Registered)	1
Dispenser (F.R.P.S.)	1
Hospital Attendants	4

Chief Steward	1
Second Steward	1
Extra Second Steward	1
Restaurant Managers	3
Head Waiters	3
Waiters & Commis Waiters	218
Officers' Stewards	36
Night Stewards	36
Public Room & Deck Stewards	36
Chef & Kitchen Staff	300
Stewardesses	46
Nursery Stewardesses	3
Laundry Stewardesses	8
Bath Attendants	10
Turkish Bath Attendants	6
Hairdressers & Shop Attendants	14
Chief Engineer	1
Staff Chief Engineer	1
Engineer Officers	80
Electrical Engineer Officers	18
Engine-Room Ratings	148
Stores & Cinema Operators	42

RMS QUEEN MARY
(Housekeeping at Sea)

During a typical 14 day 'round voyage' these are the average quantities of ship's stores consumed at sea.

Apples (40lb. boxes)	300 boxes
Apricots (dessert)	100lb.
Bananas	1,450lb.
Blueberries	100lb.
Grapes (choice)	1,500lb.
Grapefruit	90 boxes

Lemons	35 boxes
Limes	1000
Melons (various)	2,800
Nectarines	300
Oranges (various)	18,000
Tangerines	100lb.
Peaches	500
Pears (various)	1,150lb.
Strawberries (soft fruit season)	2,250lb.
Pineapples	75
Fresh Frozen Fruits	1,500lb.
Ice-Cream	4,000 quarts
Choice Loins Beef	19,000lb.
Choice Rib	1,250lb.
Choice Fillet Beef	1,150lb.
Beef (various)	2,000lb.
Beef (corned)	1,500lb.
Lamb (including Joints)	10,100lb.
Pork (including Joints	2,500lb.
Pork (corned)	1,500lb.
Veal	850lb.
Offals (various)	3,650lb.
Tongues (corned & smoked)	1,250lb.
Chickens (broiling)	1,900lb.
Chickens (squab)	175lb.
Chickens (roasting)	6,500lb.
Guinea Fowl	115lb.
Poussin	90lb.
Poullard de Bress	900lb.
Poulets de Grain	600lb.
Pigeons (various)	425lb.
Turkeys (Tom)	5,950lb.
Turkeys (Hen)	225lb.
Turkeys (smoked)	50lb.
Sausages (breakfast, etc.)	2,150lb.
Vegetables (various)	41,000lb.
Vegetables (frozen)	8,750lb.
Potatoes	55,000lb.
Biscuits	1,100lb.
Cereals (breakfast)	500lb.
Cereals (breakfast packets)	1000lb.

Cereals (cooking)	800lb.
Beans, peas (dried)	950lb.
Flour (all kinds)	20,000lb.
Macaroni, Spaghetti, Noodles etc.	550lb.
Oatmeal, Rolled Oats etc.	450lb.
Dried Fruits	1,300lb.
Fish (canned)	1,150lb.
Fruit (canned)	2,650lb.
Mustards, Peppers, Spices, etc.	150lb.
Salt (various)	2,400lb.
Conserves (Fruit)	45lb.
Honey & Ginger (preserved)	35lb.
Jams & Marmalades	1,575lb.
Jellies (various)	115lb.
Syrups (various)	30 gals
Juices Fruit & Vegetable)	2,750 cans
Nuts (various)	550lb.
Pickles & Olives	800 jars
Sauces, Ketchup, Chutney, etc.	900 jars
Salad Oil	160 gals
Turtle Soups etc.	475 pints
Cup Chocolate & Cocoa	41lb.
Coffee (various brands)	1,700lb.
Tea (various)	1,100lb.
Vinegars	200 pints
Vegetables (canned & Purée)	3,500 cans
Strained Foods (infants)	300 cans
Essences	25 botts.
Bacon	5,150lb.
Hams	2,500lb.
Cheeses	1,800lb.
Butter	5,900lb.
Eggs	70,000
Cream	3,250 quarts
Milk (fresh)	24,250 pints
Milk (evaporated)	600 gals
Margarine & Lard	2,250lb.
Fish (fresh & shell)	19,500lb.
Fish (smoked)	1,450lb.
Salmon (smoked)	425lb.
Sturgeon (smoked)	50lb.

Scallops & Clams 125 gals
Snails 300

(Other specialities, such as caviar, foiegras, truffles and oysters, lobsters, and crab, when in season. were carried as well, together with special stores to cover Kosher requirements, and special diets including a variety of Japanese stores.

	Bottles	Half-Bottles
Champagne	2,400	1,440
French Sparkling Burgundy	300	180
Red Bordeaux	900	20
White Bordeaux	720	480
Red Burgundy	600	600
White Burgundy	420	300
Rhone	60	72
Rhone Rosé	240	240
Alsace	60	--
Rhine	600	--
Moselle	300	--
Rhine & Moselle Sparkling	180	--
Chianti		132
American Wines	36	--
Empire Wines	192	--
Port	168	--
Sherry	480	--
Cooking Wines	144	
Liqueurs	672	
Cognac, Fine Champagne	180	
Cognac (3 Star)	300	
Armagnac	24	
Rum	360	
Scotch Whisky	2,400	
Irish Whiskey	120	
American Whiskey	1,200	
Canadian Whiskey	480	
Gin	1.200	
Aperitifs, Vermouths, etc.	2,504	

Ale & Beer	6,000
Stout	2,400
Lager	12,000
Lager (draught)	6,000 gallons
American Beer	2,400
Cider	240
Mineral Waters	48,000
Cordials	360
Cigarettes (No.)	1,500,000
Cigars (No.)	15,000
Tobacco	240lb.

M.V. ERRWOOD
(Registered in Guernsey)

Owners

EFFLUENT SERVICES COMPANY
MACCLESFIELD

German six-cylinder diesel-engine 280 H.P.

Shortly after the German surrender on 7th. May 1945 (my 30th . Birthday) Allied Forces discovered and confiscated a large number of brand-new diesel-engines intended for 'U-Boats'. They were later sold to various shipowners in the U.K. One of them being installed in the 'Errwood'.

I shall probably never know what kind of decision I may have arrived at before he had made that last remark. One thing I am certain, his words served to harden my resolve to see it through. I had signed Articles, I would abide by them. So, turning to face him squarely I held out my hand and said, "Skipper I'll see you at midnight." Then, turning away I slid down the bridge-ladder and at the foot of the gangway turned and gave him something between a salute and a wave before climbing into the car.

During the drive home I thought of little else other than to concede what a lucky chap I had been to meet up with Dennis Murray, skipper of the 'Errwood' and to enjoy the prospect of some pin-money. At least until such time as when I would be entitled to my 'old-age pension'. For the remainder of the drive home to 'Meadow End' I would have to decide what, and how much gear I should take with me, on my first voyage in what seamen call a 'Bovril Boat'. My main concern now was what Joan would have to say about it. On the other hand, as with all women, money is a powerful inducement!

And that was the beginning of a very happy and lucrative eighteen month stint as Mate of a 'Bovril-Boat'. That my wife Joan didn't care much for the idea was obvious - but I was sure the sight of my weekly pay-packet would help her to bear it with some semblance of equanimity and aplomb!

Later that evening I had changed from civvies into the navy blue battle-dress I had often worn on Cunard cargo-ships but considered inappropriate for cruise liners. I had wisely removed the epaulettes with four gold stripes as being too ostentatious. I had also decided to wear my beret instead of my peaked-cap with oak-leaves for the same reason. After a light snack and having watched the news on T.V. I saw no point in delaying any longer. I struggled into my warm duffle-coat then, giving Joan a kiss and a hug I climbed into the car giving her a cheery wave before letting out the clutch.

My Dear Wife had thoughtfully made a selection of sandwiches and brewed some hot tea for the thermos-flask. I was now well prepared for a trip into the unknown. It was a few minutes short of eleven-thirty when I parked the car a few yards from where the gangway had been earlier. Not very far off high-water I noticed the

'Errwood' was so deep in the water I was able to scramble over the bulwark onto the deck and aboard the little ship.

Luckily, I had come prepared with a torch as I found the ship in total darkness but I was able to find my way up to my cabin on the port side of the bridge-house. From the snores on the other side of the bulkhead I deduced the skipper was fast asleep in the adjacent cabin on the starboard side. Keeping my torch alight I found the small settee where I parked my hold-all and seated myself alongside it. A few minutes later a motor-generator started-up and lights came on, at the same time I heard movements next door. Making my way into the chartroom I was soon joined by the skipper sipping something hot from a cracked mug. With a stifled yawn he said, "Good morning G.D." It had been a considerable time since I had been thus addressed!

While still sipping the hot beverage from his mug, Dennis kept up a ceaseless chatter while busying himself switching-on the various navigational aids. First the Decca Navigator with the red, green and purple decometers flashing in sequence, then the Radar, gyro-compass and VHF radio-telephone and while doing so pointed out the positions of the various switches for each of them.

Through the wheel-house windows and in the dim orange-lighting on the quayside, I became aware of a shadowy figure for'ard on the foc'sle-head taking-off a few turns of the mooring-ropes. Seeing my interest in these operations the skipper answered my unspoken question. "That'll be Frank Baldwin one of the deck-hands reducing our moorings ready to let-go, the other chap will be doing the same aft to our stern moorings." With those remarks he then gave the engine-room telegraph a few short rings followed by the setting 'Stand-By' and the indicator immediately repeated from the engine-room.

Dennis Murray unhooked the handset from the VHF radio-telephone cradle and made a call, "Colchester Port Control - Colchester Port Control, this is 'Errwood' repeat 'Errwood' - how d'you read, OVER." and in a fraction of a second came the reply - "Hello 'Errwood' - this is Port Control - the river is all clear for your departure, Port Control, OUT."

Dennis Murray opened the wheel-house door overlooking the quay and giving a quick glance forward and aft making sure all was clear for engine-movements. A few barked orders from Dennis and the moorings were 'let go' except the forward backspring wire. He then gave me the order "Slow Ahead" and seconds later, "Stop Her". Striving to move ahead against the pull of the backspring the stern now began moving away from the quay. Dennis then told Frank to "Let go your backspring" and to me he ordered a short kick astern on the engine. The ship moved slowly into midstream. Then came "Stop" followed by "Half Ahead" and the 'Errwood' began to gather speed and away from Hythe Quay.

Steering a ship of whatever size gives one a great deal of pleasure and satisfaction. To watch the bow or the compass needle swing to starb'd or port then steady and settle in the direction required under the influence of the helm and helmsman never ceases to thrill. It must have been this emotional experience must have inspired John Masefield to write, ' I'll go down to the sea, to the lonely sea and the sky...............'

The Skipper Dennis Murray, peering into the Radar-screen would occasionally correct my steering with such remarks as, "Keep her a little more to starb'd", or, "That's fine G.D., keep her as she is." At other times he would say, "We're coming up to the bend heading straight for 'The Anchor' at Rowhedge." It had just gone one-thirty in the morning and 'The Anchor' was in complete darkness but the reflection of the street lights on the water gave me a clear indication of the bends in the river.

Shortly after passing the little yard in Rowhedge where 'R.N.L.I.' lifeboats were built and maintained the skipper rang 'Slow Ahead' on the engine-room telegraph. "There's a ship alongside the lower berth" said Dennis, "We have to watch our displacement wave doesn't snap her moorings and gangway." And as we slid slowly by the little ship alongside there came the unmistakable smell of her cargo of 'bone-meal'. I held my breath for as long as I could!

On the approach to the timber-yard in Wivenhoe we slowed-down again and kept our slow speed while passing the attractive little town with its boatyards, Yacht-Club and Brown's shipyard further down.

Then, with the lights of Wivenhoe well astern Dennis increased speed to 'Full Ahead' the river becoming wider from this point abeam of the old ballast quay on the Fingringhoe marshes opposite. From this point the lower reaches of the River Colne is well marked with with starb'd and port hand buoys and on such a clear night as this I found it easy to keep the 'Errwood' slightly to starb'd side of the channel in the event of shipping heading up-river.

It must have gone two o'clock in the morning with Alresford Creek somewhere astern on our port quarter and the lights of Brightlingsea faintly visible on the port bow. Dennis Murray left his post near the Radar and taking the wheel said, "OK G.D. I'll take her now, go and get your head down, I'll call you at six o'clock." Admittedly I was feeling pretty bushed, it had been a long day, all in all, and I was ready for bed.

It seemed more like four minutes than four hours when Dennis brought me a mug of scalding-hot tea and with a grin said, "See you in ten minutes - it's a nice, bright sunny morning and we've started pumping out." With that he returned to the wheel-house leaving me to hurriedly wash and shave while allowing my tea to cool a little. Then, 'all dressed and ready to go', I sauntered through the chart-room into the wheel-house where I found the skipper cleaning the windows and no-one at the wheel. My surprise must have been so obvious Dennis gave a short laugh and with a shrug of his shoulders said succinctly, "Automatic!"

He pointed out the 'SUNK' light-vessel a couple of miles to the east and said, "You've seen the chart G.D. whatever you do, keep her within those pecked lines or we are likely to be reported." He busied himself switching-off the automatic-pilot saying, "I think it is best to stay on the wheel until you've got the hang of it cruising up and down - we're on slow speed until Dave tells you he's finished pumping." He stopped talking for a few seconds while putting the wheel hard-a-port. I gave a quick check at the 'racon' flash across the screen of the monitor and saw we had reached the north limit of the 'area'.

Dennis dried his hands then said, "OK, I'll hit the sack, if I'm not up and about in time bring her back to the anchorage just below Pyefleet Creek opposite Brightlingsea then call me, we'll have to wait awhile for flood-tide before returning to the Hythe." And with that he was gone, leaving me alone in the wheel-house and a thousand unanswered questions!

Up and down - up and down we steamed keeping within the pecked lines on the chart and keeping a 'weather-eye' on the 'racon' splash across the Radar screen to know when to turn. And each time I turned, through the wheel-house windows I could see the grey stain in the water where the 'effluence' was being pumped out through the eight-inch pipe over the stern.

A few minutes after eight o'clock a face appeared at the door a stranger stepped smartly into the wheel-house. Thrusting his hand toward me with a broad smile said, "My name's Burton, Dave Burton, Chief Engineer", he gave a light chuckle then added, "The only engineer!" I shook his hand and replied, "My name's Williams - but the skipper has decided to call me G.D." so we grinned at each other. I had begun to like this young chap already. "We've finished pumping so you can head back whenever you like." said Dave, adding, "Have you had breakfast yet?" I shook my head. " No, I hadn't thought about it until now but I realise I'm feeling a bit peckish." - "I'll tell Frank on my way down, see you later." Then he disappeared from sight.

I gave a final check on our position and brought the 'Errwood' around to port and steadied her on a Course of 242 which would bring us to the 'Knoll' buoy eighteen miles away. A light tinkle on the telegraph told me Dave was back in the engine-room, so I rang 'Full Ahead' and I could feel the powerful surge as 'Errwood' gathered speed. A minute or so later the deckhand Frank arrived with a steaming mug of tea in one hand and a plate of bacon sandwiches in the other. "Here you are Cap'n," said Frank with a broad grin, "This'll grow hair on your chest," he deposited his load on a small shelf.

With a smile of appreciation and thanks I told Frank, "None of the Cap'n here Frank, the Skipper and Dave call me G.D. and that's good enough." He gave a little grunt and said, "OK Cap'n - I mean G.D., don't let your tea get cold." With that he opened the wheel-house door and shuffled off. The tea was hot and strong, I hadn't tasted bacon sandwiches as delicious for more years than I could tell. I was more than peckish.

There was now a clear run of sixteen miles so I put 'Errwood' into automatic-steering. This gave me more freedom to study the coastline through my binoculars. Within a few seconds I had picked out the conspicuous 'Naze Tower' to the north-west and over to the south-east the 'can buoy' marking Gunfleet Sand. The deep channel in between the coast and Gunfleet Sand banks known as 'The Wallett". Between the shoals of 'Outer Gabbard', 'Kentish Knock' and the mainland.

Then came Frinton and its conspicuous 'water-tower' - and the two 'Martello Towers' in Clacton. I noticed quite a number of trawlers working in pairs between ourselves and the coast. At a quarter to eleven I picked out the cardinal buoy 'Knoll' right ahead as expected and adjusted Course to bring it a couple of degrees on the starb'd bow. When within two miles of the buoy I cancelled automatic-steering and took the wheel myself in readiness for making the sharp starb'd turn around the 'Knoll'. Through my binoculars I could now see and distinguish the conical 'Eagle Buoy' and 'Colne Bar Number 5'.

We were now approximately at the confluence of the Colne and Blackwater Rivers and I shaped a Course of 348 to pass between 'Colne Point and the 'inner Bench Head Buoys'. I gave the engine-room telegraph a tinkle to warn Dave I would soon be reducing speed. A few seconds later the telegraph tinkled to indicate Dave was in the engine-room - probably having kept an eye on our position, so I rang, 'Stand-By' and I detected a slight change in the sound and rhythm of the diesel-motor.

I counted five ships at anchor off Brightlingsea and saw an ideal place to anchor between them and the 'Lowlands' wreck just south of Pyefleet Creek. I pressed the button for the bell in the crews' quarters to bring the deckhands out to 'anchor stations' and within a minute or so both men were seen walking for'ard to the foc'sle-head. By half-past eleven we were snugly at anchor and I stepped out of the wheel-house onto the open bridge, to breathe-in fresh clean air and to admire the view.

"Hmm, fresh air", exclaimed Dennis Murray as he joined me on the port side of the bridge nearest 'Mersea Stone', the eastern extremity of Mersea Island. He looked refreshed after nearly six hours sleep.

A wash and shave had got rid of the dark stubble on his face when I had relieved him at six o'clock that morning. "Any problems after I turned-in?" I shook my head, "No, everything has gone smoothly," I replied. Then, to change the subject I pointed to the entrance to Pyefleet Creek, "Did you know they've been cultivating oysters there ever since Roman days?" He gave a grunt and said, "Don't care much for them, reckon they're over-rated m'self." He paused then added, "I suppose you've had your fair share." I retorted, "A few haven't worked!"

For a minute I was silent, thinking and remembering then said, "I like oysters but they're much too expensive in Mersea." I told him about the voyage I had made as Master of the 'Port St. Lawrence' to Bluff, New Zealand where oysters were so plentiful and cheap Joan and I had enjoyed oysters by the score. "Oh!", said Dennis, "So your wife could accompany you on voyages then?" I nodded and replied, "Yes, but only after Trafalgar House had bought Cunard." I gave a little chuckle, "Before then, wives were allowed on board but had to be off the ship by eight o'clock in the evening." We both laughed at the absurdity of such a foolish regulation.

But seeing he was genuinely interested I went on, "You see Dennis, apart from the passenger ships and a considerable number of cargo-ships, the Cunard Group comprised the fleets of Port Line, Brocklebank and Moss Tankers a total of over sixty ships." Dennis registered his surprise pulling a face, I went on, "And when Trafalgar House bought the whole shebang they insisted Masters and officers should be prepared to sail in any ship in the group." I took a deep breath before continuing, "That is why I have been Master of both Port Line and Brocklebank ships and enjoyed a much broader outlook." I told him of voyages to The Great Lakes in Canada and America, South Africa, New Zealand, Red Sea ports, the Persian Gulf and the Bay of Bengal etc.

While the skipper and I had been gossiping the 'Errwood' had begun to swing round to the flood-tide. Dennis drew my attention to the iron framed beacon less than a hundred yards away. "d'you see the three horizontal angle-bars supporting the frames there?" I nodded my assent, and he went on, "When the tide reaches the third horizontal bar it'll be time to weigh anchor and proceed upriver." I nodded again to indicate I understood, then remembered I hadn't touched the sandwiches Joan had made for me. I invited Dennis to join me but he declined saying, "No thanks G.D., I have to bring the Log-Book up to date, you eat your sandwiches, but don't forget to keep an eye on that iron crossbar. "With that he returned to his quarters.

The water was just beginning to lap the third bar when I rang for the men to standby for'ard and I put the engine-room telegraph on 'Stand-By'. Dennis reappeared on the bridge as soon as he heard the windlass turning. When the anchor was aweigh he called out, "Half ahead - hard a'port." And the 'Errwood' began her passage upriver. It was precisely 14.55 and I made the necessary entries in the bridge log book.

Being daylight I was able to admire the scenery on both sides of the river, although I found the 'Errwood' rather more difficult to handle in her 'light' condition than when loaded. Furthermore, even with a flood-tide, there was so little water between the keel and the bottom, she had a marked tendency to veer suddenly and without warning. In fact, there were times when rounding a bend she would slice through the soft mud.

When approaching the ships alongside the Hythe berths Dennis took over the wheel saying, "From here on G.D. the steering becomes very tricky." He was quick to notice I looked a bit outraged so he added, You see, with the flood-tide up our arse we have to go very very slow, which makes steering all the more difficult and there's little room between these ships and the river bank." I was soon to appreciate what he meant!

In my book 'From the Captain's Table' I mention how much we survivors from the torpedoed ship 'Nariva' admired Lt. Commander Pat King, RNR for his great skill and seamanship. These were more than adequately displayed a few days later when, in a typical North Atlantic gale he manoeuvred his corvette alongside a lifeboat with survivors from another torpedoed ship 'Canadian Star'. And the next afternoon when the gale was at its worst he was equally skilful approaching a life-raft with another group of survivors. It must always be appreciated the great risks he took in these humanitarian gestures with enemy 'U-Boats' operating in the area.

And in a later chapter of my book I describe the high degree of skill and seamanship displayed by Captain Donald Sorrell, Extra-Master, Square-Rigged Sailing Ship, when he manoeuvred the mighty 'Queen Mary' safely alongside her berth at Pier 90 in New York without the aid of the usual six tugs that were on strike.

But even better was the way in which skipper Murray brought his ship 'Errwood' through that part of the River Colne where no less than five coastal vessels were moored bow to stern along the half-mile stretch of Hythe Quay. It has to be appreciated the flood-tide was running at approximately one and a half knots. And to ensure the 'Errwood' had sufficient steerage-way her engine had to be turning at a speed without the displacement wave disturbing the moorings of those ships. What made the manoeuvre particularly difficult was the echo wave thrown back from these ships would make the 'Errwood' veer in one direction or the other. The only way to counter this would be to give the engine a short 'Kick-Ahead' to give a greater effect on the rudder momentarily.

Then, having successfully negotiated this perilous stretch of the river we finally reached the turning area and had to make the same passage back to here berth near the sewage treatment plant. Doing so AGAINST the flood made the manoeuvre somewhat easier and my heart resumed its normal rhythm!!

Eventually 'Errwood' was moored securely alongside her allotted berth and Dennis 'Rang-Off' engines and switched-off the various electronic aids to navigation. With a broad smile he said, "Well. that's your first round trip on the 'Errwood' and what d'you say to that?" My reply was instant and sincere. "Frankly Dennis, I've never seen ship-handling so brilliantly demonstrated in all my years at sea." He gave a sheepish grin and shrugged his shoulders. "It's all in a day's work - let's have a gin."

And that was another lesson to learn. Dennis produced the bottle of gin and a tonic that seemed to have lost most of its fizz. After a couple of appreciative sips he brought back the subject of ship-handling. "You must have been in some tricky situations yourself at some time or another." I took another sip then replied. "Since becoming Master there have been a few sticky moments, I remember but they were always in the category of a 'one-off-situation' - and never repeated - you know what I mean." Dennis nodded and I continued, "So, what you did today, like threading a needle, you do almost every day." Dennis shrugged his acceptance of my comparison.

Dennis began running his finger around the rim of his glass making a high-pitched musical sound. "You mentioned a few sticky moments when you were Master." He looked up from playing with his glass. I told him of the time in Beira, Portuguese Mozambique, when I had been warned the FRELEMO insurgents had captured the town and could be in the harbour at any moment. I had little or no option but to sail immediately and how I had managed to navigate the tortuous channel out to sea without the aid of a Pilot.

When I had finished Dennis said, " You'd better push off home for a few hours, high-water will be 0215 in the morning so you needn't be back on board until 0130 if that's OK with you." I nodded and touched my forelock with an "Aye-Aye Sir." And of course that was another lesson to be learned, I was caught by the tide over the Strood and arrived home later that expected.

The welcome by my wife was as warm as if I had been away for weeks or months and the tantalising smell from the kitchen promised one of her superb meals. A shave and a hot shower refreshed me outwardly while the pink-gin Joan handed me did much the same inwardly. Meanwhile she plied me incessantly with questions, questions and more questions.

Replete after a magnificent meal, I relaxed in my favourite armchair to await 'Coronation Street'. But it had been a very long twenty-four hours since I had left home the previous evening. It was the sound of Big Ben striking the hour that awoke me in time to watch 'The News At Ten' during which time Joan made us a cup of tea. Soon after eleven o'clock I insisted she went to bed while I busied myself in the kitchen brewing another pot of tea for my thermos-flask.

It was just gone midnight when I parked the car in the usual place and , much to my surprise, saw the electric lights were on in the 'Errwood', but as there was no sign or sounds of life on board, I crept quietly into my cabin. I had no intention of sleeping but I must have drifted-off until awakened by the skipper bringing me a mug of tea and saying, "We'll be under-way in fifteen minutes."

By the time I joined Dennis in the wheelhouse, I found the weather had changed for the worse with a light drizzly rain and visibility a mere two to three miles. We kept to the same routine as previously with Dennis glued to the Radar while I took the wheel. The reduced visibility required considerably more concentration until approaching Brightlingsea. When a shift in the wind improved conditions considerably and Dennis insisted on me turning-in until arrival at the dumping-grounds as before. During my first trip in the 'Errwood' I had held certain reservations about the Skipper's ship-handling prowess but, having seen him conning his ship in that narrow channel to the Hythe I had no qualms now only complete confidence.

How often have we stopped to think how much of our civilised world and especially the scores of public amenities we take so much for granted. How many of us remember the days and weeks, not so very long ago, when local Council workers were on strike and hundreds of tons of garbage were left uncollected and bereaved families couldn't even bury or cremate their dead?

The same blind unconcern also applies to most of us who haven't a clue what happens to our body functions once the chain is pulled or the lever flushes it all away, never to be seen or heard of again! Well, dear reader, before I continue my narrative of life on the 'Errwood' let me give you some vital statistics.

In the 'flowery' language of a glossy brochure, "Aqua privies and septic tanks together with an adequate means of final effluent disposal, is required in all sewage systems!" The essential preliminary to the process of raw sewage is the removal of all gross solids such as rag, (of all description), paper and autumn-leaves all of which could cause physical blockage. For this purpose simple screens of vertical bars not more than 2.5 centimetres apart will suffice.

There are sedimentation tanks having upward and horizontal floors to assist in the removal of sludge by gravity. This sludge is allowed to ferment which will then rise to the surface as 'scum'. Stabilisation ponds or lagoons are filled with water before being used and within a week a crust forms which almost eliminates odour. The organic matter is then consumed by biological organisms and oxygen, the oxygen supply for the aerobic ponds depending largely on algae and sunlight.

When a sufficient accumulation of treated effluence is stored it is then pumped through a manifold on board ship where it is then diverted as required for 'trim' purposes to the various tanks. It is then taken out to sea where it is discharged overside in the area designated by the Authorities and marked by 'Pecked Lines' on all Admiralty Charts.

So, my second trip in the 'Errwood' was no different from the first, in that the skipper, Dennis Murray, took the helm while I 'turned-in'. And on arrival at the 'dumping-ground' I was called to con the ship while steaming up and down discharging our 'cargo' of treated effluence.

A couple of hours later Dave Burton, the engineer, appeared to report pumping completed and I brought the 'Errwood' around to the usual Course making for the 'Knoll' buoy. On this occasion Dave stayed in the wheel-house for a chat. He was very interested to learn about my years in Cunard and particularly from an engineer's point of view. His eyes bulged and his mouth opened wide as I gave him some details about the 'Queen Elizabeth'. In reply to a question I told him there were four sets of single-reduction geared turbines totalling 200,000 horse power fed by twelve water-tube boilers producing super-heated steam. The daily consumption of fuel-oil 1,200 tons at 1.76 tons per mile of distance.

Of course from time to time he would interrupt my ready flow of information to ask some specific question such as how much fuel-oil would she consume in one round voyage? To which I replied, 16,000 tons from Southampton and back. Dave literally gaped when I told him. the generators produced enough electricity to supply any city the size of Coventry. And that she carried approximately 4,500 tons of fresh-water. And that the height of the funnels were 145 feet above the waterline. The height of the masts 194 feet above the waterline on a draft of 40 feet!

I was about to confuse him with further details when he mumbled some excuse and stumbled out of the wheel-house. "Well." I thought to myself, "That'll take him some time to digest." But the arrival of Frank with hot tea and bacon sarnies brought much pleasanter thoughts to mind. That, and the need to adjust Course to avoid a couple of fishermen erased all memories of the 'Queen Elizabeth' from my mind, at least for the time-being!

After we had anchored, again not far from the old 'Lowland' wreck off East Mersea, Frank came and joined me on the bridge. "A few shackles in the anchor-chain look pretty worn", was his first comment. Then changing the subject completely added, "Would you like some coffee?" Feeling a bit fragile I nodded then said, "Thanks Frank, I'll mention those shackles to the skipper when he surfaces, then I'll take a look at them as we weigh anchor to proceed upriver." With that the deckhand scampered off to fetch me the coffee, (a brew I secretly hate, but find it to be a good stimulant).

On his return with a steaming mug full I asked Frank if he knew the length of the anchor-cable and he shook his head. "I've never seen it all out." Was all he could volunteer. I told him most deep-sea vessels had a minimum of ten shackles on each cable to which he remarked,"I don't think we have that much, 'cos when we've anchored with three shackles in the water, I know there doesn't seem too much left in the locker." I smiled and asked, "What's the weight of the anchor Frank?" He shook his head, "I dunno, about thirty hundredweights I guess."

Throwing away the rest of the coffee that had gone cold I said, "D'you know Frank, the 'Queen Mary' has a port and st'bd anchor and one spare and they each weigh sixteen tons. "He gave a loud gasp and said, "Bloody hell," and that made me laugh. I went on to say, "And each link in the chain weighs just over two hundred-weights." Frank gave a loud whistle and shook his head in disbelief. Then, to add coals to his astonishment I said, "The 'Queen Elizabeth' has the same port and st'bd anchors, but she also has a stem anchor, and a spare and they each weigh sixteen tons."

"Who weighs sixteen tons?" said a voice and Dennis Murray came through the wheel-house yawning loudly. I said, "Good morning skipper, I was giving Frank some vital statistics about the anchors and cables in the two 'Queens'. His crisp comment to that was, "All that would be enough to sink this shiteship."

RMS QUEEN ELIZABETH

PARTICULARS OF SHIP

Official Number	19th February 1940	166290
Signal Letters		GBSS
Port of Registry		Liverpool
Built & Engined by	John Brown & Company, Clydebank	
Owners	Cunard White Star Ltd. Liverpool	
Length Overall		1,031 Feet
Length between Perpendiculars		965 Feet
Breadth		118.6 Feet
Tonnage - Gross at 100 Cu. Ft. Per Ton		83,673.02
Tonnage - Nett at 100 Cu. Ft. Per Ton		41,877.28

Engines	Four Single-Reduction Steam Turbines	
Horsepower		200,000
Number and Description of Boilers -Twelve Water-Tube		336 Tons
Cargo-Winches	Laurence Scott D.C.	Electric
Moulded Depth		92 Feet
Displacement (Loaded)		77,940 Tons
Displacement (Unloaded)		62,300 Tons
Loaded Draft		39.01 Feet
Freeboard		35.5 Feet
Tons Per Inch (Loaded)		206.2 Tons
Oil Fuel Capacity		8,450 Tons
Allowance for Fresh Water (All Drafts)		9.5 ins.
Passengers 1st. Class 790 Cabin 680 Tourist 790		Total 2,260
Troops (War-Time)		14,180
Crew (Peak Travel Season)		1,276
Number of Lifeboats 28 (Total Capacity)		3,724
Life rafts (War-Time Capacity)		15,555
Height of Fore & Main Masts Truck to Keel)		233 Feet
Height of Fwd. Funnel (To 39 Feet Waterline)		145 Feet
Height of Bridge (To 39 Feet Waterline)		90 Feet
Anchors - Three Stockless		Each 16 Tons
Studded-Link Chain (At 6 Feet Per Fathom)		330 Fathoms
Weight of Each Link		2 Hundredweights
Fresh Water Capacity (Drinking)		360 Tons
Fresh Water Capacity (Domestic)		4,200 Tons

Number of Decks		12
Number of Watertight Bulkheads		18
Balanced Rudder	Weight	140 Tons

Propellors
Four Manganese-Bronze Each Eighteen Feet in Diameter   32 Tons

Power Stations Two	(Sufficient to Supply City of Coventry)	
Telephones		600
Radio Stations	(Manned Continuously)	Two
Crow's Nest	110 rungs up inside foremast 130 feet above water level. Roofed, electrically heated. Telephone Communication to Bridge.	

Carpets	(Total Coverage)	10 Miles
Cutlery		16,000 Pieces
Crockery		200,000 Pieces
Chinaware & Glassware		100,000 Pieces
Bedsheets		30,000 Pieces
Blankets		5,600 Pieces
Table-Cloths		21,000 Pieces
Towels		210,000 Pieces

Electric Lamps		30,000
Safe Deposits (Miniature Safes)		350
Kennels	Passenger Pets Various	26
Fire Hydrants		378
Promenade Deck	(Four Times Around)	Equalled One Mile

Watertight doors   43 (Two & Half Tons Each) Operated From the Bridge and Individual Local Control.

LAUNCHED BY HER MAJESTY QUEEN ELIZABETH
at 3.36 pm on September 27th. 1938

From the anchorage off Brightlingsea I again took the wheel upriver until the approaches to the Hythe berths when Dennis again chose to take the wheel. And again I was very impressed by his skill threading the narrow waterway between ships alongside on the one hand and the river bank on the other. What impressed me most was the way in which he anticipated the way the 'Errwood' veered suddenly under the influence of the rebounding displacement waves. As I said before, the return passage from the turning basin to our berth against the tide was relatively simple.

After mooring the ship in her berth Dennis invited me into his dayroom for a quick drink, but having learned by my previous mistake I declined with thanks. Just as I was about to leave Dennis said, "We won't be sailing tonight G.D. there won't be a full load ready for us, so come aboard at nine o'clock tomorrow and we'll take a look at those anchor shackles." The very thought of having a full night in our bed gave me an acute sense of relief, I hadn't realized that at 64 years of age how tired I had now become.

Joan's welcome was as warm as ever and after a shave and a shower it was good to relax with my feet up, a pink gin in my hand and to watch the six o'clock news on the 'telly'. In between frequent visits to the kitchen where she was preparing the evening meal, Joan plied me with questions. Some I answered as honestly as I could and some I didn't yet have the answers and some I pretended not to have heard in the first place.

After a lovely meal it was a godsend to relax and watch our favourite programmes on T.V. not that I saw much. I dozed off and on until, after the ten o'clock news I called it a day and slept like the proverbial log. My last conscious thought was to have a close look at those anchor shackles the next day and ensure that they were correctly marked with seizing-wire. What the rest of the day in port would bring was sheer conjecture.

Not quite certain of what the day's work would bring, I had brought a pair of overalls with me. When I arrived on board 'Errwood' at a quarter to nine the next day I found the skipper in his dayroom making entries in the Official Log. For several minutes we discussed the entries. In those days the Official Log warned shipmasters that it was illegal to perform wedding ceremonies on board and we had a good laugh at the expense of the public in general and movie-makers in particular who still believe this myth.

After a while we decided to go for'ard to examine the anchor-chains so I nipped into my cabin and climbed into my working overalls promising to join him on the foc'sle-head after I had done so. As Frank had reported earlier, some of the shackles were in a bad state so, with Frank and the other deckhand. His name I have sadly forgotten. Then we reversed the little windlass and 'flaked' the chains along the quay to examine and change shackles where necessary. Having completed these changes Dennis and the other deckhand went off to carry out some other repairs leaving Frank and I to re-mark the shackles with new seizing wire.

It was nearly one o'clock by the time the job had been completed to my satisfaction and after we had cleaned our hands with Swarfega I went looking for the others to help windlass the cables back into the chain-locker but the skipper had other ideas. He said, "No, first, we go to 'The Maltsters' for a pie and a pint then we rewind the anchor-chains when we come back." That was an idea that met with general approval, because the pub was only a few hundred yards up the Haven Road.

It took only a few minutes to get washed and changed from working gear and we were off up the road to savour a pint of the best bitter 'The Maltsters' could offer. Dennis and I chose a 'Ploughman's Lunch' while the other two ordered pork-pies. Strange as it may appear, there was no apparent air of distinction between us, reminding me of the 'Toc-H' motto "Abandon Rank All Ye Who Enter Here!"

I turned to Dennis with the question, "Where does Dave have his lunch skipper?" He put his pint down, slopping some of its precious amber nectar, "Dave always goes home, did you know he lives in an old fishing-boat?" I shook my head and he went on. "Yes, he and Kay bought an ex-French wooden-hulled trawler." he used his napkin to wipe-up the slopped beer. "It's moored just beyond the turning basin, they're very proud of their boat and would love to show you around" He paused to take a sip of his bitter then, "They work hard making it habitable for themselves and their two little'uns, a boy and a girl."

As Dennis was talking I found myself glancing across the table at the deckhand whose name I can't remember. I couldn't help but notice the resemblance between him and my dear Uncle Tom Jones, (now deceased). It was the large drooping moustache I supposed, Uncle Tom's was so luxurious he always drank his tea from a 'moustache-cup'. Funny-thing, one never sees them these days - they were made with a bar across the lips of the mug to prevent the moustache getting wet! So, unable to remember the chap's name I shall refer to him as 'Tom'.

Later on I was to learn that Tom was a 'brickie'. A professional bricklayer but trade had been pretty slack for some time and he had taken this job rather than stay on the dole with a large family to support. I made a mental note of these facts knowing that they would come in useful. Joan and I had already made plans for the patio at the rear of our bungalow!

With lunch over and our pint-pots drained of the last dregs we made our way back to the 'Errwood' and within the hour we had stowed and secured both anchors and cables on board. It was coming up to three o'clock and Dennis said we should call it a day. "By the way G.D. we're not sailing again tonight, so I'll see you nine o'clock tomorrow, OK?" I nodded acknowledgement the, checking the time of high-water I climbed into the car in the hope of crossing The Stroud before it flooded over.

Saturday morning saw us pottering around the ship aimlessly. I found a few halyards needed renewing. These modern man-made fibres of polypropylene I found very hard and difficult to splice and I broke a few fingernails while doing so. Just before eleven o'clock Dennis Murray called me to join him for coffee and I was mildly surprised when he handed me a 'pay-envelope'. My surprise soon turned to unmitigated delight when I discovered it contained £168.34p!

I looked at the Skipper and said, "There must be some mistake Dennis." For a few seconds he stared then said, "Were you expecting more?" "No, but are you sure this is correct, do you realise this is more than I was earning as Master in Cunard?" His reply staggered me, "This has been a poor week, your average earnings per week will be nearer to £200." He gave a short laugh then went on, "You see G.D. a lot of the time you put in is 'overtime', unsocialable hours and not forgetting the subsistence allowance." He paused and scribbled something on a scrap of paper, then added, "In Cunard you were being fed." Then he grinned, "And from what you've told me, you were fed bloody well!" I shrugged, there was no answer to that! But I remembered the slogan 'Gracious Living at its Best'.

"Tomorrow's Sunday", said Dennis as he produced the usual gin, tonic and glasses. "Would you like to come out to my place, Brenda would love to meet you, I know she's dying to meet a Cunard skipper, big ships and all that." I felt a bit embarrassed by his flattery but I said, "Yes thank you Dennis, would four o'clock suit you?" He nodded and replied, "Four o'clock will be fine and I'll show you some of my photos taken while I was in the Royal Marines."

Knowing from past experience how Dennis was prone to be heavy-handed with the gin, I refused 'the other wing' and with the pretext of high-water over The Strood I thanked him for his hospitality and with a final "See you tomorrow afternoon," I made my escape. On my way home in the car I couldn't help wondering what Joan would have to say about my wages - 'Pin-Money'!! Hell!

We found the Murray's home on the Ipswich Road without any trouble. It was almost next door to where Joan's cousin George Smith and his wife Margaret lived. George was employed by the Inland Revenue as a Tax Inspector. Dennis himself answered the door in response to my ring and the usual introductions made. Brenda Murray had a very slight but attractive lisp and she made us very welcome indeed and served tea with the usual choice of sandwiches and cakes to follow.

After tea Dennis brought out his collection of photographs. We all had a good laugh at some of them taken when he was an eighteen-year-old 'Teddy Boy'. With black curly hair and sideburns to match, he was wearing a three-quarter length coat, drain-pipe trousers and winkle-picking black shoes. But there was such a transformation when he produced photographs of himself in the uniform of the Royal Marines, in blues and tropical kit with white pith helmet and highly polished badge. I have always known

Marines to be among the smartest and this was Dennis Murray at his smartest.

When I asked him why he had left the Corps he gave us a graphic account of when he was stationed in Hong Kong he and three others had driven in a jeep to the top of Stanley Heights overlooking the Harbour. On their return journey down they had taken a corner too fast, skidded off the the road and had fallen hundreds of feet. I can't remember the details about the other three Marines but Dennis had suffered multiple injuries. After many months in hospital he was eventually invalided out of the service he had loved with such a passion.

I supposed it was the emotion and physical effect of telling his story that made Dennis thirsty. Be that as it may it was evidently a sufficient excuse to bring out the bottles and glasses. Brenda and Joan chose sherry while Dennis treated us both to a glass of 'single malt' whisky to which, I may add, I am extremely partial! In those days there was much less of the paranoia about drink-driving as there is today.

During a short lull in the conversation Brenda turned to me and said "Dennis tells me you were Captain of the 'Queen Mary'." I laughed and shook my head, "No Brenda, by the time I was promoted to Captain the two 'Queens' were long gone, much to my regret." "Oh", she said, "I must have misunderstood him then." Not wishing to disappoint her however I told her I had been First Officer of both 'Queens' at different times. That seemed to please her then she went on, "Which of the two did you prefer?" I replied, "Well Brenda, I preferred the 'Queen Mary' because she was the most luxurious of the two and I felt privileged to serve under Captain Donald Sorrell, who, in my opinion, was the the finest shipmaster I'd ever met."

Her next question was much more difficult to answer, "Wasn't the 'Queen Elizabeth' just as luxurious as the 'Queen Mary?" I then launched into the explanation of how the 'Q.E.' had been built in 1938 when materials were more expensive etc. Then, before she could ask another question I told them of the secret dash across the Atlantic in 1940 to escape being bombed by the Germans and that a lot of her fittings had been completed in New York, but only for the carriage of troops. I ended the story by describing how she and the 'Queen Mary' eventually carried up to 16,000 American troops on each voyage, to the various theatres of war. I ended by saying, "And it was only after the war was over that the 'Queen Elizabeth' was finally fitted-out for the carriage of passengers, and being a time of austerity the materials available were not of the high quality of the 'Queen Mary's'.

The next question Brenda asked was typical of a woman but much easier to answer. "How many women were there in the ship's crew?" I said the total crew averaged 1,285 of which there were 90 females. The look of incredulity almost made me laugh, but went on to enumerate. "44 Stewardesses, 8 Laundry Stewardesses, 6 Shop Attendants, 6 Hairdressers, 4 Telephonists, 4 Lady Assistant Pursers, 4 Nursing Sisters and 2 Physiotherapists, I think I've left out a few." Brenda was speechless, probably in shock, all I got from Dennis was, "Bloody 'ell." I turned to Joan and suggested it was time we made a move, and she nodded.

High-Water, Monday morning, was at the civilised time of eight o'clock when, loaded overnight, we slipped moorings and left Hythe Quay. Thanks to the 'Powers that be' for giving us Summer Time. Our routine was the same as on previous trips with me taking the wheel as far as Alresford Creek and 'turning-in' when Dennis took the wheel as far as the 'Dumping-Ground' when I once more had the 'thrill' of steaming up and down while discharging our cargo of chemically-treated 'porridge'.

Later in the day when 'Errwood' was anchored as before, Dennis joined me in the wheel-house for coffee. He laughed and said, "You remember when I was showing you photos of me in uniform, you remarked on the brightness of the badge on my pith helmet." I nodded and he sipped his coffee then went on, "I didn't want to tell you about it while Brenda was there but that bloody badge cost me ten days 'jankers.' (My reader will possibly know the term 'jankers', in the armed forces means punishment for offences committed by 'other ranks'.)

"Well, we were 'on parade' in Hong Kong, lining the route along which the visiting Japanese Prince, Akihito would be travelling. The Royal Marine Band was playing and there were thousands of flag-waving, cheering crowds waiting to see the cavalcade." Dennis finished his coffee and went on, "It was a week later, I was 'on defaulters' marched into the commanding officer's office, drawn to attention, saluted, gave my name and serial-number."

"In the C/O's office I saw a film projector at one end and a screen at the other. he blinds were drawn and the projector switched-on. It was the parade all over again and the camera was panning slowly along the ranks to where I was standing with my rifle at 'present arms'. Then, as the royal carriage came by I saw a flash of sunlight reflected on my badge. No further proof was needed, that I had moved my head to watch the cavalcade pass by. And THAT was how my bloody badge cost me a ten bloody days stint of bloody 'jankers'." (What could I say to that?!)

I am reasonably certain my reader will understand that from a distance in time of nearly twenty years I would find it difficult to remember accurately how many trips we would make in any particular week. It all depended on the amount stored in the 'pond' and the carrying capacity of the 'Errwood'. Be all that as it may the routine each trip was much the same except the days were getting shorter.

But it was one of those quiet days when, instead of running effluence out to the 'dumping ground' we carried out various repair jobs and doing a bit of painting overside. Anyway, one morning when the skipper had gone across to the office I had the opportunity for a long chat with Dave, our engineer, during which he invited me to inspect his engine-room.

To say he was justifiably proud would be an understatement. I found his domain clean, neat and very tidy with copper and brass piping beautifully polished and the paintwork looked as though it had been recently done. I was most intrigued with the main engine which had been made in Germany. I remarked on this to Dave who told me a strange but most interesting story. It appeared that soon after the German surrender on 7th. May 1945 and the Allied armies had overrun the ports of Kiel and Stettin they had discovered hundreds of crated diesel-motors that had been intended for U-Boats.

The U-Boats loss was the British shipowners gain. The Allies confiscated these brand-new diesel-motors and they were sold as main propulsion units for small merchant vessels and as electric-generators for larger ships. Of one thing I am pretty certain Dave was extremely proud of his main engine and rated it very highly indeed. For my part I was most impressed with it and all th auxiliary units in his engine-room and I said so. I could tell by his reaction and the way his eyes lit up he was pleased and grateful for my comments.

As I was leaving Dave's company to return to my duties on deck he asked if I would care to see his boat which was moored higher up-river. I replied I would like to very much so it was agreed I would pay them a visit the following Saturday morning. Meanwhile there were several more trips of effluence to make from the Hythe treatment plant.

Forenoon Saturday, and having found a suitable place to park my car, I made my way to where their craft ex-French fishing trawler named 'Claire de Lune' was moored. She was much bigger than I had imagined with dimensions in the region of fifty feet in length and a sturdy beam that would make her a comfortable and seaworthy craft.

I was made welcome on board by Dave's attractive wife Kay who apologised for her husband's absence saying he had gone to purchase some electric-cable. The deck was cluttered with a variety of stores and equipment, I gathered there was still a lot of conversion work in hand. We had just about finished our tour of the deck, when Dave turned up carrying coils of cable.

After exchanging a few words with his wife he led the way below pointing out the salient features of their boat and the alterations they had made or were about to make. We entered what had once been the fish-hold, now converted into a most attractive saloon-cum-lounge with well-upholstered settees either side. Seated on a low bench were their two children aged between five and seven. Stevie being the older and his pretty little sister Elizabeth had their eyes glued to the television set in the corner.

Forward of the saloon I was shown the crew's quarters and aft of the saloon the Master's cabin occupied by the largest double-bed I've ever seen. Evidently there was much work to be completed before the ex-trawler would make an ideal home. But the Burtons were still a young couple, energetic, enthusiastic and, what's more, very capable. At the end of our tour we sat in the saloon discussing plans for their boat and future.

I have previously mentioned Frank Baldwin the senior deck-hand and how, on occasions, we would work together whatever the job, such as the anchor cables. And on these occasions we would gossip and exchange facts about each other without invading each other's privacy. For instance, I learned that his wife's name was Linda and she was a registered 'foster-mother' I was particularly interested to learn that most 'foster-mothers' preferred white children which aroused a deeper loving instinct in Linda for black children. Frank told me she could always count on his support whatever children she chose and I must say I admired both of them for their humanity.

Autumn was well advanced when the 'Errwood' was replaced by the 'Scammonden II' a much larger ship with a greater carrying capacity so much so that two trips a week was ample to cope with the effluence processed. At about this time I had acquired a fair working knowledge of the River Colne and the sea passage up to Harwich and the 'Sunk' lightship area. So Dennis introduced a better-balanced routine where we would change conning the ship on alternate trips.

When I had expressed concern with my first week's pay-packet and Dennis had almost guaranteed my average pay would exceed £200, I discovered he was not exaggerating. This was certainly not 'pin-money', but a very handsome salary whatever the nature of my employment. On the strength of this we were able to have a third bedroom and bathroom built on to our bungalow.

This was the time when the residents of West Mersea enjoyed the amenities of a night-club called 'Hall Barn' which was very popular indeed and to which Joan and I belonged. During one of many chats with skipper Dennis Murray I had mentioned this establishment, describing it as having no less that three rooms of varying capacity. That it could be the ideal venue for a Christmas Party. Dennis was quite enthusiastic about it and having discussed total numbers attending I volunteered to ask the proprietor, Max Garcia for his terms and conditions.

One trip we made in late November is indelibly imprinted in my memory and my high opinion of Dennis Murray shot even higher. A blanket of wet fog enveloped the whole of Essex but in the Colne Valley, with all its marshes, it was dense. I have never known a Cunard ship sail in such conditions but Dennis Murray was not a Cunard skipper. He knew the River Colne even better than the back of his hand and, to my surprise he gave the usual orders for leaving the berth.

I took the wheel and Dennis concentrated on the radar screen giving me instructions to give more or less helm as we negotiated the bends and turns of the winding river. The worst moments came as we approached the first bend near 'The Anchor' in Rowhedge when I didn't give enough 'port helm' and we passed the pub so close I swear I heard snores from a bedroom. From Rowhedge the river becomes a little wider and we were able to relax a little. My admiration for the skipper grew every minute for the way he combined his intimate knowledge of the river and interpreting the picture on the Radar screen.

And again it was my fault for delaying a helm order, even by a whisper, when we touched the wooden pilings a glancing blow at the timber yard in Wivenhoe and slid along the wharf for about a hundred feet before gradually easing her back into mid-stream. For all the fact that the fog was cold and clammy I think we were both bathed in perspiration until we were well past Wivenhoe. Then, quite spontaneously, we burst into nervous laughter. And that was the only trip I remember when I insisted on staying at the wheel all the way to the 'dumping ground' until daylight when the fog lifted and visibility improved.

By sheer chance the only other occasions where we had fog on the river was when we were safely moored alongside in our berth on the Hythe awaiting further increase in effluence at the treatment plant. But, as I've already mentioned, 'Scammonden II' being larger and longer than 'Errwood' her stern came perilously close to touching the opposite bank in the turning basin and my heart came just as close to my mouth.

With the generous co-operation and support given by Max Garcia and his wife Rose, our Christmas Party at the 'Hall Barn' was a huge success. They had produced a magnificent buffet to which I had contributed a pound of caviar given me by Captain Arnold Krems, the Russian Master who had taken-over from me command of the Cunard liner 'Franconia' when sold to the Russians and renamed 'Fedor Shalyapin'.

There were more guests than crew at the party, but our wives, Brenda Murray, Kay Burton, Linda Baldwin, 'Uncle Tom's' wife whose name I have forgotten, and of course Joan played their part as hostesses to make everyone enjoy themselves. The 'four-piece band' organised by Max Garcia played throughout the evening like whirling dervishes and the dance-floor squeaked with dozens of happy shuffling feet.

One of the wives praised the quartet so much, I told her they reminded me of the 'Misty Group' in the 'Cunard Adventurer'. I told her they would begin playing in the 'Starlight Room' immediately above my quarters at midnight when, trying to sleep I would have willingly murdered them and the dancers. She laughed when I added, "Those shuffling stomping teenagers always have a glazed look in their eyes, as though they were giving vertical expression to a horizontal desire!"

I honestly can't remember who she was but after a fit of giggles she asked ,"And was it like that every cruise?" I told her one cruise was pretty much the same as another. Always sailing at or near midnight every Saturday and after a long hot and trying day I was always glad to get to bed eventually. Then she said, "But surely you could take it easy on a Sunday." To which I replied, "Not Pygmalion likely - at eleven o'clock every Sunday I would be conducting the Church Service." Her eyes stared with surprise and her mouth opened wide. To avoid any more questions I said, "Come on let's dance, " and I led her onto the dance-floor.

And so, Christmas 1978 came and went. But this time I was at home with my family to enjoy it. All things considered I suppose I've been luckier than most seamen having been temporarily appointed Assistant Superintendent in London on many occasions. Even now, while working as 'Mate' on the 'Scammonden II' my chances of being home for Christmas were almost 100%. Not forgetting I was being paid for it as well.

In the week between Christmas and the New Year the Murrays held a little celebration party at their home on the Ipswich Road to which Dave and Kay Burton, Joan and I were invited. While drinks were being handed around there was general consensus that the party at Hall Barn had been an unqualified success and hopes were expressed we could repeat the occasion the next year.

I think it was Kay who said, "At the Christmas Party, I overheard you describing a cruise on the 'Cunard Adventurer', were they all pretty the same G.D.?" I replied, "Yes Kay, they were pretty much the same, we sailed from San Juan at near midnight on Saturdays, having arrived there shortly after six that morning." I took a sip of my 'single-malt' then went on, "In those days the itinerary was the same, from San Juan to Martinique, Grenada, St. Lucia, St. Thomas in the Virgin Islands. We would leave St. Thomas at or near midnight and six hours later arrive back in San Juan."

Every once in a while someone would interrupt to clarify a point, otherwise I managed to satisfy their curiosity without much difficulty, besides, they were genuinely interested. Someone then said, "Calling at the same places every cruise must have been pretty boring." I nodded then continued, "Well there was one exception I shall always remember." I took another sip, while they all waited, (dare I say, with bated breath?!), Then I went on to tell them about the '1973 Eclipse Cruise'.

My very good friend, Captain Tony Braithwaite, the Company's personnel manager had persuaded Joan to fly out to San Juan, at Company expense, to join me on the 'Cunard Adventurer', So we were together on this very special '1973 Eclipse Cruise'. And I may add, as this cruise had been organised by the 'National Geographical Magazine', these were not 800 ordinary passengers. There were lecturers and students of astronomy and allied sciences. The world-famous author of 'A Space Odyssey' Arthur C. Clarke. A well-known Volcanist lecturer and Colonel Wally Scheerer the 'Apollo Five' astronaut, being among the lecturers.

We sailed from San Juan at 23.59 hours on Saturday 23rd. June for our first port of call, Martinique. The eleven o'clock Divine Service was omitted in favour of a tight schedule of lectures. At and from the very first meal the passengers at my table, and, for that matter, all others were solemn, quiet and, if I may say so, a pretty miserable crowd. As is the custom the Captain does his utmost to entertain his table companions with all the wit he can muster. Nothing worked at best all I got was a grimace which I took to be a smile. Occasionally Joan would look at me then upwards showing the whites of her eyes.

In St. Lucia the passengers were ferried ashore in our launches at Souffrier Bay where they were then taken inland to see the sulphur-springs and the 'Pitons' after which we steamed around to the harbour at Castries, thence to Port of Spain, Trinidad where we were taken to view the Asphalt Lake. On leaving Port of Spain I navigated the ship through the 'Dragon's Teeth' to give the passengers a thrill, by blowing a loud blast on the ship's whistle to disturb thousands of birds.

Now we set Course to the geographical position, Latitude 10*47' N. Longitude 44*55 W. which was our rendezvous position for the Total Eclipse of the Sun calculated to be at 07.12 on Saturday 30th. June 1973. By steaming at full speed on a certain Course totality lasted nearly three minutes longer. The special cameras, telescopes and other measuring devices owned by the passengers were insured for over a million dollars.

Perhaps I should have been afraid my fellow guests were bored out of their skulls, but, in all honesty, I could see by their rapt attention my description of that special eclipse cruise had really interested them. Be that as it may, I asked them if they wanted me to proceed and I could tell by their murmured encouragement that I could carry on. However, as Dennis was attending to everyone's drinks I waited a couple of minutes, then, with a grateful sip of my single-malt nectar I went on.

"There's not much more to tell you about the eclipse itself other than to say it was hugely successful and I have, at home, an enlarged photograph of totality with Bailey's Beads on the rim and the enormous solar-flare that gives it the appearance of an engagement ring. Then, roughly between 07.30 and 08.00, the Boffins celebrated the occasion by raising the International Eclipse Flag at the foremast after which we set Course for St. Thomas, Virgin Islands arriving there early Tuesday 3rd. July."

"What struck me forcibly was the changed attitude and demeanour of our serious-minded passengers. In fact it was something of a metamorphosis. Instead of being morose they now began behaving like excited school-children. They even laughed at some of my worst jokes. (and that is saying something!) And after dinner the Cruise Director laid-on a very special concert with our professional entertainers pulling-out all the stops."

"And right on midnight all the ships in the harbour began blowing their whistles to herald American Independence Day the 4th. July and - by coincidence - the anniversary of the foundation of The Cunard Steamship Company. Then, as if this were a signal, there was the most magnificent display of fireworks on every hillside surrounding the harbour of Charlotte Amalie, St. Thomas."

Even as I stopped, my listeners were still - listening? I took a long pull at my whisky and said, "Well, that's all folks, I hope I haven't bored you." Then, to my surprise they stood and applauded so I took another heave ho at my whisky which Dennis had surreptitiously replenished!.

There was one particular trip on the 'Scammonden II' I shall never forget. I saw something I had never seen in my life, although Dennis Murray said he'd seen it a few time before.

It was on our return from having 'dumped' another load of effluence into the North Sea and the skipper was at the wheel skilfully conning the ship along the narrow waterway between ships alongside Hythe Quay and the opposite bank. As usual, I was outside on the port wing of the bridge keeping Dennis informed of the clearance between ourselves and the ships alongside.

We were passing the last ship alongside the quay and I remarked how very low she appeared in the water. Dennis gave her a quick glance then yelled, "Watch her carefully G.D., keep looking." I saw the water-level was within inches of her Main Deck and guessed she was stuck in the mud not afloat and within a matter of minutes the rising tide would pour over her and she'd be completely submerged!

We were barely past this coaster and approaching the 'turning basin' when suddenly it happened. The ship literally popped to the surface with a loud sucking noise and all her moorings fore and aft twanging like guitar strings. For several seconds she rolled to and fro and her short gangway slipped into the water between ship and quay.

Seconds later we were at the 'turning basin' and I had to dash aft to keep Dennis informed of the distance between our stern and the opposite bank. Then, having made our turn we were heading back the way we had come towards our own berth. I returned to the wheelhouse where I found Dennis still chuckling and as we passed slowly by the little coaster for a second time I asked him to explain the phenomena we had just witnessed.

As I have said before, having turned the ship around at the basin the return passage to our berth is made relatively easier with steering against the flood-tide. So Dennis began, "The mud alongside the quay is very soft and greasy and perhaps the underwater contour of certain ships is a contributing factor". He paused a second while giving the 'Scammonden II' a little more helm than usual then went on. "These ships sit on the bottom at low water and a sort of vacuum occurs so when the water rises with the flood-tide the ship remains stuck. I've seen ships completely submerged and they had to call the fire-brigade to pump all the water out!"

I gave a low whistle of surprise then asked, "So how and why do the suddenly pop-up like a Jack-in-the-Box, like the one we've just seen?" Dennis gave an expressive shrug then went on, "I imagine it is when a ship passes by, the displacement wave somehow breaks the vacuum seal and 'POP'! up she comes!" I was still contemplating his explanation as we approached our berth and had to leave the wheelhouse to attend to our stern moorings. Afterwards, when the 'Scammonden II' was secured and not wishing to be caught by the tide over The Strood I declined the skipper's invitation to a wee snifter and climbing into the car headed for home.

From the many cozy chats I had with Dennis Murray I had gathered that his favourite 'watering-hole' was a pub called the 'Artilleryman' to which, one day, he invited me. Due to this great lapse in time I'm not absolutely certain but I had the impression he and 'mine-host' of the pub had served together in the Royal Marines.

Be that as it may, but on one of our trips from the Hythe, Dennis invited the landlord and his wife to come with us as passengers. And from start to finish, it was one of the most enjoyable parties I have ever attended. OH! how I wish I could remember their names. There was no shortage of gin and tonic but when the camaraderie is absolutely right booze is of secondary importance and I cannot remember having laughed so much before or since.

In order not to confuse my reader I feel bound to give our guests some fictitious names so I shall call them Bill and Edna. It was some innocent but witty remark made by Edna on the subject of 'tips' and 'tipping' that launched me into a description of the 'tipping' scales in big passenger liners whether cruising or on the North Atlantic.

"First of all," I began, "Experienced bedroom-stewards, stewardesses and restaurant staff know instinctively the 'type' of passenger they serve and how much they are likely to get in the way of a 'tip' at the end of the voyage or cruise." Then, seeing I had their undivided attention, I continued.

"The average American longs to be admired, even liked, for being wealthy enough to travel First Class, (on the Atlantic run) or able to take a long cruise to wherever. They are self-made men who worship their maker and, above all, big 'tippers'. Other nationals also tend to overdo their 'tipping'. Some are either too mean, and give little, others are totally ignorant of what the 'right amount' should be."

I gave a little disparaging cough, then apologised, "I'm afraid I am boring you with all this talk of 'tipping'." "No, No," protested Edna, and Bill. Dennis and I could see they were genuinely interested so I continued. "Then there are those others with hundreds of years of good breeding." I paused wondering how best to describe, what most people call 'aristocrats' but our stewards, stewardesses and restaurant staff always referred to them as 'bloods', (abbreviated 'blue-bloods'). And they 'tip' exactly the 'right amount' at all times.

There followed a heated debate among all three of my listeners about the accuracy and viability of my description with each of them in turn demanding further details. To bring more humour into the discussion I then proceeded to describe some of the 'tricks' which were played by certain members of the crew to earn favours from grateful, but naive, passengers.

I told them, in the 'Queens' there would be eight 'bell-boys' aged fifteen to sixteen. Bright-eyed, pink cheeked youngsters dressed resplendently from 'pill-box' hate, short maroon jackets buttoned down the front with white gloves tucked into shoulder-straps, black trousers and shoes. These lads would vie with each other to relieve the 'lift-attendants' for meals, and when answering a 'bell-call- would be found whistling merrily by the passenger or passengers.

"Hello youngster," would be the greeting by the passenger, "You seem chirpy this morning." "Yes Sir," would come the immediate response, "It's me birthday Sir." And a ten-dollar 'tip' would ensue! The very thought of what I'd said very nearly made me choke into my gin and tonic. "Those pink-cheeked little rascals would make more in one voyage than I would earn in a month," said I, as all three of my listeners stared, was it in disbelief? I wondered.

It was the next question that left me in no doubt that our guests were genuinely interested in my description of life on board Cunard passenger ships, and in particular, cruise-liners. It was Bill who brought the subject up, "I was looking at the one boat you have here on the 'Scammonden II' and wondered how many you had on the 'Queens'.

I scratched my head, more to collect my thoughts rather than for any other reason, then began. "Both 'Queen Mary' and her sister ship 'Queen Elizabeth' had twenty-four lifeboats, twelve on each side of the boat-deck. Numbers one and two were the 'seaboats', each certified to carry 47 persons and used primarily in emergencies, such as when taking the ship's doctor across open water in the Atlantic to attend to a sick or injured person on another ship or, perhaps when required to bring that person back on board for treatment in the ship's hospital. The two radio lifeboats were each certified to carry 136 persons, while the remaining twenty were each certified to carry 147 persons.

"Just a minute G.D." said Bill producing a small diary and pencil from his inside pocket he began jotting down the figures I had just quoted, he began adding them together. then he gave a low whistle and blurted out, "Jeeze, that makes a total of 3,306 persons." I nodded my head then went on to say, "To that lot you can add 24 inflatable life-rafts each certified to carry 20 persons." I paused to let it sink in and finish his arithmetic. Bill leaned back in the settee and blew out his cheeks then with eyes tightly closed said, "Jesus Christ that makes a total of 3,786 goddamn people."

I gave a light laugh then, tapping his knee said, "Here are some more figures to play with Bill." He shook his head in apparent disbelief but I went on, "Sixteen ounces of biscuit per person, sixteen ounces of barley-sugar per person, sixteen ounces of condensed-milk per person and one gallon of fresh-water per person in each and every lifeboat and life-raft." His only reply was, "Bloody 'ell."

They were still arguing about the totals of this and that when Edna, turned to me and said, "You mentioned condensed-milk G.D. that seems a strange sort of 'food' for the lifeboats." She looked askance, so I related the story of the Hain Steamship Company's 'Trevessa', which had foundered in the Indian Ocean during a violent storm while on passage from Australia to the UK with a cargo of zinc-concentrate. And while preparing the lifeboats before abandoning ship the Master had ordered the Chief Steward to add cases of condensed-milk. Four weeks and nearly two thousand miles later they landed on the island of Madagascar claiming it was the condensed-milk that had saved them. Since when it has been a Board of Trade statuary requirement for all British ships. To their look of utter astonishment I could not resist adding, "And the blasted condensed-milk comes in fourteen-ounce tins." My listeners simply roared with laughter.

While Dennis Murray busied himself with replenishing our glasses I went on to tell our guests about the splendid launches that were carried in the 'Green-Goddess', the 'Caronia' for use when, unable to berth alongside due to her size, her passengers would be ferried by launch to and from a jetty. I described how these cruise-launches could carry up to sixty passengers, thirty in the forward cabin and thirty aft. The coxswain steered his launch from a midship 'cuddy' or cockpit.

Suddenly remembering, I went on to describe how a few launch coxswains would have, placed carefully in front of him, a photograph of 'loved ones back home'. I paused for effect then went on, "The photograph was not necessarily HIS loved ones, sometimes they were 'borrowed'. The object of this display was to encourage some sentimental female passenger to remark on it with the obvious resultant 'present' being brought back by the same soft-hearted, cruelly deceived female as a 'gift' for the baby or child!"(did I detect a tear in Edna's eyes???)

So it went on, week after week we took the 'Scammonden II' with her porridge of treated effluence out to the dumping ground approximately eight miles off the port of Harwich from whence it would be carried northwards on the falling tide. By this time quite a bond of friendship had been forged between myself, the skipper Dennis Murray and our engineer Dave Burton. My weekly pay-packet would put Cunard to shame if it were not for the oysters, caviar and lobster-thermidor which I missed sorely.

It was at some time in the summer of 1981 that Doug and Marjorie Humphreys came to stay with us for a week or so. They were very dear friends who once lived near us in London but who now lived in Eastbourne. On my days off we would take them to all the beauty-spots around Colchester. Then, having first checked with Dennis, I invited them to take a trip with us on the 'Scammonden II' and, much to my surprise, they accepted.

Much more reserved than our previous guests on the 'Scammonden II' we enjoyed their company nonetheless and they enjoyed the novelty of a short sea trip even though they suffered a brief period of 'mal-de-mer'! And although it has nothing whatsoever to do with their short voyage I vividly remember the day we took them to 'Constable Country' to admire 'Willy Lott's Cottage' and 'The Mill' at Stratford. We had strolled over the rustic bridge and I espied two young girls seated in a boat and while slowly drifting down-stream they were licking ice-cream cones. Unable to resist the temptation I copied the TV advert to sing, "Just One Cornetto, Give it to me!" They both burst into laughter, rocked the boat and nearly fell overboard!

With the approach of Autumn the skipper Dennis Murray said that his wife Brenda had hinted for a repeat party at the Hall Barn later in the year. So, at the first opportunity I approached Max Garcia and after checking his 'fixture diary' we settled on a date in the first week of December when there were neap-tides and the 'Scammonden II' would lay idle for a few days.

The November fogs and drizzly rain meant a lot of intense concentration for the whole of the round trip from the Hythe to the dumping ground and return. On two occasions the wind was so strong we chose to anchor in the Blackwater within sight of our bungalow rather than our customary anchorage off Brightlingsea. The only bright spot on our horizon was the party at Hall Barn in the first week of December.

It seemed to be my lot again to be asked countless questions about 'big ships' and again most of my questioners were ladies at the party. However, one question was directed specifically at cruising, so I launched into the '108 Day Around the World Cruise' of the 'Caronia' which I called 'The Millionaires' Yacht'. All seven hundred passengers had to be millionaires to be able to afford the fare which, in 1959 was from $35,000 upwards.

My listeners were staring open-mouthed as I told them about Mrs Dodge, the widow of Dodge Motors, who, not only paid her own fare but that of her lady-companion, her private doctor and her private lawyer! And there was Mrs Oliver who booked three First-Class cabins, two for her luggage and one for her maid! Mrs Oliver would have for herself a State-Room. And not least Miss Clara Macbeth who, like many others, found it cheaper to live on the 'Caronia' than pay a large staff to run their mansions in and around New York.

But female curiosity knows no bounds, as soon as I had slaked my thirst I was bombarded with more, and still more questions about the 'Caronia' 'Queen Mary' and 'Queen Elizabeth'. One young lady asked if I still missed the sea and I replied, "Well, occasionally it comes over me in waves!!" Then another question (the old chestnut). "Is it true that a sailor has a girl in every port?" To which I replied truthfully, "I really don't know, I haven't been to every port -Yet!"

We were steaming slowly down the Colne with yet another load of porridge when I pointed out to Dennis Murray the rear of what had been my home for many years in Old Heath. With a bit of a laugh I told the skipper that somewhere between ourselves in the 'Scammonden II' and our house 'Normandy' across the marshes there were six .38 calibre bullets I had once fired from my 'Webley' revolver!!

As we wended our way down-river the skipper and I spoke on many subjects. Much of it, he admitted, the happiest days of his life were spent in the Royal Marines and his various postings abroad. There was no doubt the accident in Hong Kong when the 'jeep' in which they were travelling left the road and plunged over a hundred feet down the steep slopes of 'Stanley Heights' brought to an abrupt end to what had been a wonderful career. When he was invalided out of the service.

One thing led to another and I told him how within a few weeks of my apprenticeship in tramp-steamers I had fallen twenty-odd feet into a dark coal-bunker. And how my landing on a heap of small coal probably saved my life. And there was a look of utter disbelief when I told him of the collision near the entrance to Las Palmas when the Swedish tanker 'Castor' destroyed the apprentices' quarters of the 'Trevose' while I was asleep. The Captain and others expected to find my bloodied corpse among the wreckage, but apart from severe bruising I was relatively unharmed.

Dennis must have thought my imagination had run riot when I told him of when my indentures as an apprentice had expired on 31st. March 1936 while my ship was out on the Japanese Coast and I was promoted to Fourth Officer. A promotion that lasted less than a week owing to the large 'packing-case' that had fallen out of the cargo net and had fallen thirty feet on top of me. It made me burst into a fit of giggles to see the look of incredulity on the skipper's face, when I explained I had regained consciousness two days later, to find myself in the International Hospital in Kobe, with multiple injuries.

I was startled when Dennis leaned across the wheelhouse and pinched my arm. "What was that for," I asked. He replied, "I just wanted to make sure you weren't a ghost, from what you've told me you are lucky to still be alive." All I could say to that was "Amen, but the same applies to you Dennis." And we both laughed. "Do you know Dennis, "I began, "That reminds me, in every Cunard passenger ship and usually in the joiner's stores there are seven silk-lined copper 'caskets' of varying sizes." Dennis looked incredulous, so I explained. "Should a passenger or member of the crew die while on board, the Master informs head office in Liverpool who, in turn get in touch with the next of kin and conveys to the Master their wishes about disposal of the deceased. And all this takes some time."

"Meanwhile, the corpse is put into one of those 'caskets' and is stored in one of the refrigerated chambers at a temperature of approximately 41 degrees, (it shouldn't be frozen), until such time as the next of kin's wishes are known. It they wish it to be brought home the ship's doctor replaces blood with formaldehyde to preserve it, otherwise we give it a Christian burial at sea." I paused to let all this sink in, then continued, "You see Dennis, the Law forbids the Master to marry people but allowed him to bury them - always provided they are really dead!" At that, Dennis used his favourite expression "Bloody 'ell!"

After a few minutes silence, to give the skipper time to absorb all this, I went on. "The one thing I really admired about the crews of all Cunard passenger ships." Dennis gave me a funny look, anticipating another of my lurid tales, so I gave him a reassuring smile. "Each ship had a very robust and active Social-Athletic Club with a very responsible committee to run it." Dennis looked relieved I had deserted my ghoulish theme so I went on, "All the popular indoor games and tournaments are held on board in the crew's "Pig and Whistle'. Football and cricket matches were played between ship teams and between ship and shore." And I went on to describe the annual carnival and the football matches against Bergen during the North Cape Cruises.

The 'Scammonden II' was alongside her usual berth at the Hythe and due to an unfavourable neap-tide we found work for idle hands. To renew the rusty yard-arm bridle, I had brought down the old wires and set it up again with new wires. Looking at my handiwork Dennis Murray said, "If I can climb a mast when I'm your age I'll be lucky and grateful."

Dennis and I were enjoying a quiet drink one afternoon when he said, "You know G.D. you've told us quite a number of tales when

Scammonden II

you were a watchkeeping officer in the 'big ship' but what about when you were Master, I mean, what was your first command for instance?" I took a quick sip of my G & T. "It's funny you should ask Dennis because I found my first ship to be a strange coincidence. The 'Andania' and her sister ship 'Alaunia' were two of our newest cargo ships.

I took another sip then asked, "How well do you know your Bible Dennis?" He made a grimace and shrugged his shoulders. "Not much I'm afraid," he mumbled. I took yet another sip then said quietly, "Perhaps you won't believe this but I think I can repeat these verses pretty accurately from Genesis Chapter 6."

"If I remember correctly it begins with verse 14". I took a deep breath, "And God said to Noah, make thee an Ark of gopherwood, rooms shalt thou make in the Ark, and shalt cover it within and without with pitch." I paused for a second then went on, "And this is the fashion which though shalt make it of. The length of the Ark shall be three-hundred cubits, the breadth of it fifty cubits and the height of it thirty cubits." I again paused for a second or so to see if the Skipper was paying attention, and to give him credit, he was indeed listening open-eyed. So I continued - " A window shalt thou make in the Ark, and in a cubit shalt thou finish it above. And the door of the Ark thou shalt set in the side thereof, with lower, second and third stories." I remembered verse 17 clearly and vividly, "And behold I, even I do bring a flood of water upon the Earth to destroy all flesh wherein is the breath of life." I stopped deliberately for maximum effect then went on, "from under Heaven and every thing that is on the earth shall die."

I drained my glass and looked at Dennis expectantly then continued but he didn't say a word, guessing there was more to come. I didn't disappoint him, "You know Dennis, it would appear theologians, scientists and historians are all agreed the length of the biblical cubit is from a man's elbow to the tip of his middle finger, approximately sixteen inches. Which makes the dimensions of the Ark about 450 feet long by 73 feet wide by 45 feet high." Then looking him straight between in the eye I said, "Those are the exact dimensions of the 'Andania'."

As the Skipper refilled our glasses he said, "You're not joking or pulling my leg G.D. are you?" I shook my head without saying a word, then he went on, "No, I thought not," and with a long drawn, "Phew" and he sat down heavily in his chair, so I went out on deck leaving him to brood over what we had been discussing.

Some minutes later I returned to the tiny dining-saloon of the 'Scammonden II'. It was to find Dennis still seated in his chair but with his head buried in his hands as though fast asleep. Not wishing to disturb him I returned to my chair opposite and kept a discreet silence. Suddenly he looked up, and with a wintry smile muttered "Samuel Langhorne Clemens," it was something I had least expected him to say. I nodded and volunteered the information, "American who became a Mississippi River Pilot, prolific writer and author who adopted the pseudonym of 'Mark Twain'."

The Skipper nodded, then asked, "But why Mark Twain?" We stared at each other for a few seconds then I said, "Well, he knew the Mississippi River intimately and as a Pilot he would have to know the 'seven pound hand-lead' and its markings pretty thoroughly." Before

I could utter another word Dennis snapped, "Do YOU know the markings on the hand-lead?" I gave it a second's thought then replied, "I think so Skipper - I used it often enough as an apprentice".

"The hand-lead weighs approximately seven pounds - it has a small recess in the bottom which may be filled with soft-soap or tallow to pick-up a sample of the nature of the bottom of the sea or river-bed, such as mud, sand, shingle etc. The leadline is marked in fathoms, (a fathom being equal to six feet). Each fathom being either a 'mark' or a 'deep'." I paused for a moment then said, "Is that enough, or do you want me to go on?" He he said, "Carry on, let's see if you remember the rest of it."

I had no doubt Dennis didn't believe I would remember the markings on the hand-lead so all I could do was hope and pray I could. I took a deep breath and began, "One fathom is indicated by a strip of leather, a seaman taking soundings would call out, "By the deep One". Two fathoms would be indicated by two strips of leather and the seaman would call, "By the mark Two", or Twain, hence the pseudonym 'Mark Twain" Three fathoms is also indicated by three strips of leather and the seaman would call out, "By the mark Three". Four fathoms is 'deep four' but five and fifteen fathoms are indicated by a piece of white linen. Six is a 'deep' while seven and seventeen fathoms are indicated by a piece of red bunting. Nine is a 'deep' but ten fathoms is indicated by a 'hole surrounded by a piece of leather'!! Dennis held up his hand in protest and laughed as he saw my joke. "You mean a piece of leather with a hole in it." I gave a little cough then continued, "Eleven and twelve fathoms are both 'deeps' but thirteen is a 'mark' indicated by a piece of blue serge."

The Skipper held up his hands again with, "OK, OK, G.D. that's enough." But I was now in full stride, "The pieces of material were deliberately chosen so they could be distinguished at night, in the dark, for instance, white linen is soft to the touch and identified as five or fifteen, blue serge has a distinctive 'feel' to it. While red bunting is so coarse, easily identified for seven and seventeen fathoms." Dennis interrupted me with, "I wish I hadn't brought this up in the first place." He reached behind him and brought out his part-bottle of gin and a bottle of tonic water. Then, while he was pouring-out liberal measures, I suddenly remembered that

'Langhorne' was also the name of the young lady who had interviewed me at the 'Job-Centre' in Colchester and I remarked on how unusual the name was.

We then exchanged memories of unusual names and nicknames we had met during our chequered careers - 'Chalky White' - 'Dusty Miller' - 'Spider Webb' - 'Chippy' the carpenter and 'Sparks' for the radio-operator. Captain John Treasure Jones, so I was obliged to tell Dennis that 'Treasure' had been his mother's maiden name. And I went on to tell him of other names or nicknames with whom I'd sailed. 'Happy' Challoner was a morose individual, 'Corpus' Jones' family were undertakers and Bill Mort had always been known as 'Rigor'. I also mentioned my old friend Andrew Thomson who, having been born in South Africa had always been called 'Zulu'. And there were Captains 'Tiger' Evans and 'Pongo' Sargent in the cargo ships. 'Spike' Milligan one of our electricians and 'Spud' Middleton because his uncle was a well-known radio gardener.

From all this and more, I then went on to tell Dennis of the two voyages to Huelva during the Spanish Civil War. I had been Third Mate in the 'Tregenna'. One day the 'old man' returned on board to say he had just met a skipper who'd been running the blockade several times and was known as 'Potato' Jones. That was when we had discovered the currency was now not pesetas but 'Palm Olive' and 'Lux' toilet soaps. And our sailors then bought silk-stockings in Cardiff to give to the señoritas - "One at a time!" Dennis fell out of his chair and nearly suffered apoplexy laughing.

When the skipper had regained his seat and recovered his composure he blurted, "Y'know G.D. you're a tonic, when you came in earlier I was feeling morose but you've cheered me up no end." I could only think of one response to that, "Well skipper, it's something like the notice I once read in a Gents' lavatory, 'We Aim TO Please - You Aim TOO please'." And that started him off in another fit of giggles.

Becoming serious for a change Dennis said, "Passengers at your table must have laughed from the beginning of a cruise until the end." He paused for breath, "And probably still laughing as they went down the gangway!" I gave a deep sigh then replied. "Y'know Dennis, every passenger brings with them a tale about something or somebody."

I took a sip of my G & T, "I made a mental note of what they said until one day, or one mealtime, something is said to trigger it off."

Dennis nodded, the asked, "Who do you reckon the most interesting person that you met at sea?" I gave it some thought before replying, "We entertained dozens of people in the wardroom from time to time." I took another sip, "Actors and actresses, Noel Coward, Ralph Richardson, David Niven, Charles Laughton, Diana Dors, Yvonne de Carlo, Anna Neagle and dozens of others. But you said 'most interesting', I think it would be a tie between Ben Gurion, the Father of Israel, or the evangelist Billy Graham, who had the most enormous charisma.

Momentarily deep in thought, Dennis then said, "I think it's high time you wrote your memoirs G.D." I gave a little self-concious cough then, "As a matter of fact I've given it some thought from time to time." For a few minutes there was complete silence between us, then I laughed. "How about 'From the Captain's Table' as a title?" Dennis laughed, "Yes that would do, or how about, 'Tales of a Master Mariner'?" The idea stayed locked-away in my mental filing-cabinet for years until something, or someone triggered it!

Possibly too concerned with my own affairs, to date, I have omitted to mention that Jane, our eldest twin-daughter, her husband Raymond and their little son Anthony had emigrated to Australia. They had then bought a bungalow and settled-down in Thornlea, a suburb of Perth in Western Australia. If my memory serves me correctly it was only a matter of days before Christmas when Jane had written to say she was expecting their second child some time in July 1982.

This news and the thousands of miles that separated us tended to make Joan and myself nervous and without her knowing it I began making discreet enquiries about flight times and fares. As my reader probably knows, the travel brochures quote return fares for 'peak', 'shoulder' and 'off-peak' periods. So, eventually, we settled on the most reasonable 'shoulder' period of November 1982 through to May 1983 and booked our flights accordingly.

Meanwhile I very rightly told Dennis of our plans and that he should feel free to advertise for my replacement. Thanks to Dennis and his Company, Effluence Services Limited we were financially in a strong position to enjoy some months with our Aussie family and our bank manager was most helpful arranging a monthly sum to be transferred to a bank in Australia.

Having received a promising response to his advertisement Dennis invited me to attend the interview of this candidate which I considered most flattering. In fact we were both very impressed with the young man, whose name I cannot recall. But that he held a 'Master's Certificate of Competency' and had served a few years watchkeeping in the Port of London's survey ship 'Patricia' was good enough without doubt. And I was particularly happy that Dennis would have an experienced officer to support him. I had made good friends and would always remember them. I had also found there was more to effluence than meets the eye on board a 'Bovril Boat'!

Our trip out to stay a few months with our little family in Australia and the opportunity to love and cuddle our little newborn granddaughter has no place in this narrative. On our return to West Mersea there was also the expected back-log of household and garden chores that demanded my full attention. In short, it was several months before I got around to paying a visit to the Hythe Quay, only to find many changes had taken place.

Effluence Services Limited and the 'Scammonden II' no longer carried the product of the Treatment Plant out to sea. It appeared the effluence was now being taken away by road haulage, I know not where, but when driving around the countryside I often get a familiar 'tang' wafted in my nostrils!

I learned from the harbourmaster, Captain Ken Goody, that Dave and Kay Burton had taken their ex-trawler 'Clare de Lune' to Scotland where they now chartered the boat to Aqua Diving Clubs. Dennis and Brenda Murray had taken-over a public-house somewhere in Hertfordshire and I have never since been able to establish the name or whereabouts of the pub.

But now, several years later, as I tap the keys of my faithful long-suffering word-processor I have reestablished communication with Dave Burton, the brilliant engineer, who is now the owner of a large and expanding company called 'Granit Union' quarry operators and manufacturers of Scottish and imported stone for the commercial and domestic sectors.

DECLINE OF THE OLD RED DUSTER

Hindsight is not a gift – and we all experience it from time to time.. It's the delayed awakening of those little grey cells beloved by Hercule Poirrot to an awareness of an event or events not registered or recognised at the time.

Among the framed photographs in the officers' wardroom of the Cunard passenger liner 'Mauretania' was one signed by those intrepid flyers Messrs Alcock and Brown and the centrepiece a photograph of the Vickers 'Vimy' aeroplane in which they had flown non-stop across the Atlantic in 1919 from Newfoundland to Ireland With hindsight it is incredible this epic flight failed to ring 'alarm-bells' in the boardrooms of certain shipowners.

And in the first few months of the Second World War a huge R.A.F coastal-command 'Sunderland' flying-boat rescued a boat-load of survivors from a torpedoed merchant ship in the Western Approaches demonstrating the capabilities of these huge aircraft.

In the post-war years circa 1960 there were a number of Saunders-Roe 'Princess' flying-boats almost twice the size of the 'Sunderlands'; moored off Calshott in Southampton Water. They were awaiting more powerful engines to make them viable as a commercial venture. At this time I happened to attend a meeting in Liverpool between ships' officers and Company officials, which gave me the opportunity to make my views heard. I suggested these prototype aircraft could make a serious impact on the trans-Atlanic routes offering 'out by Princess, home by Queen' or vice-versa.

Much to my dismay and chagrin the deputy Chairman retorted "Rubbish Williams, we've been a successful shipping company for the past 143 years", he paused to blow a cloud of tobacco-smoke into the air then continued with "and I don't doubt we will continue to do so for another 143 years.!" My reply to that was a mumbled "that's putting all your eggs in one basket, Sir." And the subject was dropped.

It was not many years after that meeting when the Cunard Steamship Company went into partnership with British Overseas Aiways Corporation. A partnership that didn't last very long and I've often wondered why. 'Blinkered vision' springs to mind, but there – its all a matter of 'hindsight' isn't it!

The end of a costly and futile Second World War came with the surrender of Germany on the 7th.May 1945, (my 30th.birthday) followed five months later with the Japanese surrender on board the USS "Missouri" in Tokyo Bay. As soon as was practical thereafter those merchant ships that had survived the conflict were dry-docked, repaired where necessary, painted in the colours of their respective owners and returned to their peacetime trades world-wide.

Wartime shortages of raw materials were soon made good and the end-products back on the shelves. Britain's import and export trade grew rapidly with satisfactory freight-rates and revenues for shipping companies. Peoples of all nations were allowed to travel where when and how they chose and the bookings for passenger ships at an all-time high and for the next decade or so it remained that way. Even if bookings fell slightly during the winter months on the North Atlantic, itineraries were changed in favour of cruising to the sun-drenched islands of the Carribbean.

But an ominous cloud was rapidly gathering over the horizon. The war years had accelerated the design, capacity and speed of aircraft beyond even the wildest dreams of our intrepid flyers Messrs Alcock and Brown. The internal-combustion engine gave way to the 'turbo-prop' until Wing-Commander Frank Whittle perfected the ram-jet engine and commercial passenger flights an everyday phenomena. And still the alarm-bells failed to ring in the shipping offices.

Inexorably the airlines, many of them subsidised by their governments, began to take the lion's share of the passenger traffic. Whatever the destination people preferred getting there in the shortest possible time allowing them a longer stay there and incidentally avoiding the misery of seasickness and if prone to airsickness it would be of shorter duration. !

It took shipowners a long time to appreciate the threat posed by the airlines but when it came it called for drastic action. Two very ugly words came into being – "rationalisation" and "redundancy" with so-called "time and motion studies" being carried out ashore and afloat. In Britain succeeding governments - regardless of political affiliation turned a blind eye to the plight of those shipowners who had served the country so well in its hour of need.

Unyielding Ministry regulations for safety precautions quite rightly demanded a sufficient number of lifeboats, life-rafts, lifebuoys and life-jackets be maintained on board at all times. But what stuck in my craw for much of the time was all the other paraphenalia when compared to civil airlines. The equipment and supplies of each and every lifeboat and life-raft had to include; A full set of oars (with two spares) a steering oar, a sea-anchor with a gallon of oil. A mast and sails, a bucket and bailer – a lamp and a gallon of lamp oil (for the use of).

Furthermore, every lifeboat and liferaft, for every person certified to carry, must provide the following; 16 ounces (1.lb) Biscuit; 16 ozs. Barley-sugar; 16 ozs Horlicks tablets and 16 ozs of Condensed Milk (supplied by the makers in 14oz tins just to make life difficult) and one gallon of Fresh-Water. The Regulations also required every British ship to carry Two (2) sets of International code-flags and a variety of national and international ensigns. Naturally there would have to be a selection of halyards from which to fly these flags and a variety of flares, smoke-flares and distress-rockets – All at enormous expense while the aeroplane simply has its identity and nationality painted on its fuselage.

But the irony of it all was the chivalry of the seas demanded that if an aircraft is experiencing or the threat of engine-failure ships have to deviate from their Course to make a rendezvous with the machine in the event of its having to 'ditch'. In this event, and it sometimes happened, the "Queen Mary" and "Queen Elizabeth" steaming along at 1.67 tons of fuel-oil per mile would consume a considerable quantity on what often turned out to be a 'wild-goose chase'. As a matter of fact and record, both "Queens" often went to the aid of surface craft requiring Medical assistance, but that's neither here nor there (or anywhere else for that matter) !

As for the manning of ships versus aircraft the reader will readily agree the odds were stacked heavily in favour of the airlines. To refer to the Cunard "Queens" again the ships complement would vary seasonally from 1150 to 1250 a terrifying ratio of one crew-member to two passengers whereas the average crew of a Boeing 747 is in the region of ten or twelve which is a much healthier and certainly a more economic ratio.

And fully aware of the imbalance between competing airlines and shipping the British government made no effort to assist in any way with the result was shipping companies having to merge or be swallowed-up by entrepreneurial predators. The following letters from the Cunard chairman, Sir Basil Smallpeice are mute evidence to what eventually became of that once great shipping company.

So, by the 21st. August 1971 ownership of Cunard was acquired by the Trafalgar House Group who later disposed of it to the Norwegian engineering company Kvaerner who, in 1998 sold it to Carnival Cruise Line Corporation of America. Thus, the once premier British shipping company founded by Samuel Cunard in 1840 has now become a wholly-owned American company with some of its ships flying the British Red Ensign as a flag of convenience.

Furthermore, it could be one of the greatest riddles of the millennium where the 150,000 ton largest passenger-ship in the world built in a French shipyard for an American-owned British shipping company was recently named "Queen Mary 2" by Her Majesty Queen Elizabeth 2 - If that's not a conundrum I don't know what is; and it wouldn't surprise me one bit to learn that Samuel Cunard is currently turning in his grave like a whirling Dervish. !!!

THE CUNARD STEAM-SHIP COMPANY LIMITED
CLEVELAND HOUSE, St. JAME'S SQUARE, LONDON, SW1
01-930-7890

THE FOLLOWING MESSAGE HAS BEEN ISSUED BY THE CHAIRMAN TO-DAY:

Because of unforeseen and major movement in the price of Cunard shares on the London Stock Exchange this morning, I had, in accordance with the rules of the City Take-over Panel to release the following statement around noon to-day:

> 'In view of the recent untoward movement in the price of the Ordinary Stock units of The Cunard Steam Ship Company the Board announces that talks are taking place which may lead to an offer for all or part of the Ordinary Share capital of Cunard. The discussions are, however, in a preliminary stage and no indication of their likely outcome can be given. A further announcement will be made as soon as possible.

From the point of view of everyone who works in Cunard or its subsidiaries, the best thing for us all to do is to continue our efforts to make the company profitable again, not to be unduly concerned about speculative rumours, but to await further official information from me as soon as I am in a position to give it. I can assure you that, whatever developments take place, the fullest consideration will be given to the position of all staff.

BASIL SMALLPEICE
CHAIRMAN   29 June 71

THE CUNARD STEAM-SHIP COMPANY LIMITED
CLEVELAND HOUSE, St. JAME'S SQUARE, LONDON, SW1
01-930-7890

THE FOLLOWING MESSAGE HAS BEEN ISSUED BY THE CHAIRMAN TO-DAY:

Following my signal of 29 June, I can now tell you all, and particularly those of you who have not read to-day's UK newspapers, that the Chairman and the Managing Director of Trafalgar House Investments Limited informed me late Wednesday afternoon that their company had acquired on the Stock Exchange 21% of Cunard's issued Ordinary Stock and intended to make a bid for the remainder at a price of about 185 p. per £1 stock unit.

The Cunard Board is, of course, consulting its financial and other advisers. However, until the precise terms of the offer have been received, I am in no position to comment generally on the situation, and particularly as to whether the conditions are in any way adequate. Meanwhile the preliminary discussions referred to in my earlier announcement have been discontinued.

Trafalgar have said that they intend, repeat intend, that Cunard's cargo and passenger fleets should continue to operate.

Otherwise, I would like to stress what I said in my earlier signal, that the interest of all staff will be given the fullest consideration by me in any negotiations that my take place.

BASIL SMALLPEICE
CHAIRMAN

2 July 1971

CUNARD

The Cunard Steam-Ship Company Limited
Cleveland House, St. James's Square, London SW1
01-930 7890

9 August 1971

To All Staff of the Cunard Group

I am sending you a copy of the letter which has today gone out to all stockholders recommending acceptance of the offers by Trafalgar House Investments for Cunard Steam-Ship Company stock.

Although most of you may not yourselves be stockholders in Cunard, I would like you to know the reasons why the Board has decided as it has. In take-over bids, everyone has to be governed by the rules of the City Code and not by his own feelings.

You will find that the points in the letter to stockholders which are of most concern to staff are contained in the last paragraph but one.

Basil Smallpeice

Basil Smallpeice

from the Chairman, Sir Basil Smallpeice KCVO

THE CUNARD STEAM-SHIP COMPANY LIMITED
CLEVELAND HOUSE, St.JAME'S SQUARE, LONDON, SW1
01-930-7890

MESSAGE FROM SIR BASIL SMALLPEICE

To: All Cunard Group Staff

On this my last day as your Chairman and a Director of Cunard, I would like to thank you all for the loyalty and support you have given me in working to make Cunard profitable again through the various and sometimes painful steps on the road to reconstruction.

From tomorrow your new Chairman will be Mr. Victor Matthews, the Managing Director of Trafalgar House. I hope you will give him the same support you have always given me.

It is vitally important for British shipping and for yourselves that Cunard should prosper as a business. There is no reason why it should not do so - at least equally well as part of the Trafalgar House Group as independently.

Good luck to you all.

Basil Smallpeice
Chairman
25 Aug 1971

EPILOGUE

89% of Britain's import and export trade is dependent on her shipping industry. But the Merchant Navy today is a mere shadow of what it once was. Up until the outbreak of the Second World War on September 3rd. 1939 there were over two-thousand vessels on the British Register of Shipping. Today, in the year 2000 there are less than four-hundred.

Prime Minister Winston Churchill once remarked, "the only thing that really frightened me during the Second World War was the 'U-Boat' peril." He had reason for his fears because he knew if the Germans had succeeded in cutting that tenuous lifeline between the New World and the United Kingdom they would probably have won the war, or certainly prolonged it.

In those ominously dark days our merchant ships were carrying the lifeblood of our nation desperately fighting for its very existence and survival. Bringing home food for our people and those vital supplies with which to prosecute the war against Nazi Germany. Without those ships the people would have been starved into submission and the three fighting services rendered impotent – with all the dire consequences which that implies.

Between 1939 and 1945 no less than 2,420 merchant ships and the lives of 29,180 merchant seamen were lost to enemy action. In the Merchant Navy War memorial on Tower Hill in London there are bronze-panels bearing the names of ships and their crews lost in two world wars and other conflicts since. It should be appreciated that, in Korea, Vietnam, the Falkands, the Persian Gulf & even in Europe itself there have been 'powder-barrel' threats of a Third World War while the present decline of our Merchant Navy is an 'imminent' threat to our National Security and our cherished Sovereignty

Of gravest concern to us all is what would be the outcome of another World War with so few ships flying the Red Ensign (the old red duster) and now when there are so few shipyards left in which to build them. The cost of chartering foreign-flag shipping would be astronomical even if they were prepared to become involved. During the recent war in Iraq of the many ships requisitioned by our Ministry of Defence only five were British. Others flew the flags of convenience such as Malta, Antigua, Bahamas, St.Vincent, Caymen Islands, Marshall Islands and Panama. And of these 47 of them had histories of deficiency and even detention.

What a terrible indictment...